Counseling The Chronically Ill Child

Counseling the Chronically Ill Child:

Psychological Impact and Intervention

Margaret M. O'Dougherty
*Ohio State University and
Columbus Children's Hospital*

Edited by James Butcher
Professor of Psychology
University of Minnesota

The Lewis Publishing Company
Lexington, Massachusetts
Brattleboro, Vermont

The Lewis Series in Applied Clinical Psychology

First Edition

This book is manufactured in the United States of America. It is designed by Irving
Perkins Associates and Kathleen Shulga and published by The Lewis Publishing
Company, Fessenden Road, Brattleboro, Vermont 05301.

Library of Congress Cataloging in Publication Data

O'Dougherty, Margaret, M., 1950–
  Counseling the chronically ill child.

  (The Lewis series in applied clinical psychology)
  Includes bibliographies and index.
  1. Chronic diseases in children—Psychological aspects.
2. Chronically ill children—Family relationships.
3. Counseling. I. Butcher, James Neal, 1935-   .
II. Title. III. Series. [DNLM: 1. Chronic disease—In
infancy and childhood. 2. Chronic disease—Psychology.
3. Counseling—In infancy and childhood. WS 350 026c]
RJ380.036 1983   618.92'00019   83-18751
ISBN 0-86616-026-4

For my husband, Frank

*Your steady counsel has been a
harborage when things were
difficult and a brisk wind
when the sailing was smooth.*

Contents

Preface

This book was written to provide a basis for understanding the impact a chronic illness can have on children and their families and to highlight the role of the psychologist in assessment, consultation, and clinical intervention. The illnesses selected illustrate special problems that can often arise with a chronic disease. Fear of pain (juvenile rheumatoid arthritis), fear of major surgery (congenital heart defects), anxiety over disfigurement (colostomy for ulcerative colitis), guilt because of genetic transmission (hemophilia, muscular dystrophy) and coping with the depression and anxiety that accompanies a degenerative disease (muscular dystrophy) are among the issues considered. Functional problems presenting with physical symptoms (encopresis), psychological problems arising secondarily from difficulty in adapting to a chronic disease (as for asthma, epilepsy, diabetes), and problems occurring as a result of the adverse effects of a specific disease (intellectual impairment subsequent to bacterial meningitis) are included as well. The purpose of this book is to offer a practical guide to psychological management of children with such chronic disorders.

The illnesses selected were designed to be illustrative of specific problems rather than exhaustive of all pediatric problems. An attempt was made throughout the book to provide a framework for integrating biologic, psychologic and social factors and for understanding basic medical information regarding the nature of the physiologic dysfunction and recommended medical and/or surgical treatment. It is hoped that this synthesis of medical and psychological information will provide a resource for psychologists working in pediatric settings or with chronically ill children as well as a reference for other health professionals (pediatricians, social workers, nurses, teachers, child life workers) and students. Effective management of the problems presented by the children often requires close collaboration and open communication among these health professionals.

No attempt has been made to cover every area of pediatric illness or disability. Other reference books of considerable value are available which cover aspects not dealt with in this book, particularly in the area of death and dying, leukemia and other malignancies, and medical problems requiring highly complex medical technologies (such as renal problems requiring dialysis or transplantation). Similarly, mental retardation, specific sensory handicaps and acquired disabilities are not covered in this book, but are critical problem areas often requiring the combined efforts of psychologists, pediatricians and various health care professionals.

Completion of this book would not have been possible without the help and support of many people. Although space prohibits my thanking all those colleagues and friends who have given me stimulation, knowledge, and support, I wish to express my special gratitude to the following persons: Pamela Kniesel and Marilyn Hartman, graduate students at the University of Minnesota, for their help in collecting bibliographic references; Susan O'Kelly, research assistant in the section of Neurology at Columbus Children's Hospital, for her tireless assistance in compiling and proofing the references and Appendix Tables and for her concentrated effort and commitment; and Diana Rizer, Cathy Stimmel and Elaine Drenten for long hours of typing.

Among my colleagues I am particularly indebted to Dr. Norman Garmezy, whose inspiration, guidance, support, and expertise shaped my interest in clinical child psychology; Dr. Grant Morrow, III, Chairman of the Department of Pediatrics at The Ohio State University and the Columbus Children's Hospital, for his interest and encouragement in promoting research and application of clinical techniques in the area of behavioral pediatrics; Dr. James N. Butcher, who provided me the opportunity and encouragement to organize and write about my experiences in working with chronically ill children and who provided very helpful editorial suggestions, sage advice and a careful review of each chapter; and Dr. Francis S. Wright, husband, research collaborator, medical advisor and dearest friend. Without his continued involvement, thoughtful attention to the medical aspects of each disease, and faith in me, the preparation and completion of this book could not have been accomplished.

|1| Overview

Prevalence

Currently, chronic diseases constitute not only the major health problem of children, but also what some consider the nation's primary health problem (Pless & Satterwhite, 1975). Prior to the 1960s, the primary focus in pediatric medicine was on the treatment of acute infectious diseases. However, major advances in the treatment of these diseases through immunization (for poliomyelitis, diphtheria, etc.), antibiotic or antiviral agents (for bacterial meningitis, encephalitis, etc.), and improved neonatal care for infants born prematurely or at risk greatly reduced the mortality rate from these diseases for infants and children (Russo & Varni, 1982; Sperling, 1978). Now, about one child in ten experiences a chronic illness by the age of 15, and many of these children are cared for by their families in the home (Pless, Roghmann, & Haggerty, 1972). Although there is a sizable medical literature discussing the child's and the family's adaptation to various illnesses, it is frequently difficult to incorporate these findings when attempting to develop a therapeutic program for a specific child. In addition, variation in the etiology of the disease, as well as its prognosis, chronicity, severity, and associated medical and surgical treatments, has not often been outlined with respect to the most effective and needed psychological interventions.

Impact of Chronic Illness

Three recent large population surveys—the National Survey of Child Health and Human Development in England, Scotland and Wales (Pless & Douglas, 1971), the Isle of Wight Study (Rutter, Tizard, & Whitmore, 1970), and the Rochester Child Health Survey (Pless & Roghmann, 1971)—have contributed greatly to our understanding of the emotional, social, and educational impact of various chronic diseases. Evidence from these surveys documents that chronically ill children show more truancy, absenteeism from school, lower academic achievement, and more behavioral difficulties than normal children. In the Isle of Wight study, the rate of psychiatric disorder among chronically ill children was 17 percent as compared to

1

7 percent in the healthy population. Increased behavioral symptoms of nervousness, aggression, or both for ill children were noted by their teachers in the National Survey, and more frequent symptoms and increasing behavioral problems with advancing age were noted by parents in the Rochester study.

A relationship between type and severity of disorder and rate of disturbance was also found in all three surveys. Children with sensory disorders were twice as likely to be disturbed as those with physical disorders (Pless & Roghmann, 1971; Pless & Douglas, 1971). In the Isle of Wight study, the neuro-epileptic group displayed significantly more clinical and psychiatric disorders than the other handicapped group and the control children (Rutter, et al., 1970). Rutter et al. also found a high rate of specific reading retardation among children with neurological disorders (27% of the children were delayed by 28 months or more). A higher proportion of children with other chronic illnesses also showed a delay in reading (14%) when compared to normal children (5%), but not so dramatically. Such a high rate of low achievement in the neuro-epileptic group likely resulted from a combination of biological (brain dysfunction) and/or psychosocial factors.

While the type and severity of the child's disorder have been implicated as significant factors in accounting for subsequent adjustment, few, if any, studies have demonstrated a specific relationship between a particular illness and a subsequent specific emotional or social problem of adjustment. In addition, while a higher incidence of maladjustment has been found in the large epidemiological surveys of chronically ill children, smaller studies examining differences between specific illness groups or smaller groups of chronically ill children have not always found differences in psychosocial adjustment (Collier, 1969; Tavormina, Kastner, Slater, & Watt, 1976).

A surprising finding has been that increasing severity of physical disability has *not* consistently related to greater child maladjustment. In studies of children with juvenile arthritis (McAnarney, Pless, Satterwhite, & Friedman, 1974), adolescents who have generalized tonic-clonic seizures (Hodgman, McAnarney, Myers, Iker, McKinney, Parmelee, Schuster, & Tutihasi, 1979), children with hemophilia (Bruhn, Hampton, & Chandler, 1971), and children with visual and hearing handicaps (Pless & Pinkerton, 1975), those having a milder disability (or better control of symptoms) often displayed greater maladjustment. These findings have been maintained even when the effects due to intelligence or school performance have been controlled. Such findings suggest that children who have relatively mild difficulty with their illnesses may be more troubled psychologically than those with more apparent physical difficulties. The reasons for such a paradoxical finding are poorly understood. Pless and Pinkerton (1975) speculate that:

> . . . the less disabling the lesion and the more marginal its effect, the greater the challenge it may pose for the child in attempting to keep abreast of competitive society. These children are neither so handicapped as to drop out automatically, nor yet well enough equipped to compete on an equal

footing. . . . In this sense, marginality and severity represent opposite poles of a disablement spectrum each with its own special problems of management. (p. 171)

The specific management problems and the special concerns that may arise with each illness and the impact that these may have on psychological adjustment are discussed at length in the following chapters.

Diversity in Outcome

There are a number of possible explanations for such diversity in outcome. Illness related variables that seem to affect the impact of the disease on the child can include the severity of the illness; the child's age at illness onset; the illness's duration, symptomatology, visibility; and the type and extent of medical interventions (Pless & Pinkerton, 1975).

The type of stress an illness presents also differs. Some illnesses are life threatening (such as a congenital heart defect or meningitis) and the child's health is in grave danger. Special treatment procedures, such as open-heart surgery, may be employed in an effort to provide normal functioning. If the child survives the life threatening phase of the disease, he or she may assume or return to a normal life pattern. In such illnesses, the stress is very intense at first and then decelerates. The critical task for the parent and child is to cope with the crisis and, once the crisis has been resolved, return to normal activities and caretaking practices. Continuation of patterns that may have been necessary and appropriate during the acute phase of the illness (protectiveness, solicitousness, feeding and dressing the child, etc.) may result in excessive dependency and passivity if extended beyond the illness period.

In other diseases, such as the degenerative or potentially terminal diseases (muscular dystrophy, cystic fibrosis, and leukemia), the stress of the illness accelerates as the child's condition progressively worsens. Different concerns and stresses emerge during the course of the illness, each possibly leading to the use of different coping mechanisms. Several stages of coping may be observed, and the patient or family may be particularly in need of additional help during specific periods (initial diagnosis, relapse, impending death, bereavement).

Finally, in many chronic diseases the stress of the illness is intermittent, as in asthma, epilepsy, diabetes, juvenile arthritis, hemophilia, or ulcerative colitis. These illnesses combine the stress of both an acute and a chronic disease. Since the diseases are chronic, the child and family are confronted with the fact that, although the disease may be controlled through medication, injections, or diet, they may have to cope with the condition throughout life. The episodic nature of these diseases subjects the child to recurrent and unpredictable episodes of acute symptom expression which vary in frequency and severity. The unpredictability of when acute symptoms will occur often severely affects the child's and family's sense of control and can make consistent management of such illnesses difficult and frustrating. It can also aggravate adjustment to and acceptance of the illness, particularly when the manifestations are very infrequent. The treatment of some illnesses, such as bone cancer or ulcerative colitis, may necessitate disfigurement of the child's body through amputation or colostomy. This disfigurement can present major difficulties in the area of self-concept, self-esteem, and social acceptance. The management of other diseases can require strict adherence to dietary schedules (as in diabetes) or strict curtailment of exercise and activity (as in hemophilia or some seizure disorders). Failure to comply with restrictions can become salient issues throughout the treatment of the disease or can emerge as a critical issue for a child at a particular developmental stage. For example, during adolescence restrictions in diet or activities can become major battlegrounds between parent and child eventuating in nonadherence to treatment guidelines and dangerous acting out (see chapters on epilepsy, diabetes, and hemophilia for further description of problems that may arise).

Within every illness and disability area, however, examples of adaptation as well as maladaptation are evidenced. Such findings highlight that the stress is not necessarily inherent in the illness, but rather may be a function of the way in which the illness is perceived by the child and family (Lazarus & Launier, 1978; Lipowski, 1970; Mattsson, 1972; Moos & Tsu, 1977). In this conceptual framework, illness is viewed as a crisis and a challenge which create a set of adaptational tasks that, if met successfully, could result in the child's or family's psychological growth. Conversely, if the illness is viewed as extremely threatening or overwhelms the child's and family's capacity to cope, significant disruption in adjustment may result.

Coping and Adaptation

Families managing the same chronic and severe illness vary greatly in their responses. Hill's classic ABCX model can provide a framework for integrating the influence of specific disease characteristics, family resources, and the family's appraisal of the stress the illness presents on subsequent coping and adaptation (Hill, 1949). This approach focuses on an event (A) (e.g., the illness and its characteristics) which interacts with (B) (family characteristics and resources both prior to the illness and subsequently), which in turn interacts with the family's definition of the event (C) to produce the family's response to the crisis (X). Our ability to understand the impact of illness on the child's and family's adaptation will be heavily dependent upon the extent we are able to understand this evolving process.

Three separate components must be understood by the therapist before suggestions for beneficial interventions can be made for children experiencing difficulty in coping with their illness. These components include the meaning that the illness has for the child and parent (their appraisal of the stress it presents to them), the specific illness related tasks and experiences that must be mastered for effective management of the disease, and the preferred coping styles and strategies of the child and family. The child's and family's response to the diagnosis of a specific illness can vary dramatically. Lipowski (1970) describes the meanings an illness may have and how such meanings may affect subsequent adaptation as follows. An illness may be perceived as: 1) a challenge, something to be mastered; 2) an enemy (an invasion of the body by harmful forces); 3) a punishment, either unjust or as a result of previous misconduct; 4) a sign of weakness or personal failing; 5) a release or a welcome respite from the demands of work, school, or interpersonal difficulties; 6) a strategy for securing attention or affection from others; 7) an irreparable loss or a change in function; 8) an opportunity for moral growth and development.

Assessment of the different meanings the illness may have for both the parent and the child is critical in understanding the emotional and behavioral responses of the family to the adaptational tasks the illness presents. Such an assessment may also provide insight into the effect of the illness on the child's behavior and may aid in understanding why some children's behavior worsens and others' improves with a similar disability. The determinants of individual outcome are, however, extremely complex and difficult to predict without knowledge of multiple factors. In addition to the child's stage of cognitive and psychosocial development (described in Chapter 2) it is also critical to understand the variety of intrapsychic processes that may be characteristic of the child and the parents. Maddison and Raphael (1971) suggest that numerous factors, such as the extent to which dependency, regression, restriction of activity, guilt, fear of mutilation, perception of pain, fear of death, and primary process thinking are present, will have a marked impact on the child's adjustment. The presence, extent, and impact of these factors should be considered in addition to the threat or possible rewards of the illness.

The threat involved in illness can, of course, be multifaceted. Depending upon the type and severity of illness, there can be a direct threat to the child's life and bodily integrity. In addition, the various medical procedures and the illness itself are often accompanied by physical pain, discomfort, incapacitation, and limitation in activity. The physical realm is, however, not the only area affected. Onset of an illness can dramatically change the child's accustomed social activity and may necessitate separation from family, siblings, and friends. This dislocation can be accompanied by the need to adjust to a new and often frightening hospital environment, as well as by exposure to confusing words, terms, and the need to make critical decisions in a stressful and unfamiliar situation. Finally, depending upon the extent of the physical disability, the child's self-concept, future plans, and emotional and cognitive equilibrium may be markedly threatened (Cohen & Lazarus, 1979; Mattsson, 1972; Moos & Tsu, 1977; Willis, Elliott, & Jay, 1982).

Effective coping with the illness must, consequently, be evaluated in multiple domains (the physiological, psychological, and social arenas), over time, and at different stages of the disease and the child's development. For example, a child who has displayed a very good adaptation to his or her seizures may experience great frustration and resentment during adolescence if unable to drive a car or participate in valued sport activities, particularly contact sports such as football, basketball, and hockey. Similarly, a female with diabetes may become aware at the time of adolescence of some of the long-term implications of her disease on her ability to conceive and successfully complete a pregnancy and at this time may experience significant distress.

Although the specific adaptive tasks posed by each illness are presented in the following chapters, an overview of the types of adaptive tasks and psychological issues typically encountered during a chronic illness is helpful. Cohen and Lazarus (1979) summarize these tasks to be mastered during illness as follows: "1) to reduce harmful environmental conditions and enhance prospects of recovery, 2) to tolerate or adjust to negative events and realities, 3) to maintain a positive self-image, 4) to maintain emotional equilibrium, and 5) to continue satisfying relationships with others" (p. 232). Failure to master these tasks adequately can result in unnecessarily prolonged episodes of illness, diminished self-esteem, distorted body image, depression, withdrawal from satisfying peer and family interactions, frequent school absences, heightened dependency on parents, sibling rivalry and resentment, and significant family disruption.

Psychological interventions can be helpful in preventing the development of serious personal, family, or social problems and in providing direct intervention for families for whom such problems have occurred. Such intervention often requires the interdisciplinary efforts of those involved in the care of the chronically ill child, including pediatricians, nurses, social workers, child-life workers, psychologists, and psychiatrists. Major preventive health care programs have included preparation of children for hospitalization and medical and surgical procedures (Melamed & Siegel, 1980; Petrillo & Sanger, 1980), facilitating children's cognitive understanding of their illness (Bibace & Walsh, 1981), helping children and their parents cope with impending death (Kellerman, 1980; Koocher, 1981; Spinetta, Elliott, Hennessey, Knapp, Sheposh, Sparta, & Sprigle, 1982), and diverse psychotherapeutic strategies, including individual and group psychotherapy, operant and social learning procedures, cognitive and behavioral self-regulation procedures, and biofeedback. (See Appendix A for treatment studies focusing on specific diseases and symptoms.)

The following chapters provide an overview of pertinent developmental, medical, and psychosocial issues presented by many common pediatric conditions, together with a review of psychotherapeutic techniques that have been successfully employed with each condition. For a comprehensive overview of the role of the pediatric psychologist in treating these children and of the opportunities for obtaining specialized training in these areas, the interested reader is referred to Tuma's (1982) excellent handbook.

References

Bibace, R., & Walsh, M.E. (Eds.). *Children's conceptions of health, illness, and bodily functions.* San Francisco: Jossey-Bass Inc., 1981.

Bruhn, J.G., Hampton, J.W., & Chandler, B.C. Clinical marginality and psychological adjustment in hemophilia. *Journal of Psychosomatic Research*, 1971, *15*, 207–213.

Cohen, F., & Lazarus, R.S. Coping with the stresses of illness. In G.C. Stone, F. Cohen, & N.E. Adler (Eds.), *Health psychology: A handbook.* San Francisco: Jossey-Bass Inc., 1979.

Collier, B.N. Comparisons between adolescents with and without diabetes. *The Personnel and Guidance Journal*, 1969, *47*(7), 679–684.

Hill, R. *Families under stress: Adjustment to the crises of war separation and reunion.* New York: Harper & Brothers Publishers, 1949.

Hodgman, C.H., McAnarney, E.R., Myers, G.J., Iker, H., McKinney, R., Parmelee, D., Schuster, B., & Tutihasi, M. Emotional complications of adolescent grand mal epilepsy. *The Journal of Pediatrics*, 1979, *95*(2), 309–312.

Kellerman, J. (Ed.). *Psychological aspects of childhood cancer.* Springfield, Illinois: Charles C. Thomas, 1980.

Koocher, G.P. Children's conceptions of death. In R. Bibace & M.E. Walsh (Eds.), *Children's conceptions of health, illness, and bodily functions.* San Francisco: Jossey-Bass Inc., 1981.

Lazarus, R.S., & Launier, R. Stress-related transactions between person and environment. In L.A. Pervin & M. Lewis (Eds.), *Perspectives in international psychology.* New York: Plenum Press, 1978.

Lipowski, Z.J. Physical illness, the individual and the coping processes. *Psychiatry in Medicine*, 1970, *1*, 91–102.

Maddison, D., & Raphael, B. Social and psychological consequences of chronic disease in childhood. *Medical Journal of Australia*, 1971, *2*, 1265–1270.

Mattsson, A. Long-term physical illness in childhood: A challenge to psychosocial adaptation. *Pediatrics*, 1972, *50*(5), 801–811.

McAnarney, E.R., Pless, I.B., Satterwhite, B., & Friedman, S.B. Psychological problems of children with chronic juvenile arthritis. *Pediatrics*, 1974, *53*(4), 523–528.

Melamed, B.G., & Siegel, L.J. *Behavioral medicine: Practical applications in health care.* New York: Springer Publishing Co., 1980.

Moos, R.H., & Tsu, V.D. The crisis of physical illness: An overview. In R.H. Moos (Ed.), *Coping with physical illness.* New York: Plenum Medical Book Company, 1977.

Petrillo, M., & Sanger, S. *Emotional care of hospitalized children: An environmental approach* (2nd ed.). Philadelphia: J.B. Lippincott Company, 1980.

Pless, I.B., & Douglas, J.W.B. Chronic illness in childhood: Part 1. Epidemiological and clinical characteristics. *Pediatrics*, 1971, *47*(2), 405–414.

Pless, I.B., & Pinkerton, P. *Chronic childhood disorder: Promoting patterns of adjustment.* London: Henry Kimpton Publishers, 1975.

Pless, I.B., & Roghmann, K.J. Chronic illness and its consequences: Observations based on three epidemiologic surveys. *The Journal of Pediatrics*, 1971, *79*(3), 351–359.

Pless, I.B., Roghmann, K., & Haggerty, R.J. Chronic illness, family functioning, and psychological adjustment: A model for the allocation ·of preventive mental health services. *International Journal of Epidemiology*, 1972, *1*(3), 271–277.

Pless, I.B., & Satterwhite, B.B. Chronic illness. In R.J. Haggerty, K.J. Roghmann, & I.B. Pless (Eds.), *Child health and the community*. New York: John Wiley & Sons, 1975.

Rutter, M., Tizard, J., & Whitmore, K. (Eds.). *Education, health and behavior: Psychological and medical study of childhood development*. London: Longman, 1970.

Russo, D.C., & Varni, J.W. Behavioral pediatrics. In D.C. Russo & J.W. Varni (Eds.), *Behavioral pediatrics: Research and practice*. New York: Plenum Press, 1982.

Sperling, E. Psychological issues in chronic illness and handicap. In E. Gellert (Ed.), *Psychosocial aspects of pediatric care*. New York: Grune & Stratton, 1978.

Spinetta, J.J., Elliott, E.S., Hennessey, J.S., Knapp, V.S., Sheposh, J.P., Sparta, S.N., & Sprigle, R.P. The pediatric psychologist's role in catastrophic illness: Research and clinical issues. In J.M. Tuma (Ed.), *Handbook for the practice of pediatric psychology*. New York: John Wiley & Sons, 1982.

Tavormina, J.B., Kastner, L.S., Slater, P.M., & Watt, S.L. Chronically ill children: A psychologically and emotionally deviant population? *Journal of Abnormal Child Psychology*, 1976, *4*(2), 99–110.

Tuma, J.M. (Ed.). *Handbook for the practice of pediatric psychology*. New York: John Wiley & Sons, 1982.

Willis, D.J., Elliott, C.H., & Jay, S.M. Psychological effects of physical illness and its concomitants. In J.M. Tuma (Ed.), *Handbook for the practice of pediatric psychology*. New York: John Wiley & Sons, 1982.

2 | The Child's View of Illness: Interaction with Psychosocial Development

Chronic illness during childhood can have a profound effect on the child's psychological and social development. Restrictions on physical activities, need for medication, limitations or prohibitions of food intake, and diminished energy or stamina may all interfere with the child's sense of mastery and control over his or her body and life. Similarly, the child's perception of his or her own body is particularly vulnerable to disturbance and distortion during illness. The pain, malaise, fear, and anxiety that can accompany the onset of physical problems can also lead to withdrawal from ordinary activities and experiences and interfere with friendships and the development of interpersonal skills.

Children and their parents respond to these stresses and concerns with differing levels of adaptive functioning. Some of the general factors that can influence the impact of an illness on the child's subsequent adaptation have been discussed in Chapter 1. This section focuses on the child's age and level of cognitive, emotional, and social development as critical factors in assessing the psychologic impact of illness. Table 2-1 provides an overview of the developmental changes that occur from infancy through adolescence, and illustrates the types of developmental crises that can occur in various age groups.

Infancy (0–1½ Years)

The primary developmental goal at this time is to establish and develop trust in significant others. During the first few months of a normal infant's life, the infant develops a sense of basic trust that his or her needs are going to be met. For the chronically ill baby, this sense of basic trust can be difficult to establish. The baby is in a very different environment, one which is often frightening, painful, unpredictable, chaotic, and unsatisfying. It is important at this time for the ill baby to have increased contact, comfort, and expression of affection from caretakers, nursing staff, and others providing physical care. This kind of physical comfort can make the pain and suffering somewhat more bearable. When such comfort is not

TABLE 2-1

Stages in Psychological Development and Potential Developmental Problems

Age	*Psychosexual* (Freud)	*Cognitive* (Piaget)	*Personal-Social* (Erikson)	*Moral* (Kohlberg)	*Potential Adverse Impact*
Infancy	Oral	Early Sensori-Motor	Trust	No Moral Concepts	Insecure Attachment Diminished Responsiveness
Toddler	Anal	Late Sensori-Motor	Autonomy	Fear of Punishment	Excessive Maternal Control Power Struggles Passivity
Preschooler	Phallic (Oedipal)	Preoperational Thought Egocentrism	Initiative	Absolute Good/Bad	Extreme Guilt Fear of Mutilation Inhibition of Initiative
Elementary School	Latent	Concrete Thinking & Problem Solving	Industry	General Rules Obey Authority	Sense of Inferiority Feelings of Inadequacy
Adolescent	Genital	Abstract, Logical, and Symbolic Problem Solving	Identity Intimacy	Abstract Moral Code	Authority Conflict Low Self-Esteem

available because of maternal or paternal absence, because the care is inadequate, or because the condition of the child (e.g., severely burned) does not permit it, the infant or child can develop feelings of insecurity, helplessness, and in extreme cases depression and profound withdrawal from social contacts.

Parental attachment is facilitated by allowing close contact and participation in the physical caretaking of the infant. During this time the parent is in need of considerable support in order to continue parenting under the stress of the illness and subsequent disruption in family life. The medical staff can facilitate this process by establishing a trusting relationship with the parent in which they teach and model effective strategies for caring for the sick infant. For this process to be maximally effective for both the infant and the parent, it is helpful to keep the number of hospital staff interacting with the parent to a minimum. During this time the infant needs adequate tactile and sensory stimulation as well, and collaboration with other health care staff to facilitate such stimulation is often necessary in order to identify ways in which it can be provided without interfering in necessary medical management. Behavioral indications that needs for stimulation and contact are not being met can include frequent crying, restlessness, difficulty sleeping, rocking, head banging, gastrointestinal disturbances, withdrawal, and depression (Petrillo & Sanger, 1980).

Another developmental change that occurs during this very early period is a growing fear of strangers and reliance on one's parents as a "secure base" (Ainsworth, 1973). When an infant or young child is hospitalized or chronically ill, this fear of strangers can be intensified because of the child's painful and frightening experiences (surgeries, blood transfusions, isolation, injections, etc.). Continuity of maternal care is especially important at this time. Although fear of strangers and separation anxiety are normally thought to be at their peak around the eighth to ninth month of life, in the hospitalized ill infant signs of mourning and withdrawal are often seen much earlier. Alternatively, the infant can show excessive dependence on strangers and avoidance or refusal to interact with his or her parents. The clinging, demanding behavior often exhibited by the baby can be quite upsetting to the parents, and it is helpful for them to understand that this is a manifestation of separation anxiety. Since separation at this time can interfere with the parents' attachment to the baby and the development of their competence in learning necessary caretaking skills, allowing the parent to "room in" when the infant is hospitalized is particularly important. Disruptions in the attachment process may result in an infant who fails to thrive, disturbed parent-child interactions, or an increased incidence of child abuse or neglect.

Toddler Period (1½–3 Years)

The major developmental goal at this time is to establish autonomy or independence. Parental or nursing care which diminishes the child's responsibilities for feeding him- or herself, bathing, dressing, or bowel and bladder functions can be perceived as very threatening. Children in this age period may show different reactions, becoming, for example, excessively dependent and passive. This is particularly marked in a child for whom achieving independence has always been a struggle and who derives most of his or her satisfaction from passively receiving nurturance from others. This child has not yet learned to actively assert his or her individuality. The opposite reaction that can also occur during this period is defiant negativism—saying "NO" to all requests and not allowing appropriate care to be given by other caregivers. To the extent possible, it is helpful to continue familiar routines and allow the child to function independently in areas in which he or she has obtained competence.

The toddler is also likely to experience the greatest amount of regression, since separation anxiety is often most debilitating at this time. Manifestations of regression can include a return to more infantile behaviors such as soiling, wetting, thumb sucking, and bottle feedings. It is very important, however, to remember that when a child is under severe stress, regression is a coping mechanism frequently employed temporarily as a means of dealing with this stress. At such a time regression may have a very adaptive function, since it can allow the child to conserve energy and accept attention and care from others that can facilitate recovery. It is only when regression persists for an unduly long time or is too extreme in its manifestation that it becomes problematic and requires psychological intervention.

Once again, encouraging the parent to "room in" can be particularly helpful in reducing the separation anxiety. Attachment to the mother is very strong at this age, and the child is often preoccupied with fears of abandonment when separated. In order for the normal process of separation-individuation to take place successfully it is critical for the mother to be present as a secure base from which the child can explore. Petrillo and Sanger (1980) provide a variety of suggestions for reducing the stress that can accompany hospitalization, such as allowing the child to use transitional objects (stuffed animals, favorite blankets) for security, helping the parents establish a consistent pattern of visits and an effective way to manage the child's fear and anxiety at separation, and providing an extensive play program in the hospital for cognitive, social, and motor stimulation.

During this period specific parental reactions, especially if excessive or employed beyond the time period indicated, can foster pathological dependency in the child. For example, during acute phases of the illness or during the initial diagnostic period, parents are often appropriately protective of and permissive with the child. If such permissiveness extends over an unduly long period, the child can become quite dependent and demanding. The parent or others interacting with the child, when faced with incessant demands, may begin to feel resentful or hostile. In time, inappropriately harsh expressions of anger or rejection of the child may occur for which the parent often feels very guilty. This guilt can then lead to overprotective and permissive attitudes and, thus, the cycle often begins anew.

Children in this stage are most often traumatized by the separation from their parents and the stress of the procedures. They display little cognitive understanding of what is wrong with them or what caused it. While doll play with appropriate hospital-like materials may facilitate expression of concerns and fears, for most children in this age period it is best to avoid giving information about the inside of the body, since these concepts are not yet understood. Children at this age can mistakenly believe that illness is a punishment for misbehavior or a sign of rejection by their parents. This response is also common during the preschool period.

Preschool Period (3–5 Years)

From three to five the primary developmental goal is the development of conscience, a sense of right and wrong. The preschool child's idea about why illness, or the pain associated with an illness or its treatment, occurs is often related to emerging moral concepts in this regard. For example, preschool children commonly think pain is the result of mistreatment by their parents or that it is a punishment because they were bad.

Quotations throughout Petrillo and Sanger's (1980) book illustrate children's concepts of illness as punishment for their misbehavior. One little boy said, "Well, you know when you do something bad and your mother doesn't punish you? Then God has to do it" (p. 72). (Clearly, for this boy the infliction of pain was viewed as a punishment.) Or, the two year old child who screamed over and over again, "I'm sorry; I said I'm sorry" (p. 69) when the nurse started an IV in preparation for chemotherapy. Another reaction that can occur when a child is hospitalized is the feeling of rejection. "Soon after two-year-old Amy acquired a sibling, she was admitted to the hospital for repair of an umbilical hernia. She explained to her nurse that she was brought to the hospital because her mother did not want her anymore" (p. 69). Similarly, a condition may be thought to be the result of aggression and rejection on the part of a sibling.

Although many of the children's ideas seem quite preposterous, Western man's view of illness as resulting from natural causes is actually a recent phenomenon. Previously, explanations involving sin or evil spirits were common; and in many communities or for specific types of illness, such attributions still prevail. One couple from a rural county in Minnesota gave birth to an infant with a congenital cyanotic heart defect. The religious community to which these parents belonged believed that heart defects occurred as a punishment from God when a woman had been unfaithful (O'Dougherty, 1981).

Viewing illness as a punishment can produce inhibition of initiative or fear of trying new things. During the preschool years particularly, this problem can be compounded by the magical thinking characteristic of this age group. Preschool children often believe that their thoughts and wishes are so powerful that they can cause direct harm (such as hating someone can cause them to be sick or even die). This results in considerable confusion. The converse of this—believing that good thoughts will protect you from harm—also occurs. Other superstitious beliefs, particularly about specific medical procedures or the origin of a specific disease, can result in substantial misconceptions: "You get penis-illin if you touch your penis" (Bergmann & Freud, 1965, p. 82) or the belief that a CAT scan of your brain allows someone to read your bad thoughts (Petrillo & Sanger, 1980). It is apparent from these quotations that children will interpret what is happening and that their interpretations may be both very inappropriate and a source of great distress or guilt.

Another fear typical at this age is that of mutilation, a fear surgical procedures and operations often intensify. Some young children think that surgical operations are similar to actions they have performed on their own toys—cutting heads off, ripping the arms and legs off, etc. The importance of clarifying surgical procedures should not be underestimated. It is important for children to know when they are going to have an operation, what (tonsils, appendix, etc.) is going to be removed, and that that is the only thing that is going to be removed.

Bibace and Walsh (1980, 1981) have developed a classification system which combines Piagetian stages of cognitive development with the type of content typical of children's responses regarding the cause of common illnesses at different ages. The children were asked questions about the cause of a number of illnesses (e.g., colds, measles, headaches, heart attacks, cancer) and their responses were coded along a developmentally ordered scale.

In the preoperational stage, phenomenism and contagion are characteristic of the types of explanations offered. Phenomenistic explanations are characterized by defining illness by association with an external phenomenon that co-occurs with the illness, but is spatially or temporally remote. In such explanations, the child centers on one aspect of the illness based on his or her unique experience (egocentrism) and cannot specify the causal mechanism involved other than to attribute it to magic or simultaneous occurrence.

> *Example:* How do people get colds? "From the sun." How does the sun give you a cold? "It just does, that's all." How do people get measles? "From God." How does God give people measles? "God does it in the sky." (Bibace & Walsh, 1980, p. 914.)

When the explanation relies on contagion as the causal mechanism, the cause of the illness is an external object or person spatially or temporally close to, but not touching, the child. The child is still unable to describe the causal mechanism between the source and the illness, but the hypothesized causal factors are more relevant and less egocentric.

> *Example:* How do people get colds? "From outside." How do they get them from outside? "They just do that's all. They come when someone else gets near you." How? "I don't know—by magic I think." (Bibace & Walsh, 1980, p. 914).

At this age the child begins to have a rudimentary understanding of internal body parts, illness, and health. This understanding parallels the developmental progress observed in the cognitive area and is characterized by preoperational thought. As mentioned, the child's responses to questions about illness are often magical, superstitious and circular in logic. Preschool children demonstrate a global awareness of the body and body activities, but are not able to differentiate structure and function. During this period, the child does begin to identify specific body parts, but views body functioning in a global, undifferentiated manner. In Gellert's (1978) study of children's knowledge about body parts and functions she found that the mean number of body parts named increased steadily from 3.3 for preschoolers to 13 for older adolescents. Preschool children most often mention internal body parts that can be felt (bones), heard (heart), or seen (blood). Children in this age group (and some early elementary school aged children as well) often believe that what they eat or eliminate (food, liquids, bowel movements) is part of them. By age eleven these items are no longer considered to be part of the body (Gellert, 1978). Some young children, when asked to draw what is inside the body on a figure outline, indicate that the whole inside of the body is filled up with food. An example of a preoperational child's concepts in this area, obtained from a five year old boy in our hospital is illustrated in Figure 2-1.

As they get older children believe that parts of the body are dispensable. Typically, parts considered dispensable are those capable of regeneration, artificial substitution, or those for which redundancy exists (lungs, kidneys, fingers). However, some preschool children believe that *all* body parts are needed in order to live. Such a view may well contribute to the anxiety a preschooler might experience if a part of the body is injured or if a part must be removed through surgery. Gellert (1978) found in her study of 96 children that 11 believed that hair was indispensable. She speculated that this belief may relate to some children's extreme resistance to having their hair cut. Such a belief may also play a role in the anxiety children experience upon losing their hair during chemotherapy or in viewing a child who has lost all of his or her hair. The merciless teasing that sometimes follows may be a way of coping with this tremendous anxiety.

Younger children also often believe that the major purpose of the skin is to keep the body together "so blood won't fall out" and "to not make see the blood and bones" (Gellert, 1978, p. 26). Given the prevailing view of many young children that the intactness of the skin is *vital* to their bodily integrity, it is not surprising that injections, cuts, incisions, and drawing blood samples are viewed with much concern, anxiety, and distress. Children also commonly believe that a Bandaid stops the blood from coming out of the hole made by the needle and that without this Bandaid they could lose all of their blood (Petrillo & Sanger, 1980). Their insistence on this Bandaid following blood drawing likely relates to this belief. In this age period children are prone to overgeneralize and may believe that all body parts are vulnerable. Castration anxieties and mutilation fantasies prior to surgery are particularly common to this age group and indicate a tendency to view illness, damage, or removal of a specific part in an overly inclusive manner. Consequently, it is

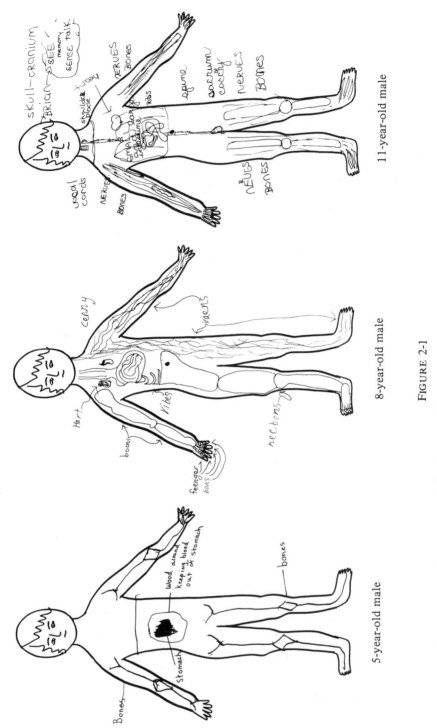

FIGURE 2-1

Developmental Changes in Children's Understanding of Internal Body Parts

particularly important to reassure the child that the illness or medical procedure is limited and specific and to discuss repair and recovery of function when possible.

The body part most frequently judged the most important is the heart; second is the brain. The eyes and parts associated with breathing (lungs, nose, throat, and mouth) are all rated important as well. While the size and location of the heart were identified quite early, preschool children could give only a general, global description of its function. Crider (1981) cites an example of a child in this stage describing the function of the heart as follows: "Something that pumps inside the body. It helps you move around so you will be living. When you breathe it pumps" (p. 56). The brain is not well understood and is often confused with the skull; consequently, many young children think that the brain is made up of bone. Finally, some young children judge a part important if they have been given instructions for careful cleaning of that body part (e.g., "the feet; you have to take good care of them," or "you have to scrub them between your toes, which is real hard") (Gellert, 1978, p. 22).

While the names and functions of external body parts are learned at an early age, children often have considerable difficulty learning about internal body parts. This may be due, in part, to the fact that these organs are hidden and not available for physical manipulation and exploration.

Children have only a very limited opportunity to observe directly how the body operates or how different systems relate to each other. Only proprioceptive, kinesthetic, tactile, and olfactory cues are directly perceived, and these cues can be misleading or confusing. Also, descriptions of complex bodily processes such as digestion, elimination, respiration, and central nervous system functions are difficult to translate into words and concepts that the young child can understand (Blos, 1978; Crider, 1981). The importance of direct observation, action, and manipulation in fostering cognitive growth in the child has been well documented. The lack of opportunity in this area may present difficult obstacles to children's conceptual growth in this area. When describing to a child the type of illness he or she has or when preparing a child for treatment, it is helpful to provide a body outline, visual aids, or a doll with visible internal parts to facilitate more accurate understanding. Following the medical or surgical treatment, doll play, utilizing toys or equipment similar to that used during the medical procedures, can increase comprehension and aid in the expression of fears and concerns (Petrillo & Sanger, 1980).

The examples in this section illustrate how important it is for the hospital support staff and parents to understand that the child's level of cognitive development strongly influences his or her thinking about illness, even after receiving factual information. Children's concepts follow a regular developmental sequence closely related to concept development in the associated areas of physical causality and physical identity. The child in this age period is, thus, particularly vulnerable to distortions and misconceptions about what is wrong, what is happening, and how it will all turn out. Support, reassurance, and specific examples and illustrations can reduce the guilt and blame the child might inappropriately feel, as well as provide the milieu for further questioning and expression of concerns.

Elementary School Period (6-12 Years)

In this age period the primary developmental goal is industry, achievement, and task accomplishment. There is still considerable overlap with the preschool period, particularly in continuing to view illness as punishment for misbehavior. During this period concerns about the cause of illness often relate to specific family interactions. For example, a ten year old with undescended testicles believed his condition was the result of his older sister having dropped him when he was two months old because she did not like him (Petrillo & Sanger, 1980). In another instance, a child who received a skull fracture while riding his bike in the street concluded that the fracture was a punishment for disobeying his parents. Typically, the parent has made a remark such as "See, I told you, you shouldn't have been riding your bike in the street." Such a pairing of comments and events often results in an association between becoming sick and the breaking of various rules and regulations. This pattern is concurrent with Kohlberg's (1976) stages of moral development in which the evaluations of the school aged child are strongly based on respect for authority and rules. During this time there is an internalization of conscience and incorporation of parents' and society's values. Fears of castration or mutilation diminish and separation anxiety is significantly reduced.

Striking cognitive changes also occur. Most children in this age group now attain concrete operational thought in which they are able to use classification and causal reasoning concretely in relation to their own experiences. Children in this stage of cognitive development have a more scientific orientation: they think in terms of cause and effect, make generalizations, understand relational terms such as "larger than" and "smaller than," and reason about real, concrete objects in systematic ways. The child clearly distinguishes between what is internal and external, is less egocentric, and can conceptualize the reversal of processes; however, difficulty in abstract thinking and an inability to consider hypothetical possibilities remain (Piaget, 1952/1963).

These cognitive advances allow for much greater understanding of the body, illness, and medical procedures. For example, Steward and Regalbuto (1975) studied how well healthy children in kindergarten (preoperational) and third grade (concrete operational) understood two commonly used medical instruments—the stethoscope and the syringe. While all of the children interviewed knew that one use of the stethoscope was to listen to the heartbeat, they differed dramatically in their understanding of why this was done. Preoperational children's explanations were characterized by magical thinking, egocentrism, and the use of either/or categories, rather than conceptualizations in terms of multiple or continuous variables. For example, kindergarten children often thought the stethoscope was used to determine life or death, to see if the heart was beating or not beating, or to see if they were happy. Few kindergarten aged children understood the reason why shots were given or how they worked. They often held a limited and specific concept of medicine ("You give it with a spoon." "You drink it." "It doesn't sting." [Steward

& Regalbuto, 1975, p. 148]) which prevented their understanding that medicine could also be in the syringe. When asked if the shot had medicine in it, one child responded, "No . . . because only the needle goes in." The shot was thought to work because "it goes in your body and it pushes your blood" (Steward & Regalbuto, 1975, p. 148). In contrast, third grade children were able to deal with several variables simultaneously in their conceptualization and showed evidence of generalization and causal thinking. For example, a third grader might respond that the doctor used a stethoscope "to see if you have too fast a heartbeat" or "to see if it's beating properly" (Steward & Regalbuto, 1975, pp. 147-148). Older children also offered more involved causal, although not entirely correct, explanations about the physiology of the heart and circulatory system and the reasons shots were given.

In the concrete operational stage children are able to differentiate the structure and function of various body parts and are able to name significantly more internal organs. (See Figure 2-1 for an example). The child is also more precise in describing the specific attributes of the different organs in terms of their shape, substance, and purpose. Typically, organs are viewed as substances or containers. For example, the lungs are for holding air, the stomach for food, the heart for blood, the brain for thoughts. Each part is treated individually, and there is little integration between the various organs of the body. Understanding or defining the processes involved in the various systems (respiration, circulation, digestion, elimination, etc.) is a very complex task that is poorly understood, if at all, by children at this stage (Crider, 1981). For example, very few children at this age understand the role of the lungs, skin, and blood in breathing. Although many children think breathing is necessary for life, they do not know why and think of it merely as taking in and expelling air with little understanding of the transformations that take place during respiration. During this age period children sometimes think eating is a function of the lungs; they may think of the air as food for the body which passes through the lungs and then assume that food must pass through the lungs as well before reaching the stomach (Gellert, 1978).

The process of digestion and the organs associated with it are also poorly understood. Under the age of 9 few children spontaneously draw the stomach, although many children have ideas about it when questioned specifically. When the stomach is drawn, it is usually placed below its correct position and its size overestimated (Gellert, 1978). This may possibly be due to an inability to differentiate the many sensations (nausea, fullness, gas, gurglings) associated with the entire gastrointestinal area from those associated with the stomach. Explanations of the stomach are often rather rudimentary, and there appears to be a great deal of confusion and misconception about what happens to food after digestion.

Although an increasing number of children at this stage do associate the heart with respiration and circulation, they do not understand the processes involved. Similarly, children are very confused about elimination processes. In Gellert's study many children considered constipation a serious—even terminal—condition and were very concerned about being able to produce sufficient amounts. The children were also surprisingly confused about the function of the bladder and its relationship to urination. Finally, although most children were able to identify separate body parts, these body parts were often thought to be made up of the same materials, typically bone, blood, skin, and flesh.

When they asked children questions about specific illnesses, Bibace and Walsh (1980, 1981) found two primary types of explanations characteristic at this age—contamination and internalization. In explanations relying on contamination, the cause of the illness is an external person, object, or action harmful to or bad for the body. The illness is transmitted through physical contact with this harmful source. Bad behavior, dirt, or germs can all cause illness; and children in this stage often believe that they can prevent illness by not allowing their bodies to touch the contaminated source:

> *Example:* What is a cold? "It's like in wintertime." How do people get them? "You're outside without a hat and you start sneezing. Your head would get cold—the cold would touch it—and then it would go all over your body. (Bibace & Walsh, 1980, p. 914)

When internalization is advanced as the explanatory mechanism, the cause of the illness is either an external contaminant (dirt, germs, etc.), which was internalized through swallowing, inhaling, etc., or an unhealthy internal body state (old age, obesity, high blood pressure). Typically, the illness is still described in global, undifferentiated terms:

> *Example:* What is a cold? "You sneeze a lot, you talk funny, and your nose is clogged up." How do people get colds? "In winter, they breathe in too much air into their nose and it blocks up the nose." How does this cause colds? "The bacteria gets in by breathing. Then the lungs get too soft (child exhales) and it goes to the nose." How does it get better? "Hot fresh air, it gets in the nose and pushes the cold air back." (Bibace & Walsh, 1980, p. 914)

For children at this stage of cognitive development, it is appropriate to continue to use body outlines to explain anatomy and physiology. It is also crucial, however, to obtain an adequate picture of the child's knowledge and understanding so that information that is not too abstract or complex can be presented. As with younger children, encouraging questions and expression of feelings, as well as active participation in the learning process, is essential. At this stage children particularly enjoy opportunities to interact with same sex peers and to meet in groups to work on projects or learn about their disease and its treatment. The experience of hospitalization can provide an opportunity for meaningful social interaction with both peers and hospital staff, if adequate preparation and support are provided. If the child is quite immature, displays significant regression, or expresses great anxiety and fear of mutilation or abandonment, the guidelines for interacting with the preschool-aged child may be more appropriate to follow in planning intervention strategies (Petrillo & Sanger, 1980).

Medical restrictions or activity limitations during this period can present difficult developmental problems by interfering with the child's sense of achievement, mastery, and skill development. Restriction of activity can impede the development of competence in the arenas of home, school, and peer relations. Similarly, restriction of play can block one of the major channels available to the child for working out tension or resolving aggressive feelings. One consequence can be withdrawal from social relationships and a retreat to a fantasy environment of unhealthy proportions. The child who complains about restrictions (although this child may present short-term management difficulties) may be coping with the situation in a more healthy way than the child who is too quiet, passive, and content to withdraw into fantasy. If an illness extends for a prolonged period, the likelihood of significant disruption of the child's peer relationships and skill development increases. It is particularly important to provide avenues to friendships and achievement, since the basis for feelings of self-esteem and confidence in one's ability to work effectively is established during this period.

Adolescence (12–19 Years)

In this stage the primary developmental task is to establish a self-identity capable of independent action. This sense of identity, feeling of security, and sense of self-worth can be difficult to establish when an illness affecting bodily functioning or appearance arises. Illness often signifies weakness for many teenagers; and in fact, it often is accompanied by loss of strength or restriction of activities. For boys, chronic illness or disability may interfere with the development of their sense of masculinity. For girls, an illness may lead to feelings of being different, damaged, without worth.

Other salient goals during the adolescent period include gradual emancipation from the family, forming heterosexual attachments, and developing a personal code of ethics and behavior, as well as consideration and preparation for a career (Petrillo & Sanger, 1980). A severe or chronic illness during this period can interfere with development in any of these areas.

Issues now emerge as primary that were of less concern during the earlier periods. Foremost among these are the needs for privacy, confidentiality, participation in decision making, consent for treatment, and deep concern over how illness or disability might affect relationships with the opposite sex, fertility and reproductive capacity, and vocational possibilities. These concerns directly relate to the developmental goals outlined above.

Adolescence is often usefully subdivided into three phases: early (12-14 years); middle (15-16 years); and late (17-19 years). Particular issues are more salient in each period. During early adolescence, for example, there is considerable vacillation between dependent and independent desires, with problems following rules, regulations, and authority quite typical. Secretiveness, defiance of traditional values, self-preoccupation, loneliness, and depression are frequently encountered. The adolescent may use hostile, provocative ways of eliciting attention, may display hypochondriacal concerns and might become quite egocentric and self-absorbed. By mid-adolescence reliance on the peer group for support, values, and recognition is more firmly established. Attempts to form relationships with the opposite sex, sexual experimentation, and reluctance to confide in parents are quite common. Finally, the older adolescent is much more future oriented and often is fairly emotionally independent from parents and peers. This is often a period in which goals are established; ideals, aspirations, and relationships are evaluated; and feelings become more manageable and under control (Petrillo & Sanger, 1980).

Important cognitive changes occur that can facilitate the adolescent's ability to cope with illness. Once the formal operational stage of cognitive development is attained, the adolescent is able to think and reason in abstract terms, to consider alternative possibilities and solutions, and to consider hypothetical possibilities as a basis for theoretical problem solving.

All of these cognitive advances facilitate understanding of the body and the body systems. During the transition from concrete to formal operational thought, the adolescent becomes increasingly able to integrate each body structure with its function. At first, the adolescent is able to conceptualize various steps in a sequence through which activities occur. For example, the process of digestion is characterized in a series of sequential spatial movements of food from the mouth through the throat to the stomach, where it is digested, and then through the bloodstream to the body and body tissues. At this stage, adolescents are able to describe these processes as involving various transformations of substances. Children and adolescents in the formal operational period are also able to provide more complex physiological explanations of the hierarchical integration of the various organs and organ systems. At this stage the body organs are differentiated, yet integrated within a system. Transformations are viewed as coordinated, reversible, and mutually interdependent (Crider, 1981).

In Gellert's (1962) study, children below the age of 8 typically thought that the food kept traveling downward to the feet and that it remained in the body or that it could only come out the way it entered (i.e., by throwing it up). In Gellert's (1962) study it was not until adolescence that the majority (67%) of children believed that some food stays in the body (and is converted to energy) and some is eliminated. Similarly, Nagy (1953) identified three concepts of digestion children have: 1) the food goes to the head or the neck; 2) the food goes to the stomach; or 3) the food goes beyond the stomach because it is assimilated by the body or evacuated. Among the school-aged children in her study, digestion was not well understood. Many children thought of digestion as food storage rather than as a transformation process.

Similarly, although many young children knew about the brain, it was not until grades 5 and 6 that children spontaneously listed cells, nerves, or the nervous system. The brain was thought to be inside the head and made up of bone, blood, skin, flesh, and cells. Confusion between the brain and the skull was apparent with many young children thinking the main constituent of the brain was bone. The brain was thought to perform a mainly intellectual activity, whereas when the nerves were mentioned, they were associated primarily with emotional functions. (Interestingly, the variety of different functions ascribed to the nerves was larger than that ascribed to any other body part in Gellert's (1962) study.) In both Gellert's and Nagy's studies, nerves were associated with negative emotional states, such as nervousness, fear, irritability, and tension. Other children thought nerves were needed to absorb shock or to stay alive. Only older children were able to explain that nerves conduct messages between the brain and the body or control and regulate mental activities and sensory experiences (Gellert, 1978). (Refer to Figure 2-1 for illustration.)

The complex interaction and hierarchical integration required to explain the functioning of most body systems are not achieved until formal operational thought is clearly established. As an example, Crider (1981) provides a description of the formal operational child's or adolescent's thought regarding nutrition, which can encompass concepts of the various organ systems involved, as well as cell metabolism, circulation, waste removal, and both neurologic and hormonal regulation.

Formal operational explanations of illness are characterized by an ability to explain illness in terms of internal bodily dysfunction, to provide differentiated explanations of the etiology of various illnesses, and to speculate and hypothesize about cause and effect relationships. Explanations of illness are typically either physiologic or psychophysiologic (Bibace & Walsh, 1980). When a physiologic explanation is provided, illness is explained in terms of malfunctioning internal organs or processes. Multiple causes for the dysfunction can be postulated and causal mechanisms are explained in a step by step sequence of events.

> *Example:* What is a cold? "It's when you get all stuffed up inside, your sinuses get filled up with mucus. Sometimes your lungs do, too, and you get a cough." How do people get colds? "They come from viruses I guess. Other people have the virus and it gets into your blood stream and it causes a cold." (Bibace & Walsh, 1980, p. 915)

Psychophysiological explanations describe illness in terms of internal physiological processes, but the individual is aware that psychological processes (thoughts and feelings) can affect bodily processes. Biological and psychological determinants are distinguished.

> *Example:* What is a heart attack? "It's when your heart stops working right. Sometimes it's pumping too slow or too fast." How do people get a heart attack? "It can come from being all nerve wracked. You worry too much. The tension can affect your heart." (Bibace & Walsh, 1980, p. 915)

Consequently, the adolescent patient in the formal operational stage is capable of understanding his or her illness at an advanced level; however, possessing the cognitive capacity to understand is not synonymous with current competence in this area. It is extremely important for those working with the adolescent to discover what information has been provided and how well it is understood. Petrillo and Sanger (1980) emphasize that in their experience adolescents are often credited with understanding they do not have. Often embarrassment about asking particular questions or confusion regarding the appropriate terms to use can block effective communication. They suggest involving the adolescent in educational meetings where information can be presented, questions encouraged, slang words translated into medical terminology, and social support provided. In addition, opportunities to talk privately (without parents present) with the physician and hospital staff can facilitate discussion of concerns, questions, or practices. Assurances of confidentiality are appropriate, provided that the adolescent is also informed that a confidence may not be held if he or she is in jeopardy (suicidal, homicidal, refusing needed treatments). If such a circumstance arises, the adolescent should be told that the confidence cannot be respected and the reasons for this discussed.

Identifying the adolescent's strategies of coping and defense, differentiating those who have a realistic acceptance of their disease and its treatment from those who are overly conforming, compliant, and submissive, or defiant and noncompliant is of great importance. Alternative coping strategies can present serious management problems, in addition to interfering directly or indirectly with treatment. These include those involving marked isolation, accompanied by unrealistic or frightening fantasies, or direct acting out, incorporating a combative, aggressive, or resistant attitude toward the treatment needed for the illness. A defense typically used by teenagers (and by adults) is intellectualization in an attempt to dissociate the physical aspects of the disease from the emotional impact of that disease. This can be an adaptive coping strategy if it prevents the individual from feeling overwhelmed by what is happening, but it can become a detriment when it blocks working through the emotions associated with the impact of the disease, or the grief associated with disability, loss of functioning, or change in physical health.

Compensation is perhaps one of the most successful mechanisms for coping with disability, particularly if the adolescent can engage in substitute activities or new ways of interaction with staff and peers. Some of the ways in which a therapist might facilitate compensation could include helping a patient select clothing that conceals disfigurement, exploring new hair fashions, promoting consultations with a beautician, work on skill improvement in areas not dependent upon physical activity (chess, reading, computers, etc.), and encouraging participation in therapeutic or social groups for adolescents with similar physical illnesses. Identification with the medical staff and interest in teaching others about illness and its treatment are other ways patients can enhance their feelings of self-esteem and competence. Some adolescents are able to express their concerns and distress directly, while others rely on artistic expression through drawing, poetry, music, or dance. Table 2-2 illustrates adaptive techniques for coping with chronic illness.

TABLE 2-2

Adaptive Techniques for Coping with Chronic Illness

Coping Technique	Illustration	Source
Artistic Expression	Pictures illustrating "sometimes you feel like a pin cushion" "some needles felt like fish hooks"	The Center for Attitudinal Healing, 1978, p. 24, 42
Humor	Sign posted outside Edward's (age 12) room: "Beware of mad dogs. Will get anyone with needles."	Petrillo and Sanger, 1980, p. 169
Forgiveness	"Forgiveness is forgiving the doctor if he puts a needle in and finds out he has put it in the wrong place and has to put it in a second time. Just letting the incident float away."	The Center for Attitudinal Healing, 1978, p. 61
Acceptance	"Don't hide yourself or the fact that you have an illness, ... You have had a little bit taken away from you, but you are still a person, . . . If others can't deal with your honesty, then it's their problem. I've been able to get close to my Mom and Dad, and we've even had a good cry together. . . ." Larianne, age 13.	Woodward et al., 1978, p. 56
Identification	"When I give myself my shot, you're doing it from both ends. You feel it from the doctor's side pushing it in, and you feel it from the patient's side going in. This way I feel the pain that you feel."	Lewis, 1978, p. 19–20
Participation in decision making	"There are lots of things you can decide, that don't interrupt the doctor. . . . Like you can sit up or lie down, or you can watch or not, or you can turn to look at TV or your Mom. . . . I always watch, after all, it's my body."	Steward & Steward, 1981, p. 76
Compensation	"Life is not a matter of holding good cards, but of playing a poor hand well."	Robert Louis Stevenson

When is it appropriate to ask for a psychological consultation regarding a patient's response to an illness? First, if depression, regression, or infantile behavior persists beyond the early stages of a disease or inhibits the child's or adolescent's return to more normal developmental pursuits, psychological referral may be indicated. Second, whenever extreme denial of the illness or acting out begins to interfere with medical management or compliance with needed procedures and treatments, psychological consultation can be helpful. Third, if suicidal ideation or marked withdrawal is observed, consultation is needed. It is, however, important to emphasize that most patients show some of these behaviors (denial, depression, acting out, aggressiveness) at various stages during an illness. It is when such responses persist, intensify, or thwart appropriate medical management of the disease, that serious maladaptation requiring psychological intervention is present.

References

Ainsworth, M.D.S. The development of mother-infant attachment. In B. Caldwell & H.N. Ricciuti (Eds.), *Review of child development research* (Vol. 3). Chicago: University of Chicago Press, 1973.

Bergmann, T., & Freud, A. *Children in the hospital.* New York: International Universities Press, 1965.

Bibace, R., & Walsh, M.E. Development of children's concepts of illness. *Pediatrics,* 1980, *66*(6), 912–917.

Bibace, R., & Walsh, M.E. Children's conceptions of illness. In R. Bibace & M.E. Walsh (Eds.), *New directions for child development: Children's conceptions of health, illness, and bodily functions* (Vol. 14). San Francisco: Jossey-Bass Inc., 1981.

Blos, P., Jr. Children think about illness: Their concepts and beliefs. In E. Gellert (Ed.), *Psychosocial aspects of pediatric care.* New York: Grune & Stratton, 1978.

Crider, C. Children's conceptions of the body interior. In R. Bibace & M.E. Walsh (Eds.), *New directions for child development: Children's conceptions of health, illness, and bodily functions* (Vol. 14). San Francisco: Jossey-Bass Inc., 1981.

Erikson, E.H. *Childhood and society* (2nd ed.). New York: W.W. Norton & Co., Inc., 1963.

Gellert, E. Children's conceptions of the content and functions of the human body. *Genetic Psychology Monographs,* 1962, *65,* 293–411.

Gellert, E. What do I have inside me? How children view their bodies. In E. Gellert (Ed.), *Psychosocial aspects of pediatric care.* New York: Grune & Stratton, 1978.

Kohlberg, L. Moral stages and moralization: The cognitive-developmental approach. In T. Lickona (Ed.), *Moral development and behavior.* New York: Holt, Rinehart & Winston, 1976.

Lewis, N. The needle is like an animal. *Children Today,* 1978, *7*(1), 18–21.

Nagy, M.H. Children's conceptions of some bodily functions. *The Journal of Genetic Psychology,* 1953, *83,* 199–216.

O'Dougherty, M.M. The relationship between early risk status and later competence and adaptation in children who survive severe heart defects (Doctoral dissertation, University of Minnesota, 1981). *Dissertation Abstracts International*, 1981, *42*(2), 782B. (University Microfilms No. 8115022).

Petrillo, M., & Sanger, S. *Emotional care of hospitalized children: An environmental approach* (2nd ed.). Philadelphia: J.B. Lippincott Company, 1980.

Piaget, J. *The origins of intelligence in children* (M. Cook, trans.) New York: W.W. Norton & Company, Inc., 1963. (Originally published, 1952.)

Steward, M.S., & Regalbuto, G. Do doctors know what children know? *American Journal of Orthopsychiatry*, 1975, *45*(1), 146–149.

Steward, M.S., & Steward, D.S. Children's conceptions of medical procedures. In R. Bibace & M.E. Walsh (Eds.), *New directions for child development: Children's conceptions of health, illness, and bodily functions* (Vol. 14). San Francisco: Jossey-Bass Inc., 1981.

The Center for Attitudinal Healing. *There is a rainbow behind every dark cloud.* Tiburon, California: The Center for Attitudinal Healing, 1978.

Woodward, K.L., Gosnell, M., Reese, M., Coppola, V., & Liebert, P. Living with dying. *Newsweek*, May 1, 1978, *XCI*(8), 52–56, 61.

|3| The Central Nervous System

Epilepsy

Epilepsy combines the stress of both an episodic and a chronic disease. In its chronic aspect, the child and family are confronted with the fact that although the seizures may be controlled through medication, all may have to cope with the condition throughout the child's lifetime. Its episodic nature subjects the child to recurrent, unexpected seizures of varying frequency and severity. The unpredictability of these seizures often severely affects the child's and family's sense of control. Such unpredictability can also aggravate adjustment to and acceptance of epilepsy, since it necessitates living with uncertainty and continuing to treat a condition which may have very infrequent manifestations. Despite the prevalence of this disease and its potential impact on cognitive, social, and emotional functioning, however, it has been relatively neglected by psychologists. This chapter presents basic information on epilepsy in childhood, including diagnosis and medical treatment, the effects of seizures and anticonvulsant medication on learning, emotional precipitants of neurogenic seizures, the differential diagnosis of neurogenic from psychogenic (pseudo or hysterical) seizures, and the social and psychological impact of seizures. Finally, specialized assessment and intervention techniques developed for use with patients with uncontrolled seizures are presented.

Definition

Epilepsy is a disorder of the brain characterized by recurring seizures that are secondary to abnormal electrical discharges from neuronal aggregates within the brain. A single seizure or a time limited episode of seizures which do not recur is not classified as epilepsy. Seizures caused by a high fever (febrile convulsions) or those which result from an imbalance in body fluids and chemicals or from alcohol or drug withdrawal are not typically classified as epilepsy.

Seizures are characterized by an episodic involuntary alteration in consciousness, motor activity, behavior, sensation, or autonomic functions (Wright, Dreifuss, Wolcott, Swaiman, Low, Freeman, & Nelson, 1982). Signs and specific symptoms of a seizure, as well as associated medical treatments, are given in Table 3-1. In 1981 the Commission on Classification and Terminology of the International

28

TABLE 3-1

Epilepsy

Definition	Major Symptoms and Signs	Possible Medical Treatment	Psychologic Issues
A condition in which there is a continuing proclivity to have seizures. Seizures are the result of sudden (paroxysmal) bursts of neuronal activity resulting from lesions or altered chemistry in the brain. Incidence: 4/1,000 Prevalence: 1–2%	Cry, sudden fall Observation of seizure *Eyes* blank stare pupils dilated eyelids flutter eyes roll, jerk, deviate *Movement* head turned body rigid or limp regular repetitive movement irregular movement automatic movement *Alteration in Consciousness* *Other Abnormal Events* flushing, sweating cyanosis salivation, tears tongue biting incontinence abnormal breathing *Post-Ictal Behavior* drowsy, or deep sleep confused physical complaint (headache)	Anticonvulsant medication Regular blood tests Hospitalization for status epilepticus Ablative surgery or cortical excision	Anxiety and fear of unconsciousness Sense of control and autonomy severely affected Social stigmatization, rejection, and discrimination Parental overprotection or rejection Heightened dependency on parents Seizures triggered by stress or hysterical in nature Learning disabilities and emotional problems associated with types of seizure disorder

League against Epilepsy published a new classification of epileptic seizures, based upon the clinical seizure type and the ictal and inter-ictal EEG manifestations. This new classification system and the older terminology are presented in Table 3-2. A behavioral description of the major seizure subtypes has been provided by the Comprehensive Epilepsy Program at Minnesota:

Generalized tonic-clonic seizure (Grand mal):
This is a generalized convulsive seizure affecting the entire body. The person may cry out. This is not a cry of pain, but is the result of air rushing out of the lungs. The person falls and becomes unconscious. The body stiffens. Then the muscles begin alternate periods of spasm and relaxation. The person may bite the tongue and pass urine. Breathing is labored or jerky and at times stops completely. If this occurs, pale or bluish complexion results. The person then regains consciousness, but is usually confused or sleepy and may experience fatigue, headache, speech difficulty, or weakness of an arm or leg. The entire seizure usually lasts one to three minutes.

Absence seizure (Petit mal):
This consists of a few seconds of loss of consciousness, during which there may be staring, eyeblinking, or mild facial twitching. The person usually maintains posture and does not fall. This type of seizure is frequently missed because it is so brief and subtle. It is most common in children. Sometimes an absence seizure progresses to a generalized tonic-clonic seizure.

Complex Partial Seizure (Psycho-motor or temporal lobe)
This type is often characterized by purposeless activity. The seizures may vary greatly from person to person; however, for each person they tend to be consistent. The person may have a glassy stare; give no response or a confused response; move about aimlessly; make lipsmacking, or chewing motions; fidget with clothes; appear drunk, drugged, or even psychotic. Emotional experiences, abnormalities in thinking, and unusual sensory perceptions may also occur during these seizures, especially at the beginning. The person is not violent, but may struggle or fight if restrained. Usually there is no memory of the seizure afterwards. Sometimes, a complex partial seizure progresses to a generalized tonic-clonic seizure.

Elementary partial seizure (Focal Motor or Jacksonian):
This is characterized by stiffening or jerking in just one extremity or one side of the body. It is sometimes accompanied by a tingling sensation in the same area. Often the person does not lose consciousness. The jerking may, however, spread to become a generalized tonic-clonic seizure.
(Comprehensive Epilepsy Progam Brochure, 1979, p. 2)

The Epilepsy Foundation of America (EFA) has estimated the prevalence of epilepsy in the general population at 1-2 percent (1975). Approximately 75 percent of all those who subsequently develop epilepsy have their first seizure before adulthood.

Cause of Seizure Disorders in Children

The specific manifestations of a seizure reflect the area of the brain in which the abnormal discharge arises. Focal seizures originate in a specific cortical area; motor and sensory symptoms ensue if the seizure discharge originates in the sensorimotor cortex (neocortex); and psychomotor symptoms predominate if the discharge originates in the limbic system or the temporal lobe. In contrast, generalized seizures are thought to involve both cerebral hemispheres bilaterally, and thus the initial neuronal discharge is widespread in both hemispheres (Commission on Classification and Terminology of the International League against Epilepsy, 1981).

In over half of the cases of diagnosed epilepsy, the cause is unknown, even after extensive clinical and EEG studies. In these instances the cause of brain damage may not be identified, evidence of brain damage may not be detected, or the seizures may be due to some unknown abnormality of brain chemistry not detectable by available assessment techniques. In the other 50 percent of the cases a known cause can be identified: problems before or during birth (infection, anoxia, trauma); head injuries; infectious diseases (meningitis, encephalitis, brain abscess); toxic factors (lead or mercury poisoning); tumors; cerebral vascular accidents; inherited or degenerative diseases; metabolic diseases; and genetic factors (Swaiman & Wright, 1982).

If the cause of the seizure disorder cannot be identified, there is a slightly higher chance the individual's offspring will have seizures. Whereas the prevalence of seizures is about 0.5-2.0 percent in the general population, about 4-5 percent of children with epilepsy have a parent with epilepsy. This figure increases slightly (10-12%) if both parents have epilepsy (Gumnit, 1981). There is an approximately equal incidence rate between the sexes (EFA, 1975).

Neurologic Evaluation

Most children with seizure disorders receive a complete neurological evaluation, medical history review, and an EEG. Special procedures that may be employed during the EEG to bring out seizure activity include hyperventilation (overbreathing), photic stimulation (flickering light), or sleep deprivation. However, the indication of paroxysmal abnormality on the EEG alone, without the clinical observation that a seizure has occurred, is not evidence of a seizure disorder. Similarly, some patients who do experience seizures do not demonstrate any abnormalities on their interictal (the period between actual seizures) EEG recording. In general, about 15 percent of normal individuals evidence some abnormality on EEG recording (typi-

TABLE 3-2

Classification of Epileptic Seizures*

I. Simple Partial Seizures (Consciousness Not Impaired)
   A. With motor signs
      1. focal motor (without spreading)
      2. Jacksonian
      3. versive (generally contraversive)
      4. postural
      5. phonatory (vocalization or arrest of speech)
   B. With autonomic symptoms or signs
   C. With somatosensory or special sensory symptoms (simple hallucinations—e.g., tingling, light flashes, buzzing)
      1. somatosensory
      2. visual
      3. auditory
      4. olfactory
      5. gustatory
      6. vertiginous
   D. With psychic symptoms (disturbance of higher cerebral function)
      1. aphasic
      2. dysmnesic (e.g., *déjà vu*)
      3. cognitive (e.g., forced thinking)
      4. affective (fear, anger, etc.)
      5. illusion (e.g., macropsia)
      6. structured hallucinations (e.g., music, scenes)

II. Complex Partial Seizures (continued)
   B. Without impairment of consciousness at onset (simple partial onset)
      1. with simple partial features (I,A (1 to 4) above)
      2. with automatisms

III. Partial Seizures, Evolving to Generalized Tonic-Clonic Seizures
   A. Simple partial seizures (I), evolving to generalized tonic-clonic seizures
   B. Complex partial seizures (II), evolving to generalized tonic-clonic seizures
   C. Simple partial seizures, evolving to complex partial seizures, evolving to generalized tonic-clonic seizures

IV. Generalized Seizures
   A. Absence seizures
      1. with impairment of consciousness only
      2. with automatisms
      3. with myoclonic components
      4. with atonic components
      5. with tonic components
      6. with autonomic components
   B. Myoclonic seizures
      1. myoclonic jerks (single or multiple)
      2. clonic seizures
   C. Tonic seizures

II. Complex Partial Seizures
A. With impairment of consciousness at onset
  1. with impairment of consciousness only
  2. with simple partial features (I,A (1 to 4) above)
  3. with automatisms

D. Tonic-clonic seizures
E. Atonic seizures
F. Infantile spasms

*Adapted from The Commission on Classification and Terminology of the International League against Epilepsy, *Epilepsia*, 1981, 22, 489-501, Raven Press Publishers, New York. Reprinted with permission.

cally slow wave abnormality), whereas 80 percent of patients with epilepsy do (Swaiman & Wright, 1982).

If a generalized seizure does occur, however, during the EEG recording the intra-ictal (the period during the seizure) EEG is invariably abnormal and is characterized by spikes, sharp waves, or spike and wave complexes. If the patient experiences an aura, attenuation of the alpha rhythm may precede the actual seizure. Slow wave activity is also seen post-ictally on the EEG. Only on very rare occasions is the surface EEG recording normal during complex partial seizures. In these rare circumstances electrical abnormality may be demonstrated by means of depth electrodes (Scott, 1982).

Since most patients experience intermittent seizures, it is not typical to have a seizure occur during the actual recording. Consequently, diagnosis of a seizure disorder relies most heavily on the family's and patient's report of the characteristics of the "episode" to their neurologist or pediatrician. Included in the differential diagnosis often are fainting, breath-holding spells, migraine, low blood sugar, anxiety, or behavioral disturbance. (The differential diagnosis between neurogenic and psychogenic seizures is covered in a subsequent section.) To rule out these other diagnoses, a comprehensive assessment, which could entail computerized axial tomography (CAT) scan, blood chemistry studies, prolonged video EEG recording, and family history assessment, may be required.

Psychologic Assessment

Impact on learning. Recurrent seizures can affect the child's sense of competence in various ways, such as limiting the number of situations in which the child can act, and thus decreasing opportunities for the development of new skills and eventual mastery of various developmental tasks. The learning disabilities which can be associated with epilepsy may reduce the child's ability to solve problems and further constrain the development of important cognitive, attentional, spatial-perceptual, memory, and linguistic skills. The psychologist needs to be alert to several critical medical variables which may mediate the child's adaptation in these areas: 1) the type and severity of underlying brain dysfunction (including presence or absence of epileptiform activity on the EEG, duration of this activity, and whether the abnormal discharge is diffuse or focal); 2) the degree of seizure control; 3) the effect of anticonvulsant medication in providing seizure control with minimal side effects; and 4) the interaction of these medical factors with individual differences in personality and coping abilities (Baird, John, Ahn, & Maisel, 1980).

Uncontrolled or undiagnosed seizures may interfere with learning in a variety of ways. Children with absence (petit mal) seizures may experience frequent episodes throughout the day. Such brief but frequent lapses in consciousness, if not recognized as seizures, may result in the child's being accused of not paying attention, not cooperating, or of misbehaving. The automatic, stereotyped, or unusual behaviors of the child with complex partial seizures can also result in censure or ridicule if not appropriately diagnosed. In addition, both the seizure and the post seizure state may interfere with learning. In such seizures, the child may respond impulsively or in an agitated, hyperactive state as part of the seizure or the post-ictal state.

Associated Learning Problems

1. General Intellectual Function. In general, the overall intellectual functioning of children with epilepsy is slightly lower than the normal population (the mean IQ score is 10–15 points below the normal population). However, the lowered overall group mean IQ score seems to be largely accounted for by an increased incidence of mental retardation in a subgroup of children with epilepsy (Wright, Schaefer, & Solomons, 1979). Factors associated with diminished intellectual functioning include earlier age of onset of the seizures, longer duration of the disease, seizure type, total number of seizures (with the exception of absence seizures), seizures of known etiology versus idiopathic seizures, slow wave EEG abnormalities, and institutionalization.

2. Specific Learning and Emotional Disabilities. In the Isle of Wight study (Rutter, Tizard, & Whitmore, 1970), children with neuro-epileptic conditions showed significantly more clinical and psychiatric disorders than other chronically ill and handicapped groups and control children. Educational difficulties have been particularly prominent, with various reports citing 33 to 70 percent of children with epilepsy experiencing some learning difficulty. One group of investigators (Baird et al., 1980) contrasted the performance of children with epilepsy who were doing well or poorly at school. Of interest was their finding that almost all the children doing well displayed as frequent, severe, and anatomically widespread sharp waves on the EEG as the children who were doing poorly. However, children doing poorly in school also had excessive activity in the theta and beta bands (particularly in the central, temporal, and fronto-temporal areas) and hyper-reactivity of evoked responses. Others (Stores, 1977, 1978) have found that children displaying a left temporal spike discharge have significantly lower reading skills, whereas children with right temporal spike discharge or generalized seizures typically do not differ from controls in reading level. The most striking and consistent finding, however, has been that boys with epilepsy, irrespective of the type of epilepsy, have significantly lower achievement, poorer concentration and attention, and increased behavior problems. Girls with epilepsy, on the other hand, typically do not differ from normal girls. All subgroups of boys studied (EEG abnormalities included generalized irregular spike and wave; generalized regular 3 per second spike and wave; right temporal lobe spike; and left temporal lobe spike) had higher scores than normal boys for anxiety, inattentiveness (with one exception—the 3 per second spike and wave group was not impaired), and social isolation. Boys with left temporal spike discharges emerged as the most disturbed and significantly more overactive. When sex of the child is not controlled, a strong association between type of epilepsy and inattentiveness typically is found. Children demonstrating

generalized but irregular seizure discharge are significantly more impaired in tasks of attention and concentration than are those having 3 per second, generalized, regular spike and wave discharge (Stores, 1973, 1976, 1977, 1978).

Psychosocial impact of epilepsy on the child and family. Like those with other chronic illnesses, children with seizure disorders vary in the effectiveness with which they can cope and adjust. There are a number of possible explanations for the diversity in adaptation. Some relate to variables associated with the seizures or to those associated with learning problems. Others relate more directly to the child's and family's perceptions and understanding of the disorder, as well as the manner in which they cope with the difficulties presented. While the type and severity of seizures have been implicated as significant factors in adjustment, the existing evidence is neither totally conclusive nor is it always in the expected direction. Hodgman, McAnarney, Myers, Iker, with McKinney, Parmelee, Schuster, and Tutihasi (1979) found that adolescents with relatively mild difficulties in controlling their generalized tonic-clonic seizures were more troubled psychologically than those with more obvious difficulties. These findings suggested that the stress of seizures is not necessarily inherent in the disorder, but might rather be a function of the way in which the illness is perceived. A mild disability may not compel the child to confront, eventually accept, and learn to cope successfully with the disease. On the other hand, if the seizures are perceived as extremely threatening or are very frequent and severe, they may overwhelm the child's or family's ability to cope. Significant disruption in adjustment may be the result.

Families of children with epilepsy are confronted with a variety of physical, social, and psychological problems that require solutions. Pre-existing cultural beliefs (such as the association of seizures with mental retardation, insanity, or possession by the devil) can present major difficulties. During a seizure self-control is lost, although the reason for this loss of control is not obvious to bystanders. Moreover, the implications of such loss of control, particularly when associated with bizarre movements and incontinence, can be very frightening and embarrassing to the child, after regaining consciousness, as well as to observers of the event. While medication provides valuable aid in maintaining a degree of control over the seizures, the amount of control that can be gained is variable. Such reliance on daily medications, frequent visits to the doctor, restriction from certain activities, and the need to rely on others for help during a seizure can interfere with a child's normal development of autonomy and independence. It can also foster for him or her maladaptive patterns of dependence and passivity, and overprotectiveness and restrictiveness on the part of the parents. The experience of a seizure might intensify the child's fear of being different, unattractive, or socially rejected because of unusual behavior. It may result in withdrawal and isolation from others as a protective defense. Such feelings and perceptions can create an atmosphere of secrecy and shame, eventuating in a poor self-image, and low self-esteem (Ozuna, 1979).

Parental expectations, attitudes, and practices may also contribute to difficulties that children with epilepsy experience in psychological, social, and academic areas. Acceptance by the parents of lower levels of performance for the child with epilepsy than for normal siblings, when not based on actual learning impairment, can result in school underachievement, lack of social interaction skills, and an increase in behavioral problems (Long & Moore, 1979).

Specific Assessment Techniques

Many children with seizure disorders require psychological assessment to evaluate cognitive, social, and emotional functioning. The child's general cognitive functioning and school performance are usually assessed by standardized, individually administered tests of intelligence and academic achievement. Other tests examining specific skills, such as perceptual motor tasks, language functioning, auditory and visual memory, and sustained attention, should also be administered when indicated. Typically, this assessment is made by a clinical neuropsychologist. If neuropsychologic dysfunction is suspected, either portions of or the entire neuropsychologic test batteries of Halstead and Reitan or the Luria Battery might be administered. This assessment should be completed prior to introducing anticonvulsant medication, with repeat testing to assess the child's performance in each of these areas once medication has been initiated. In this way improvement related to better seizure control can be documented, as well as medication toxicity detected.

A specific battery of neuropsychologic tests for assessing adult patients with epilepsy has been developed by Dodrill (1981). This battery includes tests of general intellectual functioning (WAIS), emotional adjustment (MMPI), tests of lateral dominance, subtests from the Halstead-Reitan Neurological Battery, the Wechsler Memory Scale, a modification of the Stroop Color Word Test, the Seashore Tonal Memory Test, and the Wunderlich Personnel Test. Research is in progress to determine the effectiveness of this battery with adult patients with seizure disorders. To date, the global measure obtained from this battery was found to be more effective in discriminating seizure patients from normal control persons than the Halstead Impairment Index (Dodrill, 1981). No adaptation of this battery for children with seizure disorders has been made, and work in this area is sorely needed.

The importance of simultaneously assessing the child's emotional and social functioning should not be overlooked. A variety of emotional, behavioral, and family difficulties can arise. In particular, signs of depression, mood swings, difficulty in forming peer relationships, overprotective or restrictive parent management, the presence of other physical complaints with no organic basis, or evidence for self-induced seizures should be explored. It is also very important to establish whether the child and family adequately understand the seizure disorder, since poor understanding is often associated with unnecessary anxiety and inappropriate management decisions. Balaschak and Mostofsky (1981) have created a comprehensive interview (The Seizure Disorders Survey) that can be used to collect standardized information on each seizure patient. The various sections of the inventory allow for data collection in the areas of family functioning; description of the clinical features of the seizures; possible seizure precipitants; relevant medical, surgical, and drug histories; behavioral complaints; subjective impressions; and neuropsychological assessment results. An additional semistructured interview is provided for children with an initial diagnosis of seizures. This focuses on the child's understanding of his or her disease and the potential secondary gain that might be occurring from environmental responses to the seizures. A complete copy of these questionnaires is available in a comprehensive chapter by Balaschak and Mostofsky (1981). They further recommend providing the child and family with a weekly chart to record seizures, an example of which is included in the chapter.

Facilitating Understanding of Epilepsy

An epilepsy education program has also been developed by the Comprehensive Epilepsy Program, directed by Robert Gumnit, M.D., at the University of Minnesota. Three films were developed and used in the hospital and in schools throughout the state. These films ("Epilepsy Is," "Epilepsy: First Aid for Seizures," and "Anti-epileptic Medications: Why?") describe what happens when a person has a seizure and provide information about seizures, appropriate first aid and precautions, the purpose of medication and how the medication works, social reactions, and the need for compliance. The latter film includes discussion of seizure threshold, therapeutic range, and steady state in relation to the need for taking medication regularly. These materials are now available from the Epilepsy Foundation of America.

Differential Diagnostic Issues

Environmental determinants of seizures. When medication has not been successful in adequately controlling the seizures, an attempt is often made to identify additional factors that may be triggering or aggravating the seizure disorder. A variety of physical (fever, allergy, physical exhaustion, menstruation, infection) and psychological (emotional stress, denial of the illness, noncompliance, misunderstanding of the importance of medication, psychiatric disturbance) factors should be considered when the child's seizures are not adequately controlled by medication alone. It is in this area that the clinical psychologist can play a particularly important role. Critical diagnostic issues include: 1) determining whether the seizures represent neurogenic seizures (seizures associated with CNS paroxysmal activity) alone with no contributing psychogenic factors; 2) determining the possible role of emotional stress in precipitating or exacerbating neurogenic seizures; 3) determining whether the patient is experiencing hysterical or pseudoseizures in addition to neurogenic seizures; and 4) identifying factors that may allow for differential diagnosis between episodes of pseudoseizures and neurogenic seizures. Clinical assessment and psychological interventions can be particularly important once these questions have been resolved.

Emotional stress precipitating neurogenic seizures. With any type of neurogenic seizure disorder, it is important to determine to what extent emotional factors play a role in precipitating the seizures. Of primary importance is the determination that the patient is experiencing neurogenic rather than hysterical or pseudoseizures. (This question of differential diagnosis is addressed in the next section.) Here, only cases with documented EEG recordings indicative of seizure disorders will be discussed. The literature in this area is quite sparse, with most studies dealing primarily with adult seizure patients or employing experimental paradigms with animals. Studies using animals have documented the interaction of a physical predisposition to seizures and stress. Genetically susceptible dogs, rhesus monkeys with epilepsy, and mice treated with pentylenetetrazol have exhibited seizures when exposed to various forms of environmental stress. Minter (1979) reviewed those studies assessing the impact of emotions in precipitating seizures in human patients and found that 15-53 percent of individuals surveyed in various studies reported stress as a precipitant or triggering factor. Another approach has been to induce emotional reactions during EEG recordings experimentally, typically by conducting a stressful interview. Using this method, increased EEG abnormalities have been identified in 25-33 percent of the patients (Minter, 1979).

Although the precise mechanism through which emotions precipitate seizure activity is not understood, such reactions are thought to stimulate the sympathetic nervous system in patients who have a low seizure threshold. Although such findings have implications for psychotherapeutic interventions, there are a number of difficulties and limitations in the present studies. One overriding confounding factor is the inability to distinguish whether the emotional reaction (fear, tension, anxiety, etc.) precipitates the seizure or is the result of ongoing seizure activity and abnormal electrical discharge. In addition, typically only the patient's report of emotional reactions is used; there is no blind interpretation of the EEG following the stress interviews; and emotional triggers are not differentiated from other types of environmental or physical stresses.

Differentiating neurogenic and pseudoseizures. One of the most difficult diagnostic problems in treating a patient with seizures is the differentiation between genuine neurogenic seizures and seizures of psychogenic origin. A pseudoseizure (alternatively called psychogenic, hysterical, or conversion seizure) is a clinical event that superficially resembles a neurogenic seizure. Such seizures are psychologically determined; and although often involuntary, they are not caused or accompanied by abnormal paroxysmal discharge from the brain. Mostofsky and

Williams (1982) have subdivided seizures of primarily psychological origin into several different categories, based on the diagnoses present in the third edition of the *Diagnostic and Statistical Manual of Mental Disorders* (DSM-III), published by the American Psychiatric Association (1980). These categories are not mutually exclusive, and in fact, may coexist with a true neurogenic seizure disorder. The various types are:

Factitious Seizures

In this disorder the physical symptoms are voluntarily produced by the patient. When this is done in pursuit of a specific goal, such as missing school, avoiding responsibilities, obtaining drugs, etc., it is called malingering. When there is no apparent goal other than to assume the role of patient, the individual is considered to have a factitious seizure disorder. This is usually symptomatic of a severe underlying personality disturbance.

Somatization Disorder

This is a disorder which simulates an organic illness. No evidence of organic disease to explain the symptom can be found, and there is positive evidence that the symptoms are related to psychological factors. In contrast to factitious disorders, the patient is not consciously aware of producing the symptoms and has no voluntary control over them. There are two major subtypes: conversion (hysterical seizures) and Briquet's Syndrome. In conversion seizures, the seizurelike phenomena are an expression of psychological conflict. The symptoms serve to reduce anxiety by keeping the conflict out of the patient's conscious awareness, while at the same time allowing expression of the conflict through physical symptoms. Conversion seizures are the form of pseudoseizures most frequently found in children and adolescents. They often develop in a setting of severe psychological stress.

Meir Gross (1979) has studied the occurrence of hysterical seizures in adolescent females following incestuous relationships with their fathers or father surrogates. In the presence of these hysterical seizures the patient often displays *la belle indifference*, a relative lack of concern over symptoms that appear very disabling. Significant secondary gains, such as attention from others, sympathy, and maintained dependency are often apparent. (See the section later in this chapter on special considerations in assessing the adolescent female patient.)

Briquet's Syndrome is a chronic disorder, often beginning in childhood or adolescence, characterized by multiple or recurrent somatic complaints for which no apparent physical basis can be found. Pseudoseizures can appear as one of many physical symptoms. For this diagnosis to be made, 14 symptoms for women and 12 for men must occur in the areas listed in DSM-III (conversion or pseudoneurological symptoms, gastrointestinal symptoms, female reproductive symptoms, psychosexual symptoms, pain, or cardiopulmonary symptoms). This syndrome is most common in adolescent girls and women and is often associated with a histrionic personality disorder.

Intermittent Explosive Disorder (Rage Outburst)

This disorder is associated with episodes of loss of control and aggressive impulses, resulting in personal assault or property destruction. Impulsivity or aggressiveness between episodes is not observed, and these outbursts are sometimes confused with true neurogenic seizures. Williams, Gold, Shrout, Shaffer, and Adams (1979) have found that this disorder is most often encountered in children and adolescents with organic brain syndrome, including seizures.

Diagnostic guidelines. Treatment recommendations differ dramatically depending on whether the seizures are diagnosed as true neurogenic seizures or as seizure-like phenomena of psychogenic origin. A misdiagnosis of neurogenic seizures in a patient with pseudoseizures will unnecessarily subject the patient to anticonvulsant medications at high, and potentially toxic, doses for many years until the correct diagnosis is made. The patient-doctor or doctor-parent relationship is also jeopardized as each becomes increasingly frustrated with the inability to achieve seizure control. Differentiation between these seizure types is often quite difficult, although during the last decade there has been increasing sophistication in making this differential diagnosis. Table 3–3 summarizes the differential characteristics between neurogenic and pseudoseizures. Few of the criteria listed in this table, when viewed in isolation, can discriminate between neurogenic and pseudoseizures. The more the pattern conforms to the total picture presented in Table 3–3, however, the greater the likelihood that a pseudoseizure rather than a true seizure has occurred.

To be certain about the distinction between a seizure-like episode and a neurogenic seizure, it is critical to have the benefit of ongoing EEG video monitoring. If a seizure episode can be recorded during the EEG monitoring, the subsequent EEG records can provide the data needed to make the differential diagnosis. For a true neurogenic seizure, the intra-ictal EEG is invariably abnormal during a generalized seizure episode. During a pseudoseizure, the EEG reveals a quite different pattern. No spikes or other rhythmical seizure elements occur. The patient exhibits muscle activity which is random or from side to side, unlike that seen in neurogenic seizures in which the muscle activity is organized into clusters in relationship to the seizure discharges. Cohen and Suter (1982) have utilized saline injection, accompanied by the suggestion that the patient will very likely experience a seizure, as a provocative test to induce seizure-like phenomena in suggestible patients. If the "seizure" was both induced and terminated by suggestion and the simultaneous EEG record during the episode shows no EEG abnormalities, conclusive evidence of pseudoseizures is obtained. In Cohen and Suter's experience, neurogenic seizures have never been precipitated by this method.

When an ictal EEG cannot be obtained, the inter-ictal EEG can be used as a guide.

TABLE 3-3

Comparison of Characteristics of Neurogenic and Pseudoseizures*

Clinical Variables	Neurogenic Seizures	Pseudoseizures
Seizure type	All types	Resemble complex partial or generalized tonic-clonic seizures
Seizure pattern	Similar	Variable
Onset	Commonly sudden	Often gradual
Duration	A few minutes	Many minutes, often much longer
Frequency	Rarely more than one a day (except absence)	Often, many in one day
Place	Can occur anywhere	Indoors, often at home
Presence of others	Occur sometimes when alone	Occur often with others (parents, friends) present
Behavior during seizures:		
Movement	Stereotyped, never directed violence	Combative, alternating from side to side
Scream	At onset	During attack
Speech	Rare, if occurs is confused, repetitive	Frequent, swearing, yelling, etc.
Biting	Tongue only	Lips, hands, other people
Incontinence	Common	Rare
Self-Injury	Can occur	Rare
Consciousness	Always impaired except in simple motor seizures	May appear impaired, but no actual alteration in consciousness
Recovery	Frequently period of confusion	Usually rapid
Post-ictal phenomenon	Always in generalized tonic-clonic; occasionally after complex partial	None
Response to suggestion (saline infusion test)	Does not occur	Seizure begins and terminates with suggestion
Environmental interruption	Very rarely possible	Seizure may be interrupted by external stimuli (loud speaker, cry, etc.)
Stress	Occasionally exacerbates	Frequently exacerbates
Electroencephalogram	Usually paroxysmal during ictus, post-ictal slowing	No ictal or post-ictal changes

TABLE 3-3 **Comparison of Characteristics of Neurogenic and Pseudoseizures** (*continued*)

Clinical Variables	Neurogenic Seizures	Pseudoseizures
Improvement with medication	Frequent	Infrequent
Level of control	Usually intermittent periods of partial or complete control	Prolonged period without control (frequently years)
Sex ratio	No definite predominance	Females predominate
Family history of psychiatric disorders	Occasionally	Frequently, particularly alcoholism or affective disorder
Sexual abuse	Rarely	Often found in histories of adolescent girls
Patient history of psychiatric disorder	Occasionally	Frequently, including attempted suicide, promiscuity, running away, sexual maladjustment, depression
Associated problems	No specific type	Hysterical neurosis, occasional psychosis, depression, or intellectual deficiency

*Modified from G.L. Holmes, J.C. Sackellares, J. McKiernan, M. Ragland, and F. Dreifuss, "Evaluation of childhood pseudoseizures using EEG telemetry and videotape monitoring" *The Journal of Pediatrics*, 1980, *97*, 554–558 and from D.F. Scott, "Psychiatric aspects of epilepsy" *British Journal of Psychiatry*, 1978, *132*, 417–430.

While a randomly administered EEG will often show abnormalities in a patient with true neurogenic seizures, it may be completely normal. Similarly, a patient with pseudoseizures may have evidence of abnormality on routine EEG recordings, although the abnormalities are usually mild despite the presence of very frequent and prolonged seizure-like activity (Scott, 1982). It is important, however, to remember that a normal EEG recorded during an inter-ictal period, neither confirms pseudoseizures nor rules out epilepsy, just as an abnormal inter-ictal EEG does not confirm epilepsy or exclude pseudoseizures (Ramani, Quesney, Olson, & Gumnit, 1980). The relationship of seizure frequency to anticonvulsant medication levels can also be a useful diagnostic criterion. Patients who have neurogenic seizures tend to have fewer seizures when treated with anticonvulsants in a dosage appropriate to ensure a therapeutic level. Patients with pseudoseizures show a poor or inconsistent response to medication, and typically their seizures do not increase in frequency when the medication is reduced.

As discussed earlier, the clinical characteristics of the seizure also provide clues to the diagnosis of neurogenic or pseudoseizures (see Table 3-3); however, reliance on clinical characteristics alone can result in an incorrect diagnosis. This is particularly the case when a complex partial seizure is in question, because the clinical manifestations of such seizures can be quite atypical.

Finally, it is important to re-emphasize that pseudoseizures may occur in a patient who also has a neurogenic seizure disorder. Of 53 pediatric patients whose seizures had not been adequately controlled by anticonvulsant medication, Holmes, Sackellares, McKiernan, Ragland, and Dreifuss (1980) identified pseudoseizures as a component in 11. However, for 8 of these 11 patients, true neurogenic seizures were also evident in conjunction with pseudoseizures. All of the patients with documented pseudoseizures showed a marked decrease in the pseudoseizures after the diagnosis was made. Such evaluations require the close collaboration of a pediatric neurologist, an electroencephalographer, and a clinical psychologist. Close observation of the events preceding the seizures, the clinical characteristics of the seizure itself and EEG recording of seizure pattern and the delineation of current psychological and environmental stresses are often required before an adequate diagnosis can be established.

Special considerations in assessing adolescent female patients. As indicated in Table 3-3, pseudoseizures are more typical in adolescent females than in males. Sexual exploitation, incestuous relationships with the father or father figure, and a pre-existing hysterical personality disorder have been identified as predisposing factors. Patients with pseudoseizures often differ significantly from patients with neurogenic seizures on a variety of psychiatric variables, including family history of psychiatric disorders, personal history of past psychiatric disorder, attempted suicide, sexual maladjustment, and clinical diagnosis of depressive disorder (Roy, 1982). Based on these findings, Roy suggests that when a young female patient with a history of one or more psychiatric symptoms presents for evaluation of uncontrolled seizures, the patient should be comprehensively evaluated to rule out psychogenic seizures *before* a trial of anticonvulsant medication is undertaken. The pseudoseizures may represent a "signal of distress" in a patient who cannot cope with the stress in her life, but is also unable to verbalize the stress she is experiencing or to seek help in an appropriate manner. The pseudoseizure, which is typically accompanied by a loss of motor control and memory for the event, can become a mechanism for releasing tension and reducing overwhelming anxiety. It may also be a way of fulfilling dependency needs or expressing infantile desires or regressive impulses. For some adolescents, the achievement of independence and identity can be thwarted because of fear of giving up the security of a dependent relationship with parents and family. Illness during the adolescent years also can allow the teenager to avoid interacting with peers or pursuing heterosexual relationships and establishing intimacy outside the family.

Psychotherapy is the primary treatment of choice for such patients. Typically the patient is suggestible and can benefit initially from hypnotherapy in which the underlying conflict can be brought into the patient's awareness. Psychotherapy can then be directed toward establishing more adaptive ways of handling such conflicts and examining situations that produce stress and discomfort (Mostofsky & Williams, 1982). If the pseudoseizures are a response to an incestuous relationship or sexual exploitation, the parents must be involved in treatment, with appropriate steps taken to protect the adolescent patient (Gross, 1979; Gross & Huerta, 1980).

Medical Treatment Approaches

Pharmacologic treatment. When a diagnosis of neurogenic seizures is made, anticonvulsant medication is the principle therapeutic agent in treating the seizure disorder. With the proper selection of anticonvulsant medication and the correct dosage about 60 percent of patients with epileptiform seizures obtain satisfactory control, and in an additional 20-25 percent of patients the seizures are decreased but not completely suppressed. Approximately 15-20 percent of patients do not respond to any combination of drugs.

The most important initial issue is to determine the seizure type. Recently, a number of new drugs have been introduced for the therapy of epilepsy that are specifically effective in controlling a particular subtype of seizures. For example, drugs useful for the treatment of absence seizures are not useful in the treatment of complex partial seizures, indicating a need for a distinction among these seizure types. (If an underlying cause of the seizure disorder can be identified, it is important to initiate therapy directed at this cause, e.g., removal of a brain tumor, treatment of metabolic derangements, etc.)

Although recent pharmacologic advances have resulted in a more accurate detection of drug concentrations in plasma and other body fluids, as yet the precise mechanism of action of the anticonvulsant drugs is poorly understood. However, improvement in pharmacokinetic techniques and understanding of drug interactions have provided important guidelines to the pediatric neurologist in the administration of anticonvulsant drugs. The specific drug, typically chosen on the basis of seizure type, is administered alone until a steady-state blood level is obtained or until signs of toxicity prevent further increases in drug dosage. Change in drug type or the addition of alternative medications should be initiated only after an adequate trial of the initial anticonvulsant has been completed (Wright et al., 1982).

Each child's response must be evaluated individually, since the rate of metabolism of anticonvulsants varies considerably from person to person. Typically, it may take several days or weeks for plasma and brain levels of the drug to reach the desired steady state. Dosage of the medication, time of day at which it is administered, as well as the rate of metabolism of the drugs are all factors implicated in achieving an appropriate medication level. Before any medication change is made, blood level estimations should be obtained to determine whether an adequate trial of the drug has taken place and to determine whether or not the child has actually been taking the prescribed medication. If the seizures are controlled, the physician must determine how long to continue drug treatment. In general, the patient continues to take medication for a period ranging from two years to four years. At such time, if the EEG is impoved, a reduction in medication may begin with the hope of discontinuation. Holowach, Thurston, and O'Leary (1972) found an overall relapse rate of 24 percent in children who had had seizure control for four years. They also identified some factors associated with continued remission versus those associated with relapse. Early age at onset (prior to 8 years of age); early control; as well as absence, tonic-clonic, and febrile seizure patterns were associated with continued remission. Late onset of seizures (after 9 years of age), Jacksonian seizures, neurologic deficit, and a severely abnormal paroxysmal EEG were factors related to relapse. If adequate seizure control is not obtained within a reasonable period of time, it is important to refer a child to a center that has a comprehensive epilepsy program with intensive video monitoring and telemetry capabilities, as well as extensive capabilities to monitor physiologic and pharmacologic indices.

Medication side effects range from benign to serious and can have an important consequence for the child's learning, attention, and memory. The detection of these side effects on cognitive function is described in the section on the effects of anticonvulsant medication.

Surgical treatment. Only a small proportion of individuals with epilepsy are candidates for brain surgery. The surgical procedures typically involve removal of a circumscribed area of the brain which has an epileptiform focus. This type of surgery is referred to as ablative surgery. Another form of surgery is restorative and involves the removal of tumors or cysts, draining of abscesses, bypassing of ventricular obstructions, or evacuation of subdural hematomas. Hemispherectomy was developed in 1950 for the treatment of intractable convulsions in children with congenital or acquired early onset hemiplegia, but this procedure has been associated with long-term complications of sufficiently great extent to limit its use. The most common form of surgical excision involves the temporal lobe in which the EEG disturbance is confined to one temporal lobe. Local cortical excision of small areas of the cortex and a commissurotomy to prevent the spread of seizure discharge from one hemisphere to another are other surgical approaches. The seizure focus must be in an area that, if removed, would not cause serious language problems or other neurologic deficits. This type of treatment has limited applicability and often requires the collaboration of neurosurgery, neurology, clinical neuropsychology, and psychiatry (Wright et al., 1982).

Cerebellar stimulation has been attempted on an experimental basis for the control of seizures. This technique involves the implantation of electrodes in the cerebellum, which is then stimulated. It is thought that such stimulation might reinforce the brain's inhibitory mechanisms and, consequently, might limit seizure discharge. The long-term risks and benefits of this procedure are unknown, and the exact mode of action has not been established. In preliminary work, however, Cooper, Amin, Riklan, Waltz, and Poon (1976) reported that 10 of 15 patients with epilepsy, treated with cerebellar stimulation, did show a diminution of their clinical seizures and improved study and work concentration. In addition, patients who had exhibited uncontrolled inter-ictal rage reactions showed a suppression of this activity following the cerebellar stimulation. This technique is considered experimental at the present time.

Psychological Intervention Strategies

Assessing anticonvulsant medication effects. The continual problem in managing children with seizure disorders is the determination of an optimal dosage of anticonvulsant medication to control the seizures and yet minimize medication side effects. With the development of serum anticonvulsant blood concentration determinations, it has been possible to determine the anticonvulsant level. Daily seizure recording techniques also provide a fairly accurate assessment of seizure frequency. Table 3-4 lists the most common antiepileptic medications, describes the type of seizures for which these drugs are most commonly prescribed, and the possible side effects.

Studies assessing the specific effect of various anticonvulsant medications have been limited to date, because of the variety of methodological problems present in this area. Most studies include only adult patients who have been receiving anticonvulsant medication for many years. There is often little assessment of pertinent factors prior to initiating anticonvulsant medication. Table 3-5 lists many of the pre-existing factors that can confound and confuse interpretations of medication effects on cognitive function. Dodrill (1981), in an excellent review of studies to date, also cites a number of critical factors that confound the findings and conclusions in this area: 1) simultaneous changes in seizure frequency and anticonvul-

TABLE 3-4

Most Common Antiepileptic Drugs*

Trade Name	Generic Name	Common Use	Possible Side Effects	Serious Side Effects
Clonopin	clonazepam	absence akinetic myoclonic	lethargy dizziness nausea/vomiting	hypersensitivity allergic reaction
Depakene	valproic acid	absence generalized tonic-clonic	nausea/vomiting, indigestion sedation hair loss dizziness tremor	hypersensitivity allergic reaction liver toxicity bone marrow suppression
Dilantin	phenytoin	any seizure except absence	body hair increase gum overgrowth nausea/vomiting tremor	hypersensitivity allergic reaction bone marrow suppression lymphoproliferative disorder anemia loss of coordination double vision confusion slurred speech
No trade name commonly used	phenobarbital	most types of seizures	drowsiness lethargy hyperactivity irritability aggressiveness depression	hypersensitivity allergic reaction impaired concentration loss of coordination

Mysoline	primidone	complex partial generalized tonic-clonic simple partial	drowsiness appetite loss irritability nausea/vomiting	hypersensitivity allergic reaction dizziness loss of coordination
Tegretol	carbamazepine	complex partial generalized tonic-clonic simple partial	drowsiness dizziness lethargy	hypersensitivity allergic reaction liver toxicity bone marrow suppression blurred vision, double vision
Zarontin	ethosuximide	absence	drowsiness hyperactivity nausea/vomiting sleep disturbance	hypersensitivity allergic reaction liver toxicity bone marrow suppression

*Modified from *Epilepsy: Medical Aspects*. Comprehensive Epilepsy Program, University of Minnesota, 1979. Reprinted with permission of the Minnesota Comprehensive Epilepsy Program, funded in part by federal funds from the Department of Health and Human Services (DHHS).

TABLE 3-5

**Factors Interacting with Cognitive and
Behavioral Function in Patients with Epilepsy**

1. Type of seizure disorder
2. Age at onset of the seizure disorder
3. Duration of the seizure disorder
4. Degree of seizure control
5. Localization and degree of EEG abnormalities
6. Pre-existing neurologic abnormalities
7. Degree of neurologic impairment
8. Associated learning disabilities

sant medications; 2) difficulty in evaluating changes in performance when a second medication is added to a drug regimen, since any additional drug tends to decrease performance when compared to a placebo group; 3) a limited assessment battery, which often does not cover the range of abilities possibly affected by the medications; and 4) evaluation of drug effects using normal control subjects who may metabolize the drugs differently from seizure patients who have taken the medication for many years. Given these limitations, the adverse side effects typically found for each of the most common drugs are listed in Table 3-4.

More recently, investigators have examined the relationship between serum anticonvulsant level and psychological and neurological impairment. In general, poor performance on a variety of psychological tests (vigilance, reaction time, memory, cognitive function) has been found in patients exhibiting toxic serum levels, and psychologic test performance has correlated negatively with medication dosage. Impaired performance on these psychological tests has also been found among patients exhibiting serum anticonvulsant levels within the therapeutic range. Such preliminary findings suggest the importance of a comprehensive neuropsychological assessment to evaluate possible adverse side effects even when therapeutic blood levels have been obtained. Blood level determination may, thus, need to be combined with psychometric performance to determine the optimal dosage for seizure control and adequate cognitive and behavioral functioning (Reynolds & Travers, 1974; Dodrill, 1975).

Assessing medication noncompliance. Another type of difficulty in obtaining or maintaining seizure control occurs when there is medication noncompliance, either deliberate or accidental. When a patient has achieved adequate seizure control with anticonvulsant medications in a therapeutic range, an episode or period of uncontrolled seizures may be associated with subtherapeutic or absent serum anticonvulsant levels. At such a time, or when seizure control is not initially obtained with anticonvulsant medication, it is important to consider a number of possibilities, including poor drug absorption, rapid drug metabolism, irregular administration of the medicine by parents, or patient noncompliance.

Consistent and reliable plasma drug level determinations are needed to evaluate the factors implicated in the poor seizure control. Guidelines for the neurologist and pharmacologist in evaluating rapid drug metabolism and poor absorption are available to rule out and/or correct for these factors. When these factors do not account for the low serum level, irregularity in taking the medication may account for the finding. For patients living at home with their parents, missing a single dose or a few doses of medication may be accidental. If, however, a marked decrease in a patient's serum anticonvulsant level is obtained despite the parent or patient's report of taking or giving the medication, the possibility of medication noncompliance must be pursued. Desai, Riley, Porter, and Penry (1978) outlined a number of possible reasons for such noncompliance: passive noncompliance (forgetfulness), chaotic living situation, denial of the illness, or deliberate noncompliance (fear of drug addiction, dislike of various medication side effects, or the need to dramatize the physical problems seizures present.) Another possibility could be that the child or adolescent has actually become toxic by purposely ingesting excessive amounts of the anticonvulsant medication in order to exacerbate the illness or as an expression of underlying depression and despair. Other problems can occur when the patient or parent believes that the medication does not need to be taken unless the child continues to experience seizures. Here an educational and informational approach, clarifying the need for medication to obtain an appropriate steady state and adequate therapeutic level, can be helpful in achieving compliance (see the section on facilitating understanding of epilepsy above).

Ketogenic diet. The ketogenic diet has been used as a treatment for absence seizures that have not responded to appropriate medications and occasionally for myoclonic seizures in children over one and half years of age. This diet includes a high intake of fats, typically three to four parts fat to one part carbohydrate, plus protein. The primary advantage of this diet is that the child may need little or no medication and consequently avoids medication side effects. Typically, the patient is hospitalized when the diet is initiated to monitor for evidence of hypoglycemia and dehydration and to check for the presence of ketosis. After the diet has been established, the parents are instructed in food preparation and in twice daily urine testing (morning and afternoon) for the presence of ketone bodies. The reason the diet improves seizure control is not well understood, and the diet carries with it some risk because of its potential to impair growth and to predispose to hypoglycemia (Swaiman & Wright, 1982).

Psychotherapeutic strategies for achieving seizure control. Mostofsky and Balaschak (1977) have written a comprehensive review of the literature on behavioral approaches to controlling or reducing seizures. The techniques and procedures employed were grouped into four categories: behavioral conditioning, self-control, habituation, and biofeedback techniques. Representative studies in each of these areas are presented in the Appendix, Table A-1.

Behavioral Therapy

Behavioral techniques typically include reward management (such as overt or covert reward programs and/or withdrawal of positive reinforcements), punishment paradigms (electric shock), and avoidance procedures. As yet, there are no controlled research studies comparing these techniques; rather, all of the studies are case reports on one or several patients. The most striking examples of success with operant conditioning have occurred using punishment to alter self-injurious behaviors. In one instance, operant conditioning was employed to eliminate self-induced absence seizures in a mentally retarded child. This child was triggering seizures by waving his hand in front of his eyes and blinking while looking at a light. Aversive conditioning with electric shock was selected in an attempt to reduce the seizures. Two inpatient hospital treatments, each lasting three or four days, successfully eliminated the handwaving and decreased the blinking behavior by approximately 90 percent from the pretreatment base rate. A followup at seven months showed continued success, with no negative side effects from the aversive procedure (Wright, 1973). Similarly, a combination of reinforcement and punishment was used to decrease the frequency of falling which caused bruises in a child with generalized (absence and tonic-clonic) seizures. The falls were found to relate to social reinforcement and not to actual seizures (Adams, Klinge, & Keiser, 1973). The success of these approaches with individual patients (see Table A-1 in the Appendix) highlights the importance of carefully assessing possible individual, social, and environmental determinants of seizures and subsequently providing immediate consequences in an effort to alter this extremely maladaptive behavior.

Self-Control Techniques

These techniques include relaxation, desensitization, and insight oriented psychotherapy. From case reports, it appears that relaxation, even when used alone, may be an important component of intervention and is particularly useful in reducing anxiety. Psychotherapy has been employed and appears to be indicated primarily when major emotional conflicts interact with and affect seizure frequency. (Illustrative studies are reported in Table A-1 in the Appendix.)

Hypnosis may be very useful as both a diagnostic and therapeutic tool. Gross (1979) employed hypnosis successfully with four adolescent girls who presented with hysterical seizures following sexual molestation and rape by alcoholic fathers or father surrogates. The symptoms served two primary purposes: 1) they allowed the adolescent to be removed from the threatening father figure by hospitalization; and 2) they allowed the girl to receive sympathy, support, and attention. In each case, Gross combined psychotherapy with hypnotherapy and in two instances also included treatment of the family. During the assessment and treatment period the adolescent was able to achieve better understanding of the symbolic meaning of her symptom. Other examples of each of these self-control techniques are presented in Table A-1 in the Appendix.

Habituation or Extinction

This technique has been used primarily with seizures precipitated by sensory stimuli. In this technique the precipitating stimuli (lights, sounds, etc.) are presented until habituation occurs. The objective of the treatment is to desensitize the patient to the trigger stimuli and to alter the critical trigger threshold. Work in this area has been done primarily by Forster (1977).

Biofeedback Procedures

EEG biofeedback procedures have only recently been employed with patients with seizure disorders (see Table A-1 in the Appendix). Subjects chosen for such procedures often have severe and uncontrolled seizures. In such a procedure, the patient is instructed to generate or to avoid generating specific types of brain activity (e.g., alpha and theta activity, sensory motor rhythms, spike and wave paroxysms) during EEG monitoring. Visual or auditory signals typically provide feedback for desired or undesirable bioelectric patterns. A theoretical rational underlying EEG biofeedback is provided in Lubar and Shouse's (1977) review of its use for seizure disorders and hyperactivity. They view biofeedback as a form of operant conditioning that involves rewarding or punishing specific electrophysiological patterns of activity within the brain. Alpha and theta activity and sensorimotor rhythms are most frequently targeted for training. In their conceptual framework, alpha and theta activities are associated with relaxation and a low level of arousal in general. The sensorimotor rhythm is associated with the inhibition of motor responses and the generation of spindles during sleep. Increased sensorimotor rhythm is hypothesized to increase the seizure threshold through an inhibition of motor responses. Alternatively, such an increase may facilitate inhibitory processes to uncontrolled discharges in the brain. Such biofeedback training has proved more successful for seizures with motor components, such as Jacksonian, psychomotor, or generalized seizures of the tonic-clonic, atonic, or akinetic types.

Although EEG changes have been obtained with some biofeedback training and have related to improved seizure control, controlled studies with larger sample sizes are needed. There are several areas in which the current data are limited; for example, the amount of time required to achieve some degree of improvement for particular seizure subtypes has not been established, nor have specific indicators or contraindicators for this type of treatment been well delineated. Systematic work with various subgroups of seizure patients differing in seizure classification, frequency, and severity is needed. In addition, the indirect effect of such frequent treatment (often 3 times a week for several months) must be evaluated. Mostofsky and Williams (1982) write that the various techniques may not be mutually exclusive, but rather appear to combine a number of therapeutic methods: "They may, indeed, share common features—such as progressive relaxation, attention activation, generation of positive expectancies, implicit or explicit reward/punishment features, and emotional support—that are more uniformly operative in each than the proponents of the different methodologies might readily acknowledge" (p. 181).

Comparative studies systematically evaluating the efficacy of the various approaches for specific seizure types are needed. Some progress has been made, particularly in the pharmacologic area. Specific anticonvulsant medications most effective with specific seizure subtypes are now being identified and employed with specific patient subgroups, although multiple trials are often required to establish the appropriate type, combination, or dosage of medication. Similarly, specific psychological interventions may be more effective with particular seizure types, at a specific age, or for specific seizure related difficulties. Identifying the appropriate combination of pharmacologic, behavioral, psychophysiological, and intrapsychic treatment approaches for specific patients will require extended observation and clinical research on diversified patient populations.

Tic Disorders

The American Psychiatric Association's recent *Diagnostic and Statistical Manual of Mental Disorders*, 3rd Edition (DSM-III) (1980) has identified a variety of disorders in which an abnormality of gross motor movement is the predominant feature. These disorders have been classified into five major subcategories: transient tic disorder, chronic motor tic disorder, Tourette's disorder, atypical tic disorders, and atypical stereotyped movement disorder. Large gaps in knowledge still remain regarding each of these disorders, but clinical and research investigations during the last decade have provided new etiologic diagnostic, and treatment insights. Current information in each of these areas will be presented with a focus on the tic disorders. It is still unknown whether the three major tic disorders delineated in DSM-III represent distinct clinical conditions or represent a continuum of severity of tic disorders. This section will deal primarily with transient tic disorder, chronic tic disorder, and Tourette's Syndrome. Other abnormal involuntary movement disorders are described in Table 3-6 and should be considered in the differential diagnosis. Many of these clinical signs are associated with other neurological diseases.

Definition

Transient tic disorder. This disorder is characterized by recurrent, involuntary, repetitive, rapid movements, typically of the eye, or part of the face. Occasionally, the entire head, torso, or limbs may be involved. The age at onset is childhood or early adolescence and typically the onset is sudden. Such tics are more common in boys, with an increase in incidence at 6-7 years of age (Schowalter, 1980). The tics vary in intensity and duration over weeks or months, but by definition have a duration of not more than one year. Some voluntary control over the movements

TABLE 3-6

Movement Disorders

Athetoid movements:	Slow, irregular, writhing movements most frequently in the hands and other parts of the extremities.
Choreiform movements:	Rapid, irregular, jerky movements that are involuntary and arhythmic.
Dyskinesia:	Silent, oral-buccal-lingual, masticatory movements in the face and choreoathetoid movements in the limbs.
Dystonic movements:	Slower, twisting movements interspersed with prolonged tonic muscular contraction, involving several muscle groups such as head, limbs, or torso.
Hemiballismic movements:	Intermittent, coarse, jumping and flinging unilateral movements of the limbs, most marked in the upper extremity.
Hemifacial spasm:	Irregular, repetitive, unilateral jerks of facial muscles.
Motor tic:	Involuntary rapid movement of a functionally related group of skeletal muscles.
Myoclonic movements:	Brief, shocklike contractions of a portion of a muscle, an entire muscle, or a group of muscles, generally restricted to one area of the body.
Myokymia:	Brief, spontaneous contractions or twitching of muscle fibers, frequently eye muscles.
Phonic tic:	Involuntary production of noises or words.
Spasms:	Stereotypic, slower, and more prolonged than tics; involve whole groups of muscles.
Stereotyped movements:	Voluntary, brief, or prolonged habit or mannerism that is often experienced as pleasurable.
Synkinesis:	An unintentional movement accompanying a volitional movement (e.g., movements of the corner of the mouth when the individual intends to close the eye).
Tremor:	An involuntary trembling or quivering, often of the head or extremities that is stereotyped and rhythmic.

for brief periods (minutes to hours) is also apparent. Often, however, a rebound in tic activity occurs following such an attempt at suppression. In addition, stress or excitement often exacerbates tics; during periods of intense concentration or sleep, tics often abate. Vocal tics are less common, but may occur as throat clearing or other noises (DSM-III, 1980). A summary of the signs and symptoms, as well as a comparison with the other tic disorders, is presented in Table 3-7.

Although no formal statistics have been reported for the incidence of transient tic disorder, surveys of school children indicate that from 12-24 percent of children surveyed have a history of some kind of tic; however, these surveys did not indicate either a minimum or maximum duration of such tics. Tics also may remit spontaneously and subsequently reoccur under periods of stress. In other instances, the

TABLE 3-7

Stereotyped Movement Disorders

Type and Definition	Major Symptoms and Signs	Possible Medical Treatment	Psychologic Issues
Transient Tic: Sudden onset of involuntary, repetitive, rapid movements Duration less than one year, tic intensity varies, some suppression possible	Eye blink or facial tic Tic involving head, limbs, or torso Throat clearing	Usually none	Identify environmental stress precipitants Transient anxiety Social embarrassment
Chronic Motor Tic: Similar to above except: duration of tics at least one year, symptoms constant over time, and movements involve no more than three muscle groups	Combination of the above tics	Muscle relaxant drugs Valium	Environmental or family stress Chronic anxiety and tension Social stigma Peer rejection
Tourette's Syndrome: Recurrent, involuntary, repetitive, rapid, and purposeless motor movements affecting multiple muscle groups	*Most Common* Multiple involuntary muscular tics Vocal tics (barks, sniffs, snorts, grunts, sounds, throat clearing) *Associated Criteria* Coprolalia Echolalia Palilalia Echokinesis Obsessive or compulsive impulses to touch self or others	*Neuropharmacologic* Dopamine blocking agents Haloperidol Medication to reduce side effects Cogentin Drugs impacting adrenergic transmission Clonidine	Symptoms are bizarre, frightening, and socially inappropriate Isolation, ridicule by peers Family conflict Low self-esteem Obsessions and body image confusion Associated problems of hyperactivity or learning disability

individual may subsequently develop Tourette's disorder. Finally, there does appear to be an increased incidence of tics among family members of individuals with transient tics (DSM-III, 1980).

Chronic motor tic disorder. This disorder is differentiated from transient tic disorder primarily on the basis of the duration of symptom expression. In the chronic motor tic disorder, the duration of tics must be at least one year, and the duration of symptoms is constant over weeks or months. The essential feature of a chronic motor tic is the presence of recurrent, involuntary, repetitive, rapid, purposeless movements that involve no more than three muscle groups at any one time. As in the transient tic disorder, there is an ability to suppress movements voluntarily for a short period of time. Age at onset is typically childhood or after the age of 40 (DSM-III, 1980) (see Table 3-7).

Tourette's Syndrome. This is the most severe of the tic disorders, and is accompanied by multiple tics, early onset age, and often lifelong affliction. It was first described in 1885 by Gilles de la Tourette; its clinical description has not varied substantially since that time. Shapiro and Shapiro (1980) provide a typical developmental sequence for patients eventually diagnosed with Tourette's Syndrome.

> At approximately 7 years of age the patient developed an eye tic. Two or three months later, facial grimaces and head jerks either replaced or were added to the initial tic. This history, coupled with the fact that the patient controlled the tics during the initial evaluation, suggested to the physician that the complaints were caused by over-controlling parental attitudes or attention seeking behavior in the child. Parents were told to ignore the "habits" that they would go away in time.
>
> However, the symptoms persisted and varied. Vocal tics developed—sniffs and throat clearing. These vocal symptoms suggested possible allergic rhinitis and consultation with an allergist and ENT specialist was recommended.
>
> The parents then noticed repetitive types of behavior, such as touching others, repeating things—not only the patient's own words, but the words or movements of others. The child even began to curse—explosively and involuntarily. Perplexed by the bizarre nature of the symptoms, severe psychopathology, encephalitis or other serious illnesses were considered and several consultations were recommended, including psychiatric evaluation. No diagnosis resulted (p. 3).

Such a delay in diagnosis is not atypical. Golden (1977) in his study of children with Tourette's Syndrome found an age of onset at 6 years, but a correct diagnosis occurring on the average 4 years later. Some patients experience a delay of at least 10 years between symptom onset and correct diagnosis.   The revised DSM-III provides clinical criteria for the diagnosis of this disorder and the differentiation of it from other tic disorders, summarized in Table 3-7.

Diagnostic Criteria for Tourette's Syndrome

The usual age at onset is between 2 and 15 years of age, and the disorder often lasts throughout the individual's lifetime. It consists of multiple muscular and often vocal tics which vary in intensity over weeks and months. As with the other tic disorders, the patient is often able to suppress the movements voluntarily for a short time, and they typically disappear during sleep or during an absorbing activity.

In the first stage of the disorder, tics involving the eyes, face, neck, or shoulders are often observed. Shapiro and Shapiro (1980) report that the first symptom in almost half the patients is a single motor tic such as an eye blink. Other patients experience multiple tics from the onset. Periods of remission may occur, or different types of tics may replace the earlier symptoms. Remissions are typically short (a week to several months) and more common in the early phase of the illness. During the second phase the motor tics may be accompanied by inarticulate noises or cries. These might include throat clearing, sniffing, coughing, barking, clicks, yelps, or grunts. Vocal tics are always present and may include multiple forms. In the final stage, the vocal tics may extend to coprolalia (involuntary utterance of obscene words), echolalia (repetition of another's words), or palilalia (repetition of one's own last words), but these symptoms are not uniformly present. Coprolalia, the symptom most distressing to parents, teachers, peers, and the patient, is present in approximately 50 percent of the cases. Other symptoms such as echokinesis (imitation of other's movements); mental coprolalia (thinking about obscene words); compulsive impulses to touch oneself or another person (often in the genital areas); or unusual movements, such as squatting, twirling, deep knee bends, retracing steps, or other complex rituals may also occur. The presence of such symptoms may confirm the diagnosis of Tourette's, but is not essential.

Prevalence of Tourette's Syndrome

The disorder is three times more common in boys than in girls and more frequently found among members of the same family than in the general population. Although no incidence or prevalence figures currently exist, incidence is estimated to be 0.1-0.5/1000, with a prevalence of approximately 22,000 to 110,000 in the United States population (Shapiro & Shapiro, 1980).

Etiology and Genetics

There have been a variety of psychological explanations of tics (which were formerly described as nervous habits). Early explanations of transient or chronic motor tics typically can be placed into one of three major categories: 1) psychoanalytic explanations in which the tic was viewed as a motoric expression of a neurotic or aggressive impulse; 2) learning theory explanations in which tics were viewed either as learned responses maintained through positive reinforcement or as normal responses that have become exaggerated or repetitive because of social contingencies; or 3) psychosocial explanations that viewed tics as a response to environmental stress and tension.

Since tics are quite commonly found in the general population (estimates range from 12-24%) and range dramatically in severity, duration, and number of muscle groups involved, the possibility of diverse etiologies for various subtypes of tic disorders should be investigated.

The most comprehensive genetic and epidemiologic studies have focused primarily on patients with Tourette's Syndrome. An increased family history of tics, a higher Tourette concordance rate in identical than in fraternal twins, an increased risk of Tourette's in relatives of females with this disorder, and an increased risk to siblings of identified cases when one parent is affected have been demonstrated. The additional finding that females with Tourette's Syndrome were more likely to transmit the disease to their offspring than were similarly afflicted males suggested that the disease may be related to a threshold effect. Since males predominate (3:1), the occurrence of this disorder in a female may require a higher genetic loading. This may explain the increased incidence of Tourette's among the offspring of females with this syndrome (Kidd, Prusoff, & Cohen, 1980; Shapiro & Shapiro, 1980).

Finally, some evidence that chronic motor tics may be a milder form of Tourette's Syndrome was obtained by epidemiological studies demonstrating that both disorders can be transmitted in the same families (Pauls, Cohen, Heimbuch, Detlor, & Kidd, 1981). While this suggests that these two disorders may be part of a spectrum of movement disorders, with multiple motor tics representing a less severe form of the disorder in these families, other investigators have found that multiple tic disorders alone, without Tourette's Syndrome, cluster in families. More extensive genetic and epidemiologic studies of families with multiple tics, Tourette's Syndrome, and combinations of both of these will be needed to determine whether this is a homogeneous disorder differing in severity or whether there are heterogeneous subtypes.

Most evidence to date suggests that the etiology of Tourette's Syndrome is an impairment (either biochemical or neuroanatomic) in the central nervous system. Currently, a dysfunction of the basal ganglia is hypothesized as the most likely explanation for the Tourette Syndrome, but experimental evidence for this is not yet available. Shapiro and Shapiro (1981a) have provided an excellent summary of the evidence supporting this and other etiologic hypotheses. Although the evidence supporting a specific neuroanatomic or neurochemical theory is inconclusive to date, the primary hypotheses include: 1. an increased level of dopamine or norepinephrine at presynaptic neurons; 2. an increased sensitivity to normal amounts of these neurotransmitters at postsynaptic neurons; 3. a decreased level of serotonin or acetylcholine, or gamma aminobutyric acid; or 4. an abnormal metabolism of neurotransmitters (Shapiro & Shapiro, 1981a). While the effectiveness of haloperidol provides some support for the role of dopamine either in excessive presynaptic levels, or postsynaptic sensitivity to normal levels, the clinical effect of other drugs also thought to affect specific neurotransmitters has not supported the hypotheses for abnormal dopamine levels.

Assessment Issues

When chronic motor tics or Tourette's Syndrome is suspected, the child should receive comprehensive neurologic and neuropsychologic assessment. Patients with Tourette's Syndrome have been shown to have a higher percentage of abnormal electroencephalograms (48.8% compared to 15% in the normal population); soft neurological signs on examination (57% compared to an expected 20% in normal children); and minimal brain dysfunction (68% compared to 3-7%) (Shapiro & Shapiro, 1980). Evidence of neuropsychologic impairment has also been demonstrated. Although children with Tourette's Syndrome typically obtain average overall intelligence scores, when more comprehensive assessment is performed, deficits in written arithmetic, copying tasks, and speed of learning and writing symbols have been identified (Incagnoli & Kane, 1981). Whether difficulties in these areas are due to sensory or motor dysfunction or the integration of these functions and whether such dysfunctions are due to a primary lesion or are secondary to neurophysiological and neurochemical irregularity still have not been determined.

Finally, emotional problems may also be associated with this syndrome or may develop as a reaction to the behaviors and responses of others (see Table 3-7). Many parents, teachers, and peers find the symptoms of the disorder particularly distressing. When coprolalia is evident or if the child touches either himself or other persons on the breast and genital areas, severe social censure and punishment may ensue. Such behaviors are considered very inappropriate in the social environment and are thought to be under voluntary control. Education of not only the family, but also the school system, is of great importance in preventing the development of serious secondary emotional problems. Children with Tourette's often can be the target of ridicule, teasing, and shaming. The extended period of time that often lapses prior to correct diagnosis and appropriate treatment can present major obstacles in the child's development of an adequate self-concept and peer and family relationships. Once a diagnosis has been made, the patients and their families often benefit greatly from participation in a local chapter of the Tourette Syndrome Association (TSA). The TSA chapters provide patient and parent support groups, facilitate education regarding the symptomatology and treatment for the disorder for parents, school personnel and health care providers, and provide a quarterly newsletter discussing current treatments, research progress, and current information about this disorder.

Current Medical Treatment

A variety of drugs known to effect specific neurotransmitters have been tried in the treatment of Tourette's Syndrome, and of these, haloperidol has been found to be most effective. In their (1981a) review article, Shapiro and Shapiro reported that of 59 patients on haloperidol, there was an 80 percent reduction in symptoms in 80 percent of the patients. This was in contrast to an average symptom decrease of only 24.3 percent in patients who were not on medication. Their clinical experience with over 600 patients on haloperidol indicates that this should be the drug of choice for patients whose tic disorder significantly interferes with social function or emotional adjustment. Similarly, Abuzzahab and Anderson's 1973 review of 430 case histories indicated haloperidol to be the treatment of choice.

The major limitation to use of this medication is its significant side effects. These can include extrapyramidal signs, such as akinesia, tremor, rigidity, depressed looking expression, drooling, shuffling gait, and a loss of coordinated movements. These side effects are most often dose related, can be minimized with the addition of anti-Parkinsonian agents (e.g., Cogentin) to the drug regimen, and may disappear after 3-4 months of treatment. Other side effects, such as cognitive blunting, lethargy, muscular weakness and fatigue, tardive dyskinesia, acute dystonia, and other physical problems (dry mouth, tachycardia, hypotension, congestion, etc.) may occur. Recently, Mikkelsen, Detlor, and Cohen (1981) found that school avoidance and social phobia developed in 15 of their child patients with Tourette's treated with low doses of haloperidol for short periods of time. They found that the symptoms abated when the medication was discontinued.

The presence of such significant side effects in some patients, as well as haloperidol's inability to reduce symptoms in other patients, has resulted in an effort to find other drugs that may be either more effective or associated with fewer side effects. Both Pimozide and penfluridol (also dopamine antagonists) have been reported as effective in treating Tourette's Syndrome and have somewhat fewer side effects; however, the Food and Drug Administration has restricted the use of the latter in the United States. Clonidine has been tried with patients who were previously treated unsuccessfully with haloperidol or who developed significant side effects (see Table A-2 in the Appendix). Although of the patients studied, 70 percent responded positively, the symptoms most improved were compulsivity, aggression, and behavioral and attentional problems. Thus, this drug may be more effective in treating some of the associated behavioral problems of this syndrome, but not necessarily the tics themselves.

A variety of other drugs have been evaluated and found ineffective in treating this disorder. Included among these are the antianxiety, sedative, hypnotic, antidepressant, and anticonvulsant medications. These drugs consequently are typically not used in treating patients with this disorder.

Stimulant medications precipitating tics or Tourette's Syndrome. Recently there have been clinical reports that a minority of patients treated for hyperactivity and attention deficit disorder (ADD) with stimulant medication have developed severe motor and verbal tics. These children have subsequently developed a severe tic disorder requiring haloperidol. Such reports (Lowe, Cohen, Detlor, Kremenitzer, & Shaywitz, 1982) suggested that, for these children, treatment with stimulant medication may have altered receptor functioning or altered the synthesis and release of dopamine or norepinephrine. Their finding suggests the need for caution in prescribing stimulant medication for the alleviation of hyperactive behaviors in any child who currently shows evidence of tics or has a history of tic disorder in the family. Similarly, once stimulant medication is prescribed for a child with hyperkinesis or ADD, careful follow-up is needed to detect the emergence of motor or verbal tics, with stimulant medication withdrawn immediately if tics develop.

The Shapiro's, who have been extensively involved in clinical and research activities involving patients with Tourette's Syndrome, however, have not found that adding stimulant medication to the treatment regimen increased tics in their patients with Tourette's Syndrome. They have found stimulant medication useful in counteracting some of haloperidol's side effects, particularly lethargy and impaired cognitive functioning. The possibility that stimulant medication can precipitate the onset of Tourette's Syndrome in an asymptomatic patient does, however, merit further study. The clinician needs also to be aware of the possibility that such medication may precipitate or exacerbate tics, although to date the evidence is not conclusive (Shapiro & Shapiro, 1981b).

Psychological Treatment

Simple transient tics. A variety of psychotherapeutic approaches have been attempted with children who have tics. These have included traditional insight oriented psychotherapy, self-control and relaxation therapy, reciprocal inhibition, massed practice, self-monitoring, and a variety of other approaches. Specific studies examining the effectiveness of these techniques are outlined in Table A-2 in the Appendix.

A treatment program for simple "nervous habits," such as nail biting, thumb sucking, shoulder jerking, tongue pushing, lip and eyelash picking, has been developed by Azrin and Nunn (1973). These nervous mannerisms are viewed as strongly established habits that have become automatic and outside the person's awareness. The suggested treatment for such tics is a habit reversal procedure in which the patient practices muscle contraction movements that are the reverse of the nervous habit, such as depressing the shoulders in response to shoulder jerking. In this treatment program the child is asked to describe and demonstrate the habit. The purpose of this demonstration is to alert the child to the early indicators (precursors) of the habit in order to learn how to detect preliminary signs of the tic. The patient is then instructed to tense muscles incompatible with the habit. After these exercises, discussion aimed at identifying situations in which the habit typically occurs is pursued and the social stigma of the habit discussed in an effort to increase motivation in complying with the procedure. Using this procedure, all patients (three of whom were children) obtained at least a 90 percent reduction in the nervous habit after one or two sessions. Although Azrin and Nunn were concerned that the alternate behavior might become a nervous habit, they did not find this to be the case on follow-up. This method appeared to be a very quick and effective method of treatment for patients with simple nervous habits. For two patients, in whom the symptoms re-emerged, a brief telephone contact or a follow-up visit was all that was needed to eliminate the habit.

Stress induced tics. When it is apparent that emotional stress is precipitating or exacerbating tics, it is important to identify the source of psychologic discomfort and distress. The child may be anxious and tense in a home environment that is punitive, restrictive, or overly demanding. Efforts directed toward changing family interactions and reducing negative parent-child interactions may be effective in reducing the motor tic. In other instances, the child may respond with excessive anxiety to normal developmental tasks and experiences. In this case, psychotherapy may be helpful in reducing the tension the child experiences. Jacobson's relaxation procedure (which incorporates antagonistic responses to relaxation) may also be effective with tics related to muscular tension by alerting the child to the preliminary signs of the tic or heightened muscular tension.

Methodologically rigorous treatment studies comparing the behavioral therapies have not yet been systematically employed with patients having either chronic or transient motor tic disturbances. Consequently, an ordering of the effectiveness of specific behavioral treatments for specific types of motor tics is not yet available. Studies comparing the relative effectiveness of habit reversal, relaxation, or hypnosis would provide much needed information in this regard. Also needed are specific guidelines concerning the need for more intensive psychotherapy or family intervention when a child presents with a transient tic disorder.

Combined medical and psychological treatment programs have been initiated for patients with Tourette's Syndrome, particularly when treatment with haloperidol alone is unsuccessful. Often these patients have been involved in a variety of treatment programs to no avail. In general, the available reports employing psychological interventions have found that behavioral approaches are somewhat more successful in reducing a child's vocal tics rather than reducing motor tics. The latter seem to respond best to treatment with haloperidol; however, self-control, self-monitoring, and relaxation techniques have been somewhat successful in reducing coprolalia or gutteral sounds (see the Appendix, Table A-2). The clinical reports indicate that, when medication is not successful or only partially successful in reducing verbal tics, these approaches may achieve additional success. All of these studies, however, have employed only a single patient, and more comprehensive investigation of the response of groups of patients with Tourette's is needed.

Some negative findings regarding behavioral approaches have also been demonstrated. Following an early report (Tophoff, 1973) on the successful use of massed practice as a method for reducing the frequency of verbal tics, other investigators attempted this procedure with other Tourette's patients. These subsequent attempts have not been successful; in fact, in one instance massed practice actually increased the habit strength of the tics. Each study employed slightly different procedures with the patient and so direct comparisons are not possible, although the lack of success of the later studies highlights potential problems in applying the technique. In Canavan and Powell's (1981) study, the patient (24 years of age) received mass practice of a single obscenity, of multiple obscenities, and also received relaxation therapy. Oral feedback ("no") was provided whenever an obscenity occurred. The patient had to converse as long as possible without emitting any tics. Feedback and time out occurred following one minute of silence. In this treatment procedure, massed practice of a single tic did not result in a change in the mean number of tics, nor did massed practice of multiple tics achieve a decrease in frequency. Although oral feedback did result in a significant *immediate* effect, this did not carry through the treatment session and was not maintained after sessions. Hollandsworth and Bausinger (1978) incorporated a massed practice procedure with monetary rewards for an 18 year old patient. In their treatment procedure the patient's father deposited $30.00 with the therapist. The patient received $2.00 for completion of each treatment session and incurred monetary fines within a session if coprolalia occurred. After eight treatment sessions the patient displayed an increase in and an improved articulation of the obscenities and therapy was terminated. At 6 months follow-up, there was a return to the baseline frequency in the coprolalia. The one successful reported case occurred for a 13 year old boy who had previously received haloperidol, psychotherapy, and progressive relaxation therapy with no effect. The treatment program included two sessions per week in which massed practice of the tics as well as assertiveness training occurred. The parents were instructed to ignore the tics when they occurred at home. Although the verbal tics decreased to zero and subsequently the motor tics also disappeared, it is difficult to attribute the success of the program solely to massed practice of the tics. The assertiveness training and parental ignoring of the tics may have played a pivotal role. Clearly, further work comparing the various procedures and combinations of procedures is needed in addition to efforts to identify subgroups of patients for whom specific treatment approaches have demonstrated effectiveness.

Bacterial Meningitis

Definition and Etiology

Bacterial meningitis is an inflammation of the three membranes surrounding the brain and spinal cord resulting from bacterial infection of these meninges. During the past two decades there has been a dramatic reduction in mortality from meningitis with antibiotic drug therapy; however, follow-up studies indicate evidence of adverse psychologic and neurologic sequelae in some of the survivors. These sequelae result from extension of the bacteriologic infection to involve brain tissue, either directly by bacteria invasion or secondarily from brain edema or vasculitis. Ninety percent of the reported cases of meningitis occur in infants and children between one month and five years of age (Feigin, 1981); children between one month and one year of age are affected more frequently and often more severely. Boys are affected somewhat more frequently than girls in ratios approximately 1.7/1 (Feigin & Dodge, 1976; Feigin, 1981). (See Table 3-8 for a description of signs, symptoms, and medical treatments.)

Despite the marked improvement in the treatment of infectious diseases, meningitis has increased in frequency during the last several decades because of an increase in the frequency of Hemophilus influenzae and Streptococcus agalactiae. Most cases in normal children above one month of age are caused by one of three organisms, clinically referred to as Hemophilus Influenzae, Pneumococcal Meningitis, or Meningococcal Meningitis. Any factor that predisposes the child to infection in other body sites can also predispose to central nervous system (CNS) infection. This is particularly apparent in the newborn infant in whom a number of factors, reflecting possible physiological deficiencies or immaturities of the infant's immunological (defense) mechanisms, may heighten the risk of infection. When the disease occurs, it often follows an upper respiratory infection. This may occur because a common route of infection is through the venous channels that drain the upper respiratory tract and are close to the meninges. Other routes of infection can include generalized septicemia, skull fracture, and infection of other sites (endocarditis, pneumonia, thrombophlebitis, sinusitis, mastoiditis, osteomyelitis) (Feigin, 1981; Wright, Schaefer, & Solomons, 1979). Other children who are vulnerable to this illness are those with sickle cell anemia, other hemoglobinopathies, malignancies (particularly of the reticuloendothelial system) congenital deficiencies of immunoglobulin systems, congenital asplenia or splenosis, diabetes or renal insufficiency, malnutrition, and possibly irradiation or treatment with immuno-suppressive agents or antimetabolites (Feigin, 1981).

Signs and Symptoms

Symptoms that parents should be alerted to include neck rigidity, fever, resistance to cuddling or diapering, irritablity or lethargy, vacant stare, anorexia, bulging or tense fontanel, and a rapidly spreading purple rash. Signs noted on physical examination include an inability to passively extend the legs when the hips are flexed (Kernig's Sign) and flexion of the hips when the neck is flexed (Brudzinski's Sign).

Medical Treatment

A lumbar puncture procedure is performed to obtain a small amount of cerebro-spinal fluid from the lumbar space. The fluid is then cultured in order to identify

TABLE 3-8

Bacterial Meningitis

Definition	Major Signs and Symptoms	Possible Medical Treatment	Psychologic Issues
An inflammation of the three membranes surrounding the brain resulting from bacterial infection	Irritability and lethargy Anorexia Fever Neck rigidity Bulging fontanel Rash	Lumbar puncture Blood culture Spinal fluid culture Antibiotic therapy Respiratory isolation Treatment of increased intracranial pressure	Fear of the child's death Fear of residual brain damage Coping with residual deficits: Mental retardation Seizures Hydrocephalus Hemiparesis Learning disability Deafness

the specific infecting organism so that appropriate antibiotic therapy can be administered. Blood culture to identify septicemia, electrolyte determinations, and complete blood count to observe the body's response to infection are sometimes needed. Once the diagnosis is made, hospitalization with respiratory isolation is needed. A number of complications can occur during the acute phase of the illness. These include cerebral edema, stupor, coma, seizures, changes in respiratory rate and rhythm, focal neurologic signs, and obstructive or communicating hydrocephalus (Bell, 1982).

Prognostic indicators. Focal neurologic signs (seizures, hemiparesis, ataxia) at the time of admission are often associated with a poor prognosis and correlate with mental retardation following discharge, as well as continued abnormalities on neurologic examination on followup visits at 1, 3, 6 months and 1 year. Although seizures that occur prior to or during the first several days of hospitalization for meningitis may not have prognostic significance, seizures that persist beyond the fourth hospital day, that are difficult to control, or that develop late in the hospitalization have been associated with permanent neurologic sequelae (Feigin, 1981).

A number of other factors have been implicated in the child's prognosis. These include: 1) the age of onset of the disease; 2) the specific microorganism causing the disease; 3) the number of bacterial organisms present in the meninges and cerebrospinal fluid; 4) the duration of the illness prior to effective antibiotic therapy; 5) the presence of other pre-existing disorders or immaturities that may compromise the child's response to infection; 6) the presence of focal neurologic abnormalities prior to admission in patients who are not post-ictal; and 7) the occurrence of prolonged, poorly controlled seizures (Wright et al., 1979; Feigin, 1981).

Psychological Assessment

Psychological evaluation of developmental functioning is frequently of benefit if the infant or child displays a marked change in developmental status during the recovery period. In such instances the psychologist should meet with the parents to assess the child's pre-illness development using a standardized developmental history questionnaire. Completion of the Adaptive Behavior Inventory or the Denver Developmental Screening Test scored by interview with the parents could also provide a useful guide to pre-illness level of adaptive functioning. The child's assessment should include measures of general intellectual function using age-appropriate tests, measures of perceptual-motor, attentional, memory, and language function, as well as standardized infant or child behavior rating scales. If abnormalities are detected during the hospitalization, extended follow-up examinations should be scheduled and parent counseling regarding appropriate cognitive and intellectual stimulation initiated to facilitate recovery of function.

Long-Term Outcome

Recent studies examining the long-term effects of meningitis on cognitive development have demonstrated significant differences in the subsequent intellectual functioning of the postmeningitic child and sibling or control children (Sell, Merrill, Doyne, & Zimsky, 1972; Wright & Jimmerson, 1971). Typically, postmeningitic children obtain IQ scores significantly lower than either their siblings or an age-matched classroom control child. Attempts to identify a specific learning disability following meningitis have met with mixed results. Frequently, more global signs of cognitive impairment are identified, accompanied by poor attention span, easy fatigability, changes in activity level, and behavioral problems. Evidence of later differential impairment of auditory abilities was obtained by Feigin and Dodge (1976) who found deficits in auditory nerve function (determined by evoked response audiometry) for 66 percent of the patients following recovery from meningococcal meningitis. This corresponded with deficits obtained by Sell et al. (1972) in psycholinguistic abilities, suggesting possible language impairment as a sequelae to meningitis. Before any conclusions can be drawn about the specificity of any learning disability following meningitis, however, it will be important to examine the type and severity of the bacterial infection, as well as the child's chronological age at illness onset, in relation to later cognitive disability.

Summary

Although antibiotic treatment of acute bacterial meningitis has significantly reduced the mortality of this potentially life-threatening disease, persistent neurologic abnormalities and psychologic dysfunction can remain as major long-term sequelae. Diverse neurologic abnormalities which reflect widespread damage to the central nervous system include: hearing impairment, visual loss, hydrocephalus, seizure disorder, or motor disabilities such as hemiparesis or quadriparesis, cranial nerve deficits, and ataxia. Psychologic dysfunction in the postmeningitic child may include: mental retardation, learning disability, language impairment, and behavioral disturbances. The incidence of subsequent neurologic dysfunction following meningitis in Feigin's recent prospective study was reported to be as high as 28 percent, indicating that these infants and children should certainly be considered an "at risk" population.

The extensive diversity of abnormalities emphasizes the need for a broad, extensive study of the possible adverse effects of meningitis. In addition, a sufficient follow-up period is necessary in order to detect those neurologic and psychologic deficits that will endure. The goal of the development of new antibiotic therapies for bacterial meningitis is to provide a more effective and safer therapeutic regimen. An equally important goal should be to ascertain that the new therapeutic drugs will both further reduce the mortality associated with acute bacterial meningitis and improve the long-term neuropsychologic outcome of the surviving children.

Infants and children hospitalized with meningitis may well benefit from neurologic and psychologic evaluation, particularly if risk factors such as focal neurologic signs, seizures, young age of onset, stormy hospital course, and development of neurologic complications occur. In such instances the children may require a comprehensive neurologic examination including an electroencephalogram (EEG), a brain stem auditory and visual-evoked response procedure, a hearing evaluation, as well as an assessment of developmental status and cognitive functioning.

References

Epilepsy

Adams, K.M., Klinge, V., & Keiser, T.W. The extinction of a self-injurious behavior in an epileptic child. *Behaviour Research and Therapy*, 1973, *11*, 351–356.

Baird, H.W., John, E.R., Ahn, H., & Maisel, E. Neurometric evaluation of epileptic children who do well and poorly in school. *Electroencephalography and Clinical Neurophysiology*, 1980, *48*, 683–693.

Balaschak, B.A., & Mostofsky, D.I. Seizure disorders. In E.J. Mash & L.G. Terdal (Eds.), *Behavioral assessment of childhood disorders*. New York: Guildford Press, 1981.

Cohen, R.J., & Suter, C. Hysterical seizures: Suggestion as a provocative EEG test. *Annals of Neurology*, 1982, *11*, 391–395.

Commission on Classification and Terminology of the International League Against Epilepsy. Proposal for revised clinical and electroencephalographic classification of epileptic seizures. *Epilepsia*, 1981, *22*, 489–501.

Comprehensive Epilepsy Program. *Epilepsy: Medical aspects*. Minneapolis: University of Minnesota, 1979.

Cooper, I.S., Amin, I., Riklan, M., Waltz, J.M., & Poon, T.P. Chronic cerebellar stimulation in epilepsy. Clinical and anatomical studies. *Archives of Neurology*, 1976, *33*(8), 559–570.

Desai, B.T., Riley, T.L., Porter, R.J., & Penry, J.K. Active noncompliance as a cause of uncontrolled seizures. *Epilepsia*, 1978, *19*, 447–452.

Dodrill, C.B. Diphenylhydantoin serum levels, toxicity, and neuropsychological performance in patients with epilepsy. *Epilepsia*, 1975, *16*, 593–600.

Dodrill, C.B. Neuropsychology of epilepsy. In S.B. Filskov & T.J. Boll (Eds.), *Handbook of clinical neuropsychology*. New York: John Wiley and Sons, 1981.

Epilepsy Foundation of America. *Basic statistics on the epilepsies*. Philadelphia: F.A. Davis, 1975.

Forster, F.M. *Reflex epilepsy, behavioral therapy and conditional reflexes*. Springfield, Illinois: Charles C. Thomas, 1977.

Gross, M. Incestuous rape: A cause for hysterical seizures in four adolescent girls. *American Journal of Orthopsychiatry*, 1979, *49*(4), 704–708.

Gross, M., & Huerta, E. Functional convulsions masked as epileptic disorders. *Journal of Pediatric Psychology*, 1980, *5*(1), 71–79.

Gumnit, R.J. (Ed.). *Epilepsy: A handbook for physicians* (4th ed.). Minneapolis: University of Minnesota, 1981.

Hodgman, C.H., McAnarney, E.R., Myers, G.J., Iker, H., with McKinney, R., Parmelee, D., Schuster, B., & Tutihasi, M. Emotional complications of adolescent grand mal epilepsy. *The Journal of Pediatrics*, 1979, *95*(2), 309–312.

Holmes, G.L., Sackellares, J.C., McKiernan, J., Ragland, M., & Dreifuss, F.E. Evaluation of childhood pseudoseizures using EEG telemetry and videotape monitoring. *The Journal of Pediatrics*, 1980, *97*(4), 554–558.

Holowach, J., Thurston, D.L., & O'Leary, J. Prognosis in childhood epilepsy. Follow-up study of 148 cases in which therapy had been suspended after prolonged anticonvulsant control. *The New England Journal of Medicine*, 1972, *286*, 169–174.

Long, C.G., & Moore, J.R. Parental expectations for their epileptic children. *Journal of Child Psychology and Psychiatry and Allied Disciplines*, 1979, *20*, 299–312.

Lubar, J.F., & Shouse, M.N. Use of biofeedback in the treatment of seizure disorders and hyperactivity. In B.B. Lahey & A.E. Kazdin (Eds.), *Advances in clinical child psychology* (Vol. 1). New York: Plenum Press, 1977.

Minter, R.E. Can emotions precipitate seizures—a review of the question. *The Journal of Family Practice*, 1979, *8*(1), 55–59.

Mostofsky, D.I., & Balaschak, B.A. Psychobiological control of seizures. *Psychological Bulletin*, 1977, *84*(4), 723–750.

Mostofsky, D.I., & Williams, D.T. Psychogenic seizures in childhood and adolescence. In T.L. Riley & A. Roy (Eds.), *Pseudoseizures*. Baltimore: Williams & Wilkins, 1982.

Ozuna, J. Psychosocial aspects of epilepsy. *Journal of Neurosurgical Nursing*, 1979, *11*(4), 242–246.

Ramani, S.V., Quesney, L.F., Olson, D., & Gumnit, R.J. Diagnosis of hysterical seizures in epileptic patients. *American Journal of Psychiatry*, 1980, *137*(6), 705–709.

Reynolds, E.H., & Travers, R.D. Serum anticonvulsant concentrations in epileptic patients with mental symptoms: A preliminary report. *British Journal of Psychiatry*, 1974, *124*, 440–445.

Roy, A. Psychiatric concepts: Definitions and diagnosis of hysterical seizures. In T.L. Riley & A. Roy (Eds.), *Pseudoseizures*. Baltimore: Williams & Wilkins, 1982.

Rutter, M., Tizard, J., & Whitmore, K. (Eds.). *Education, health and behaviour; psychological and medical study of childhood development*. New York: Wiley, 1970.

Scott, D.F. Psychiatric aspects of epilepsy. *British Journal of Psychiatry*, 1978, *132*, 417–430.

Scott, D.F. The use of EEG in pseudoseizures. In T.L. Riley & A. Roy (Eds.), *Pseudoseizures*. Baltimore: Williams & Wilkins, 1982.

Stores, G. Studies of attention and seizure disorders. *Developmental Medicine and Child Neurology*, 1973, *15*, 376–382.

Stores, G. The investigation and management of school children with epilepsy. *Public Health*, 1976, *90*(4), 171–177.

Stores, G. Behavior disturbance and type of epilepsy in children attending ordinary school. In J.K. Penry (Ed.), *Epilepsy, the eighth international symposium*. New York: Raven Press, 1977.

Stores, G. School-children with epilepsy at risk for learning and behaviour problems. *Developmental Medicine and Child Neurology*, 1978, *20*, 502–508.

Swaiman, K.F., & Wright, F.S. (Eds.). *The practice of pediatric neurology* (2 vols., 2nd ed.). St. Louis: C.V. Mosby Company, 1982.

Task force on nomenclature & statistics of the American Psychiatric Association. *Diagnostic and statistical manual of mental disorders* (3rd ed.). Washington, D.C.: The American Psychiatric Association, 1980.

Williams, D.T., Gold, A.P., Shrout, P., Shaffer, D., & Adams, D. The impact of psychiatric intervention on patients with uncontrolled seizures. *Journal of Nervous and Mental Disease*, 1979, *167*(10), 626–631.

Wright, F.S., Dreifuss, F.E., Wolcott, G.J., Swaiman, K.F., Low, N.L., Freeman, J.M., & Nelson, K.B. Seizure disorders. In K.F. Swaiman & F.S. Wright (Eds.), *The practice of pediatric neurology* (Vol. 1, 2nd ed.). St. Louis: C.V. Mosby Company, 1982.

Wright, L. Aversive conditioning of self-induced seizures. *Behavior Therapy*, 1973, *4*, 712–713.

Wright, L., Schaefer, A.B., & Solomons, G. *Encyclopedia of pediatric psychology*. Baltimore: University Park Press, 1979.

Tic Disorders

Abuzzahab, F.E., Sr., & Anderson, F.O. Gilles de la Tourette's Syndrome international registry. *Minnesota Medicine*, 1973, *56*, 492–496.

Azrin, N.H., & Nunn, R.G. Habit-reversal: A method of eliminating nervous habits and tics. *Behaviour Research and Therapy*, 1973, *11*, 619–628.

Canavan, A.G.M., & Powell, G.E. The efficacy of several treatments of Gilles de la Tourette's Syndrome as assessed in a single case. *Behaviour Research and Therapy*, 1981, *19*, 549–556.

Golden, G.S. Tourette Syndrome: The pediatric perspective. *American Journal of Diseases of Children*, 1977, *131*, 531–534.

Hollandsworth, J.G., Jr., & Bausinger, L. Unsuccessful use of massed practice in the treatment of Gilles de la Tourette's Syndrome. *Psychological Reports*, 1978, *43*, 671–677.

Incagnoli, T., & Kane, R. Neuropsychological functioning in Gilles de la Tourette's Syndrome. *Journal of Clinical Neuropsychology*, 1981, *3*(2), 165–169.

Kidd, K.K., Prusoff, B.A., & Cohen, D.J. Familial pattern of Gilles de la Tourette Syndrome. *Archives of General Psychiatry*, 1980, *37*(12), 1336–1339.

Lowe, T.L., Cohen, D.J., Detlor, J., Kremenitzer, M.W., & Shaywitz, B.A. Stimulant medications precipitate Tourette's Syndrome. *Journal of the American Medical Association*, 1982, *247*(8), 1168–1169.

Mikkelsen, E.J., Detlor, J., & Cohen, D.J. School avoidance and social phobia triggered by haloperidol in patients with Tourette's disorder. *The American Journal of Psychiatry*, 1981, *138*, 1572-1576.

Pauls, D.L., Cohen, D.J., Heimbuch, R., Detlor, J., & Kidd, K.K. Familial pattern and transmission of Gilles de la Tourette Syndrome and multiple tics. *Archives of General Psychiatry*, 1981, *38*, 1091-1093.

Schowalter, J.E. Tics. *Pediatrics in Review*, 1980, *2*(2), 55-57.

Shapiro, A.K., & Shapiro, E.S. *Tics, Tourette Syndrome and other movement disorders: A pediatricians guide*. Bayside, New York: The Tourette Syndrome Association Inc., 1980.

Shapiro, A.K., & Shapiro, E. The treatment and etiology of tics and Tourette Syndrome. *Comprehensive Psychiatry*, 1981a, *22*(2), 193-205.

Shapiro, A.K., & Shapiro, E. Do stimulants provoke, cause, or exacerbate tics and Tourette Syndrome? *Comprehensive Psychiatry*, 1981b, *22*(3), 265-273.

Task force on nomenclature & statistics of the American Psychiatric Association. *Diagnostic and statistical manual of mental disorders* (3rd ed.). Washington, D.C.: The American Psychiatric Association, 1980.

Tophoff, M. Massed practice, relaxation and assertion training in the treatment of Gilles de la Tourette's Syndrome. *Journal of Behavior Therapy and Experimental Psychiatry*, 1973, *4*, 71-73.

Bacterial Meningitis

Bell, W.E. Bacterial infections of the nervous system. In K.F. Swaiman & F.S. Wright (Eds.), *The practice of pediatric neurology* (Vol. 2, 2nd ed.). St. Louis: C.V. Mosby Co., 1982.

Feigin, R.D. Bacterial meningitis beyond the neonatal period. Unpublished manuscript, Baylor College of Medicine, 1981.

Feigin, R.D., & Dodge, P.R. Bacterial meningitis: Newer concepts of pathophysiology and neurologic sequelae. *Pediatric Clinics of North America*, 1976, *23*(3), 541-556.

Sell, S.H.W., Merrill, R.E., Doyne, E.O., & Zimsky, E.P., Jr. Long-term sequelae of hemophilus influenzae meningitis. *Pediatrics*, 1972, *49*(2), 206-211.

Wright, L. A method for predicting sequelae to meningitis. *American Psychologist*, 1978, *33*, 1037-1039.

Wright, L., & Jimmerson, S. Intellectual sequelae of hemophilus influenzae meningitis. *Journal of Abnormal Psychology*, 1971, *77*(2), 181-183.

Wright, L., Schaefer, A.B., & Solomons, G. *Encyclopedia of pediatric psychology*. Baltimore: University Park Press, 1979.

4 | The Cardiovascular System: Congenital Heart Defects

Congenital heart defect (CHD) is a descriptive phrase used to denote a structural defect of the heart or its great vessels present at birth. This abnormality in the cardiovascular system is thought to occur during the first trimester of pregnancy (by the ninth gestational week), since by this time the formation of the heart is virtually complete. Although in the vast majority of cases (over 95%) the cause of the abnormality is unknown, in some instances CHD occurs following maternal rubella or in conjunction with other syndromes such as Marfan's, Turner's, Hurler's, or Holt-Oran Syndrome. The incidence of CHD is 6 to 8 of every 1,000 live births. Despite this relatively low incidence, cardiac defects are one of the leading causes of death in infancy.

Diagnosis and Classification

In order to understand the types of circulatory problems that can arise when a child has a heart defect, it is helpful first to review normal blood circulation, illustrated for reference in Figure 4-1. In the normal circulation of blood, the right and left sides of the heart are connected through the lungs in which blood receives its oxygen supply. After leaving the lungs, the blood returns to the left heart and is pumped via the aorta to the brain and body tissues to supply the oxygen necessary for metabolism. Blood then returns to the right heart to be pumped via the pulmonary artery to the lungs, thus completing the circulation cycle.

Nadas (1963) provided a useful grouping of the heart defects according to their physiological consequences. A heart defect may create: 1. insufficient oxygen in the blood; 2. overwork on the heart by an overload of blood in the chambers; 3. an inadequate output of blood by the heart (resulting in physical underdevelopment); and 4. high blood pressure in the blood vessels of the lungs leading to damaged blood vessels in later life (pulmonary arterial hypertension). Heart defects are typically subdivided into two major groups (acyanotic and cyanotic) depending on whether the heart defect results in adequate or inadequate oxygen in the blood. Table 4-1 presents the major signs and symptoms of each of these subtypes.

Schematic Diagram of a Normal Heart

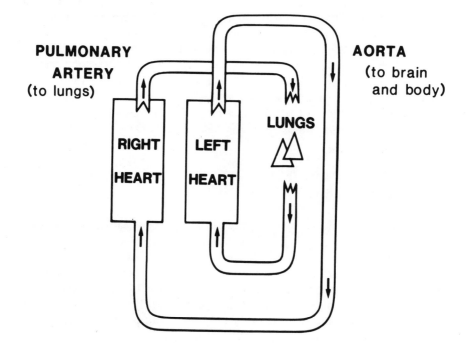

Figure 4-1

*Courtesy of Francis S. Wright, M.D. Based on a flow diagram of abnormal heart functioning from R.J. Vanden Belt, J.A. Ronan, Jr., and J.L. Bedynek, Jr. *Cardiology: A clinical approach*. Chicago: Year Book Medical Publishers, Inc., 1979.

TABLE 4-1

Congenital Heart Defects

Definition	Major Symptoms and Signs	Possible Medical Treatment	Psychologic Issues
Acyanotic Congenital abnormalities of heart structure in which there is adequate oxygen in the blood	Often asymptomatic Exercise intolerance (shortness of breath [dyspnea]) Growth failure Heart murmur Repeated pneumonia Congestive heart failure (sweating, fast breathing [tachypnea])	Antibiotics Digitalis for heart failure Catheterization for diagnosis and treatment Palliative surgical procedures Open and closed heart corrective surgery	Parental guilt and depression over defect Coping with a life threatening illness Combination of other handicaps (e.g., mental retardation) or malformations Extensive, painful procedures Prolonged separation during infancy
Cyanotic Congenital abnormalities of the heart in which there is insufficient oxygen in the blood	The above symptoms and bluish color (cyanosis) of mucous membranes, lips, fingertips, skin, etc. Squatting spells Alterations in consciousness Clubbing of toes and fingers		Difficulty disciplining child (fear of precipitating symptoms) Child's fear of pain, mutilation, death

While over 40 different defects have been identified, there are about 9 types that constitute 90 percent of all CHD. The most common types are ventricular septal defect (a hole in the wall separating the ventricles): atrial septal defect (a hole in the walls separating the atria); coarctation of the aorta (constriction of the aorta); aortic stenosis (obstruction of blood flow at any of the aortic valves due to a narrowed opening); truncus arteriosus (aorta and pulmonary arteries arise from a single artery connected to the heart); transposition of the great arteries (alteration in the position of the pulmonary artery and the aorta); patent ductus arteriosis (a persistence of a blood vessel between the aorta and pulmonary artery); pulmonary stenosis (an impediment to blood flow at the valves in the pulmonary artery); tetralogy of Fallot (a ventricular septal defect, in conjunction with pulmonary stenosis, right ventricular hypertrophy, and origin of the aorta from both ventricles).

Impact On the Parents

The outlook for survival of a child with a congenital heart defect has drastically changed over the last fifteen years. The infant no longer must establish his or her viability before aggressive surgical management intervenes. Improved surgical techniques and new methods of anesthesia have allowed earlier operative intervention and dramatic improvement in longevity. For many infants, corrective or reparative open heart surgery is possible using the technique of cardiopulmonary bypass with or without hypothermia. There are varying degrees of difficulty in repairing the different heart defects. Some, such as patent ductus, simple atrial or ventricular defects, and simple coarctation have been operated on successfully and with lesser surgical risk. Others, such as tetralogy of Fallot, pulmonary stenosis, aortic stenosis, transposition, and total anomalous venous return, are considered to carry increasing surgical risk, with tricuspid atresia one of the most difficult to correct (Travis, 1976). As the mortality rate improves, these children and their families must cope with the stresses of a chronic physical problem, poor health of the child prior to reparative surgery, repeated hospitalizations, repeated surgical intervention, and uncertainty of outcome.

When an infant is diagnosed as having a congenital heart defect, both the parents and, for some families, the siblings, must cope with the stresses associated with serious illness and the possible death of a family member. The seriousness of these heart conditions varies, depending upon the specific heart defect, the presence of associated anomalies, and the surgical risk. Discussing the consequences of such congenital heart defects, Travis (1976) writes:

> The psychosocial ramifications may be long and continuous, repeatedly crisis-centered, or minimal until time for surgery, when the major crisis exists. The condition is usually life-threatening, and often creates medical emergencies that alter social plans. Destructive psychological effects require skillful handling by all who may be concerned with the child and his family. (p. 233)

A review of the major findings on the impact of congenital heart disease indicates that there is a widespread potential impact of such a disability on the parents. These effects are mediated, in part, by the severity of the defect, whether it can be corrected, the extent of restrictiveness it places on the child, and the adequacy of existent medical care. Compounding these factors is the interaction of the parents' response to the disease, their ability to cope and to normalize their child's life, and the attitudes of the other children and extended family members toward the child.

Initial reaction. Giving birth to a child with a congenital defect creates a crisis situation for most parents. Many feel a sense of guilt that they may have been responsible for the child's abnormality. Prolonged grief, loss of self-esteem, shock, disbelief, initial attempts to deny the severity of the defect or the child's possible mortality are frequently observed. Solnit and Stark (1961) hypothesize that when a "defective" child is born in place of the wished for normal child, the mother often reacts as if the hoped for normal child had died and grieves, mourning this loss. Many of the families of children with congenital heart disease interviewed by Garson, Benson, Ivler, and Patton (1978) displayed a process similar to mourning both at the time of the initial diagnosis and at the time of reparative open heart surgery. These authors report that:

> The parents needed to be able to live with their loss of the normal child in order to achieve a realistic adaptation to that child. . . .The failure of some parents to deal with their feelings successfully and to complete this mourning process led to a disordered emotional and cognitive response to their defective children. (pp. 91–92)

It is these frequent affective responses (fear, anger, guilt, anxiety) that can form the base for the protective attitudes and restrictiveness of some of the parents of children with congenital heart defects. The possible adverse consequences for the child can reside in prolonged dependency, a failure to achieve autonomy, or the modeling of the parent's anxieties and fears.

Helping the Parents to Cope

All these factors have increased our awareness of the specific impact of a cardiac defect and the potentially detrimental effects such a disease may have on the child's subsequent psychological development. Ways in which the parents can be helped to cope effectively with the diagnosis of a heart defect and the variety of medical and surgical stresses related to it have just begun to be addressed. Studies exploring physician-parent communication about the child's congenital heart defect have met with some success in outlining problems that frequently arise in such dialogues. When physician communication to the parents is overly academic or technical, parental stress is increased. Often the physician's assumptions or expectations of the parents' knowledge and the parents' actual understanding differ markedly. Intervention strategies involving clarification of medical information and open discussion of psychological issues have been effective in helping the parents gain an accurate understanding of the diagnosis, prognosis, and specific treatment procedures. With such understanding, parents and patients tended to be less anxious, more satisfied and more receptive to medical recommendations (Kupst, Blatterbauer, Westman, Schulman, & Paul, 1977; Kupst, Dresser, Schulman, & Paul, 1976).

Also prominent in the literature on congenital heart defects is the clinical observation that many parents respond adaptively to this life-threatening crisis. Given the severe stresses to which parents of children with congenital heart disease are exposed, the resilience of some, as observed by Travis (1976), is remarkable:

> Problems abound, but some families have unusual strengths. They are able to cope with the anxiety related to all heart ailments, the parental guilt constantly encountered in congenital defects, the great demands in caring for symptomatic infants or small children prior to surgery, the intense emotion inherent in submitting the child to an operation of great risk, some psychological crippling in the child, and the strain on family relationships. However, other families need help if the experience is to be weathered with minimum trauma. Most of the children are young, in the life-shaping age and vulnerable to family attitudes. Thus the family experience leaves a permanent imprint on the child. . . . Whatever the financial or educational status of the family, they can and do have problems during the period a child is in physical jeopardy. Support should be available to them. (pp. 247–248)

Fishman and Fishman (1971a, 1971b) have provided some clues to the adaptive mechanisms employed by well adjusted children with birth defects (various types included) and their mothers. These mothers assumed certain attitudes and behaviors that included: a) positive regard directed to the child; b) active confrontation of the reality of the defect; c) open communication with the child about the nature of the defect; d) a positive view of the future; and e) encouragement of the child's independence and achievement. Those children showing positive adjustment also showed active cognitive confrontation, seeking an accurate and comprehensive understanding of their defect and open communication with their mothers and peers regarding it. This study examined factors relating to successful adjustment in children with a variety of birth defects; its results are provocative and may also characterize effective coping strategies for children with CHD and their mothers. It also suggests the necessity not only of pursuing the qualities of adaptive children and their mothers, but also of taking account of the entire familial and social matrix of which these families are a part.

A family coping assessment interview can provide a framework for examining a family's ability to cope with an illness experience. Important factors to consider in assessing a family's ability to function as a unit throughout a stressful experience might include: the characteristics of the pathology (type of disability, prognosis, family's perception of the illness, etc.), how the family perceives the illness event in terms of family relationships and goals, the social and financial resources available to the family, and the family's pattern of handling previous crises (MacVicar & Archbold, 1976). These guidelines are based on clinical experience and observation; there is little correlated evidence available about the specific resources and coping skills needed of parents who have a child with a congenital heart defect.

Impact on the Child

Intellectual impairment. While there is no question that children with CHD have benefitted from the medical advances and technical progress of the past two decades, the total impact of these new surgical techniques on the child's neurological and psychological development must be evaluated. Research has documented that a significant proportion of children with CHD evidence mental retardation. This may result from an associated anomaly of the brain or possibly from long term insult to the brain from chronic hypoxia, CNS infection, or stroke. Early reports (Silbert, Wolff, Mayer, Rosenthal, & Nadas, 1969; Linde, Rasof, & Dunn, 1970) and informal observations of a higher than expected incidence of mental retardation among children with congenital heart defects prompted systematic studies of the intellectual development in these children.

These studies verified that, while the majority of cardiac children have an IQ above 90, the general distribution of IQ scores is not normal. Rather, there is marked variability and a higher incidence of children at both the low and high ranges of ability. The causes of intellectual deficits, when they do occur, are difficult to interpret. They could be related to a variety of factors specific to the heart defect and its physiologic consequences (e.g., fatigue, slowness of response, lethargy, lack of stamina on tasks requiring a motor response) or could relate secondarily to the child's or family's attitude and adaptation to the disease. Poor school attendance because of repeated illnesses or numerous hospitalizations must also be considered as potential contributors to the child's low functioning.

Recent studies of the intellectual development of children with CHD have compared the functioning of children with cyanotic congenital heart disease, acyanotic cardiac disease, and normal or other control children. A summary of these studies is presented in Tables A-3 and A-4 in the Appendix. In general, the cyanotic children score lowest in developmental and intelligence tests. There is, however, great individual variation amoung cyanotic children, some obtaining IQ scores in the superior range. The most marked deficit of cyanotic children is found on tasks requiring gross motor ability. This is illustrated by later age of walking, which in the cyanotic group is typically achieved at a mean age of 16 months, as opposed to 13 months in acyanotic children with heart failure, and 12 months in acyanotic children without heart failure. Similarly, cyanotic children often perform most poorly on perceptual motor tasks, while those having acyanotic heart disease and a history of congestive heart failure perform significantly better than cyanotic children, but more poorly than acyanotic children with no history of heart failure (Silbert et al., 1969; Linde, Rasof, & Dunn, 1967).

Growth failure. Children with CHD typically show a retardation in height and growth prior to reparative surgery. The extent of this growth failure varies, depending on the specific type of cardiac defect and its functional effects. Such growth delay is quite common among infants and children with transposition of the great arteries (TGA) prior to open heart surgical repair. The major factors associated with growth retardation in TGA children prior to surgical correction are age, subpulmonic stenosis, and increased pulmonary and systemic flow often manifested clinically by congestive heart failure (Levy, Rosenthal, Castaneda, & Nadas, 1978). The mechanisms by which growth is delayed are not yet clearly understood, although Rosenthal and Castaneda (1975) offer a hypothesis: they propose that the infant with a cardiac defect may not receive sufficient nutrient and caloric intake because of a variety of factors such as fatigue due to excessive respiratory effort, recurrent infection, cardiac decompensation, or psychologic factors which may emerge as a result of chronic illness. Such malnutrition during the period of rapid brain growth may result not only in retarded physical growth, but in permanent anatomic or functional brain impairment as well. This hypothesis received support in an autopsy study of infants with congenital heart disease which revealed that the brain weights of these infants were approximately two standard deviations below the mean (Naeye, 1965). Thus, in addition to the cardiac benefits of early reparative surgery, there may be great potential neurologic benefit as well, since 50 percent of normal postnatal brain growth occurs in the first year of life, while only 20 percent occurs during the second year.

The role of chronic hypoxia (which exists until the time of corrective surgery) in producing growth failure remains unclear. Cyanotic children have not been consistently shown to have poorer growth than acyanotic children; and among cyanotic groups, the presence of congestive heart failure rather than severity of cyanosis has been associated with serious growth retardation in children. However, delayed skeletal maturation and growth have been related to severity of hypoxia for cyanotic *adolescent* patients. Rosenthal and Castaneda (1975) speculate that with increased duration and chronicity, hypoxia may interfere with growth. Reports on delayed growth and skeletal maturation in animals and humans living in hypoxic environments provide further support for this view (Frisancho, Thomas, & Baker, 1975).

Significant improvement in growth often occurs following reparative surgery, particularly if the defect is corrected at an early age. The prognosis is best for infants without other cardiac anomalies who have normal birth weight and relatively uniform hemodynamics. Risk factors for postoperative growth failure include older age at time of repair, significant residual hemodynamic abnormalities, and preoperative growth failure (Rosenthal & Castaneda, 1975).

Chronic hypoxia. Children with cyanotic CHD are exposed to low oxygen levels (chronic hypoxia) until corrective or reparative open heart surgery is performed. Since open heart surgery is performed after different intervals of time, children with cyanotic CHD may be at varying levels of risk for developing future neurologic and/ or psychologic disabilities. The developing brain can be deprived of oxygen by two mechanisms: 1) decreased oxygen concentration in the blood supply (hypoxia) and 2) decreased blood perfusing the brain (ischemia). Acute severe hypoxia produces profound biochemical change within the brain, leading to diminished energy supply and brain dysfunction. The neurological sequelae of such acute hypoxia include neuronal damage in the cerebral and cerebellar cortices leading to atrophy, neuronal cell loss, and scarring within the brain (Volpe, 1976).

Animal studies have indicated that experimentally induced differing patterns of brain injury occur depending upon the circumstances under which the hypoxia occurs. Total acute lack of oxygen (anoxia) leads to brain stem damage. The pathology seen in the brain stem following sudden total oxygen lack reflects susceptibility to injury related to blood flow rate and the high metabolic requirements of these tissues. Partial oxygen lack (hypoxia) associated with acidosis produces widespread brain swelling and neuronal cell death. The entire cerebral cortex may be affected or the injury may be confined to the paracentral or posterior parietal cortices bilaterally (Myers, 1975). These pathological changes can produce mental retardation, seizures, and/or cerebral palsy. Hypoxia without acidosis leads to cerebral hemisphere white matter injury, especially in the prefrontal and posterior parietal regions. Lesions in these areas can produce motor and/or intellectual deficits. Finally, hypoxia followed by complete anoxia leads to injury of the basal ganglia structures. Abnormal movements would be the expected clinical outcome of such injuries.

While the effects of acute hypoxia on the central nervous system are well known, the metabolic and pathologic sequelae of chronic hypoxia are largely unknown. The cyanosis that accompanies several congenital heart defects may well provide a model for the central nervous system effects of chronic hypoxia. Based on the animal experimental studies described above, it might be anticipated that the effects of chronic hypoxia would approximate those changes seen in the animal models of acute hypoxia, at least with respect to location of injury but not necessarily the severity. This suggests that children with cyanotic heart defects may be at risk for motor, perceptual, attentional, and/or general cognitive disabilities.

Despite the consistent finding of intellectual deficits, and particularly motor deficits, among cyanotic children, early efforts to evaluate the effect that the chronic hypoxia associated with cyanosis has on the child's intellectual development have met with mixed success. Early investigations found no relationship between arterial oxygen saturation (severity of cyanosis) and IQ. Later studies by Silbert, Rosenthal, Aisenberg, and colleagues (1967, 1969, 1977) at the Children's Hospital in Boston and by O'Dougherty, Wright, Garmezy, Loewenson, and Torres (in press) at the University of Minnesota have, however, found a relationship between cyanosis and impaired central nervous system function. The Boston group demonstrated that intellectual and perceptual motor differences between cyanotic and acyanotic children were maintained, even when the child's physical activity level was held constant. Additional deficiencies evidenced by cyanotic children were slow visual reaction time, lower critical flicker frequencies, and increased reflex duration in older cyanotic children. Low perceptual sensitivity, problems in sustained attention, poor spatial and perceptual-motor skills, and more frequent abnormalities on neurologic examination were identified by the Minnesota group for children with transposition of the great arteries (TGA). Difficulties in these areas increased with longer duration of hypoxia.

Unsuccessful palliation. While initial palliative procedures substantially reduce the mortality rate of cardiac infants, they do not always provide satisfactory amelioration of the severe hypoxia of some infants and do not necessarily prevent a stroke from occurring. Mortality rate also increases considerably when initial palliation is unsuccessful. Some children die before alternative palliation or corrective surgery can be performed. Further surgical interventions, such as a Blalock Hanlon (surgical atrial septectomy), are necessary, but carry a risk of mortality; risk of neurologic (stroke) or other complications (pulmonary vascular disease) increase as well (Zavanella & Subramanian, 1978). If the palliation is successful, subsequent intellectual function may be facilitated. Finley and colleagues (1974) examined children who had tetralogy of Fallot. They found that those patients who had received a Blalock Hanlon obtained higher preoperative IQ and greater gains in their IQ scores following corrective surgery than children who had not.

Neurological complications. Among the more severe neurological disturbances that may result from complications of congenital heart disease are seizure disorder, alterations in consciousness, cerebrovascular stroke syndromes, and brain abscess. These neurological complications are a significant and at times life-threatening event.

Alteration of Consciousness

Episodic alterations in consciousness occur most frequently in the cardiac infant and young child between the ages of 6 months and 3 years. These episodes are associated with severe cyanosis accompanied by rapid breathing. These attacks are frequently brought on by exertion and may be associated with eating and bowel movements. The cyanotic attacks are thought to represent a sudden increased shift of blood from right to left circulation, producing the severe cyanosis and hypoxia. Characteristically, the infant during an episode involving exertion becomes markedly more cyanotic, breathes rapidly, and loses consciousness, becoming limp. If the episode of unconsciousness is severe, the child may have a generalized seizure (Tyler & Clark, 1957). The significant clinical feature in differentiating this type of loss of consciousness from a primary convulsive disorder is the appearance of the cyanosis and rapid breathing preceding the loss of consciousness. In a severely cyanotic child, however, this differentiation may be impossible to make.

Seizure Disorder

The diagnosis of a seizure disorder in a child with congenital heart disease may be very difficult. The nature of the onset of the disturbance may readily point to a seizure rather than a hypoxic episode. The EEG may be helpful in pinpointing a convulsive disorder, although many cardiac patients (approximately one-third) have abnormal EEGs, but not a seizure disorder. This high incidence of abnormal EEGs may relate to interference in the normal maturation of the electrical brain rhythms because of the alteration of cerebral blood flow secondary to the heart defect (Torres, Frank, Cohen, Lillehei, & Kaspar, 1959).

Cerebrovascular Stroke Syndrome

There appear to be several factors important in the pathogenesis of cerebrovascular stroke syndromes. In cyanotic patients there is considerable hemoconcentration with an increased number of red blood cells, increased blood viscosity (thickness), and low oxygen saturation. It is thought that the combination of all these factors results in cerebrothrombosis (obstruction of the blood vessels in the brain). In addition, any condition causing dehydration such as diarrhea or excessive vomiting can rapidly lead to a worsening of the hemodynamic factors resulting in the likelihood of thrombosis (Wright & O'Dougherty, 1979). Cerebrovascular accidents in children less than 4 years of age have been associated with anemia, while cerebrovascular accidents in older children have been associated with increased number of red blood cells and hypoxia. Precipitating factors can include sudden fever, cardiac catheterization, and episodes of rapid breathing. A common manifestation of a stroke in these children is the sudden onset of hemiplegia (Phronphutkul, Rosenthal, Nadas, & Berenberg, 1973).

Brain Abscess or Central Nervous System Infection

These problems are relatively uncommon in children with CHD; when they do occur, they present serious difficulties. In addition to jeopardizing the infant or child's health, the risk of later neurologic or psychologic sequelae is enhanced. In our study of TGA children, those who had experienced a central nervous system infection were significantly compromised at follow-up in cognitive, attentional, and perceptual-motor functioning (O'Dougherty, et al. in press).

Biomedical risks associated with open heart surgery. Corrective open heart surgery is made possible through the technique of cardiopulmonary bypass with or without hypothermia. Deep or profound hypothermia has gained wide popularity among surgeons because it provides a flaccid motionless heart in a bloodless operative field. In addition, the duration of cardiopulmonary bypass is often reduced using this method. Nevertheless, hypothermia is a most unphysiologic state, and consequently it has introduced a new set of potential medical and neurological complications.

During the last decade, various research investigators have explored the possible deleterious or advantageous effects of particular types of cardiac surgery, for example, cardiopulmonary bypass with or without deep hypothermia and with or without circulatory arrest. The findings from these studies are summarized in Table A–5 in the Appendix. The studies indicate that, although the beneficial effects of adequate physiologic heart functioning and the resulting decrease in mortality are abundantly clear, the risks of these procedures for subsequent neuropsychologic functioning have not been clearly delineated for specific groups of cardiac patients. Although the studies report infrequent injury to the central nervous system when deep hypothermia and circulatory arrest are employed, the data are limited for a variety of reasons: 1. a focus only on immediate postoperative results or cursory neurological exams; 2. inadequate sample sizes; 3. lack of comprehensive psychological assessment; 4. inclusion of subjects having very heterogeneous congenital heart defects; 5. lack of long-term follow-up assessment of young children whose IQ score in infancy often bears little relation to future intellectual functioning; and 6. failure to identify and differentiate children who have sustained central nervous system damage prior to corrective surgery from those whose damage resulted from the surgery. Further evaluation of these techniques is needed, particularly among and between subtypes. Abnormal neurological findings and EEG recordings are apparent for a significant proportion of these children in the immediate postoperative period, and many studies do report an increased proportion of children showing subsequent intellectual retardation when compared to the normal population.

Single vs. cumulative risk. Understanding the multiple factors that can jeopardize the growth and development of an infant with a congenital heart defect is essential in planning appropriate follow-up assessment to identify infants at risk for future disability. Our study of the later outcome of infants born with TGA indicated that parental concerns about the possible impact of specific individual medical risk factors (such as the occurrence of congestive heart failure, the need for additional palliative and surgical procedures, or lengthy cardiac repair) could be assuaged. Similarly, the presence of seizures during or following open heart surgery was not associated with an unfavorable outcome, but severe neurologic insults such as a stroke or brain infection did compromise intellectual functioning. When multiple risk factors occurred prior to reparative surgery or if the risk factors had a prolonged duration (chronic hypoxia) or impact on growth, the outcome was less favorable. The psychologist should be alerted to the possible deleterious effects that these multiple risk factors can exert, especially in the areas of learning, academic achievement, and neurologic integrity. Infants and children with cardiac defects who experience multiple risk factors may require detailed neurologic and psychologic evaluations in order to plan for appropriate educational interventions at an early age (O'Dougherty et al., in press).

The Psychological Stress of Congenital Heart Disease on Child and Family

Separation from parents during hospitalization. Bowlby's (1969) extensive clinical and naturalistic observations of how young children respond while away from home and cared for in a strange place by a succession of unfamiliar people and of how they respond to the mother during and after return home has greatly enhanced our understanding of the problems of separation. He has written at length about the distress during separation and the anxiety often evident following reunion with parents. During the separation, the child is usually acutely distressed for a period of time and not easily comforted. After return home he or she is likely to be detached from the parents or excessively clinging for a while. Another common pattern is for detachment to precede the period in which the child becomes very demanding of parental attention.

Following these early observations, investigators have examined numerous additional variables—the specific illness, strange surroundings, extent and quality of substitute care, types of relationships before and after the separation—to explore the extent to which these other factors can intensify or mitigate the child's response to a separation. The work of Ainsworth (1975) and Sroufe (1979) on the nature of the infant-mother relationship has contributed greatly to our understanding of infant exploration, reaction to separation, and attachment to mother. Such separation can lead to serious later adjustment problems. Work is underway to examine the psychological reactions that may evolve from a pathogenic early occurrence (such as a long separation or loss) to a particular type of clinical disturbance (such as depression or an anxiety state).

This work has raised the critical issue of the stress-inducing nature of any hospitalization for a child, irrespective of the specific procedures encountered. At present, there is no consensus on the effects of hospitalization and surgery on children's psychological adjustment. Both adverse and, for some children, beneficial effects have been obtained. Differences in the medical settings, the child's previous family environment, and varied assessments of the type or amount of stress experienced all contribute to making definite conclusions difficult.

In response to these concerns, there has been a surge of interest in the psychological and social impact of illness and hospitalization on children. During the past two decades, many hospitals have instituted programs designed to lessen the possible deleterious effects of hospitalization and to alleviate the anxiety children may experience while in the hospital (Petrillo & Sanger, 1980; Melamed & Siegel, 1980). Some of the unique programs instituted include: preadmission orientations, parents sleeping in, formation of Ronald McDonald houses and many other support groups, care by parent units, modification of visitation restrictions, play programs, etc.

Many of these programs have been designed to meet the specific developmental needs of children (see Chapter 2).

Painful, frightening surgical and medical procedures. The various surgical and medical procedures may also place the child at risk for developing behavioral adjustment problems. Two procedures, cardiac catheterization and open heart surgery, can be particularly stressful. In one study of the sequelae of cardiac catheterization nearly all (93%) of the preschool children and slightly less than half (43%) of the older children reacted with emotional symptoms of varying degrees of severity following catheterization. The younger children displayed regression, aggression, and negative affect and attitude for several weeks following the procedure. Boys typically expressed their aggression physically, while girls more often responded with aggressive verbalization. Both older and younger children became more anxious (Aisenberg, Wolff, Rosenthal, & Nadas, 1973).

In an effort to reduce the stress of this procedure, Petrillo and Sanger (1980) have provided a set of guidelines for preparing the child for cardiac catheterization and for cardiac surgery. First, it is important to determine the child's understanding of the reason for the hospitalization and to elicit through interview, drawings, or puppet play what he or she thinks may have caused the problem. Once the child's understanding, concerns, and misconceptions have been identified, clarification of the purpose of the immediate hospitalization and reassurance that nothing anyone did or thought was responsible for the problem should be provided.

Cardiac Catheterization

Strategies for describing the catheterization procedure ("You need to have a special test and pictures of your heart so that your doctor can discover what the problem is and how to treat it." [p. 257]) and explaining the steps involved in the procedure so that children of different ages can understand it are well delineated in Petrillo and Sanger's book. A body outline, visual aids, or a patient doll (especially for younger children) can provide an opportunity for further discussion of fears and concerns and also facilitate understanding of the anatomy and physiology of the cardiac system. Preoperative visits can provide an opportunity to familiarize the child with the equipment and hospital environment prior to the time they are actually needed. Instruction immediately prior to a frightening procedure often arouses so much anxiety that coping is diminished rather than enhanced. Scrapbooks showing doctors and nurses at work, children being cooperative with treatments, going to the operating room, waking up in the recovery room, using the equipment, and receiving ribbons or trophies for bravery can provide concrete models of adaptive coping. Visual aids and dramatic play materials also facilitate preoperative teaching. Use of puppets and puppet play can depersonalize teaching for a child who is very anxious about discussing his or her concerns or fears. Allowing the child to talk about how the puppet feels about the ordeal or what the puppet thinks is happening may provide a more open medium for sharing concerns (Petrillo & Sanger, 1980).

Cardiac Surgery

Psychological disturbances associated with open heart surgery have been well described in adults, but little has been written on children. In general, the increased incidence of acute postoperative psychotic reactions among adults who have had open heart surgery has not been observed in children. In the most comprehensive study of the postoperative reactions of children (46 of whom had open heart surgery and 22 of whom had thoracotomies without extracorporeal circulation) only four children had grossly abnormal reactions, and all of these children had had open heart surgery. Predisposing factors in three of these children (such as deception regarding the surgery, inability to speak English, and previous mumps encephalitis with personality changes) could be identified. All but four of the children displayed reactions considered normal, but included expressions of anxiety, anger, restlessness, and fearful withdrawal. Ten children were overtly angry and combative during most of the time they spent in the intensive care room. This group of children had a higher percentage of medical complications. Younger children evidenced a moderate degree of separation anxiety which appeared to be related primarily to the experience of hospitalization rather than to the surgery (Danilowicz & Gabriel, 1972).

Many of the children found other hospital procedures more frightening than the open heart surgery per se. Degree of pain was not always the determining factor as evidenced by the finding that many children feared the oxygen micro-mist tent more than blood drawing or tracheal (throat) suctioning. Specific procedures may well carry symbolic meaning which varies among children. The importance of eliciting the child's own fears and fantasies in order to provide appropriate intervention is well illustrated by these findings.

Petrillo and Sanger's guidelines for preparing a child for open heart surgery address many of the developmental issues that can arise when a toddler, preschooler, elementary school aged or adolescent patient faces cardiac surgery. Examples of how to provide explanations about what will happen during surgery and about new devices the child will encounter on his body or in the recovery room (catheters, nasogastric tubes, intravenous infusions, ECG leads and monitors, endotracheal tube, pressure/volume control respirator, mistifier, blow bottles, suction machine, etc.) are given in this excellent resource manual accompanied by numerous illustrations and specific examples.

The importance of working through this experience was highlighted in my own work with a 14 year old boy referred to me for evaluation because of recent school failure and behavioral problems. This boy had undergone open heart surgical repair of a ventricular septal defect the previous summer. During the surgery, he experienced a stroke which resulted in right sided weakness and speech impairment. Because of the cardiac surgery, he was temporarily restricted from sports in which he formerly had excelled. His drawing, a former hobby and source of great satisfaction, was impaired from the stroke, leaving him with few outlets and significant frustration. Although he demonstrated substantial recovery of function in the months following surgery, his behavior at home and school became increasingly disruptive and noncompliant. He formerly had rarely argued, but he now found daily opportunities. His fear of dying if hit in the chest prevented him from directly expressing his anger at peers, but indirect expressions (stealing from parents and peers, lying, noncompliance) were frequent. During therapy, the experience of open heart surgery and the subsequent impact this surgery had on his life became a focal point. Peter (pseudonym) perceived the surgery as a vicious attack on his body from which he was powerless to protect himself (see Figure 4–2) and which left him unable to perform in areas vitally important to him (soccer, gymnastics, drawing). The restrictions enhanced his feelings of inadequacy as a male. His drawings (see Figure 4–2) beautifully reflect his sense of powerlessness, isolation, assault, and overwhelming fear. Gradually, he overcame his frustration with his fine-motor impairment and found that time and effort spent on artistic tasks resulted in gradual improvement. Alternative sports (swimming, roller skating, tennis) were slowly introduced; and, in time, Peter developed more direct ways of expressing his fears, concerns, and anger. Throughout therapy, opportunities for discussion of the surgery itself, the tremendous anxiety he experienced prior to surgery, and the rage he felt at the loss of his "masculinity" after surgery were provided. Clarification of the actual losses sustained following the stroke and surgery (temporary speech impairment, difficulty with fine-motor coordination, need for caution in selecting physical activities), and exploration of his "fantasied" losses (virility, brains, ability to defend himself) were critical in helping him to gain mastery over this overwhelmingly stressful experience. Having major surgery at the beginning of adolescence had a profound impact on Peter's sense of self-esteem and identity. The perceived threats to his life and to his masculinity and his total defenselessness against this attack precipitated a crisis in which his behavior and achievement dramatically deteriorated.

In other age periods, or with children whose vulnerabilities lie in other areas, different problems may arise, accompanied by various coping techniques. The psychologist can play a critical role in helping the child reintegrate this experience in a manner that fosters effective coping and enhances self-esteem through the mastery of difficult life experiences.

Adverse parental attitudes and management. Poor adjustment in a cardiac child has often been shown to relate more to the mother's anxiety, overprotectiveness, and pampering than to the child's degree of physical incapacity. Although increased protectiveness and pampering are more characteristic of mothers of cyanotic infants (who are more obviously symptomatic), the difference in anxiety between mothers of cyanotic and acyanotic infants is small compared to the large difference in physical capacity. Interestingly, most studies have demonstrated that maternal anxiety is related to the *presence*, rather than to the *severity*, of the heart defect.

Relief following surgery and improvement in both emotional adjustment and intellectual development have been particularly characteristic of cyanotic children. This improvement is also often reflected in general family functioning and adjustment. Parents of cyanotic children who have had surgery become less anxious and

Figure 4-2 *Open Heart Surgery as Remembered by a 14-year-old Boy.*

overprotective and show greater postoperative relief when compared with those whose children did not have surgery (Linde et al., 1970). For some parents, the presence of concrete symptoms (e.g., increasing cyanosis, exercise intolerance) may actually facilitate adaptive coping by forcing the family to acknowledge and deal with the reality of defective heart functioning. For the parents of acyanotic children, the lack of objective signs of illness likely leads to uncertainty. The subsequent often observed overprotection may develop as a response to the anxiety such uncertainty evokes. Support for this hypothesis is provided by Garson and colleagues (1974, 1978) who have worked extensively with tetralogy of Fallot cardiac patients. They report that the greatest degree of psychological symptomatology is often found in those patients who show the *least* physical symptomatology. Problems typifying these patients include dependency, self-indulgence, little ambition, restrictiveness, and lower general information. The study suggests that an "invisible" defect may be more difficult to cope with adaptively than one that presents more visible signs and symptoms.

A follow-up study of children who received a misdiagnosis of a congenital heart defect provides further information in this regard. When such defects were misdiagnosed and the parents were mistakenly asked to restrict their children's physical activity, the children subsequently displayed overall full scale IQ scores lower than the control children. Children who were misdiagnosed but not restricted in their activity demonstrated lower verbal, but not performance, IQ scores (Cayler, Lynn, & Stein, 1973). The importance of physical activity as a means of fostering cognitive growth and the impact of both restriction and misdiagnosis are highlighted in this work. Since parental anxiety may well be heightened if their infants are asymptomatic, there was likely considerable stress and confusion for those parents whose children were both restricted and erroneously diagnosed.

Another task the parents must face if the child's surgery is successful is to alter their responses in a number of domains. Restrictions or limitations that once may have been indicated because of the child's physical incapacities now should be put aside. Many mothers who coped successfully with the demands of caring for their symptomatic infants often found satisfaction and heightened self-esteem from these activities. Garson et al. (1978) emphasize that, following successful surgical correction of the heart defect, mothers often experience a second mourning process, showing signs of depression, missing the closeness the child's presurgical condition allowed. These authors stress that it is important to mourn the loss of the previously defective child before the healthy child can be responded to appropriately. The inability of some parents to alter their overprotective, solicitous behavior toward the child following surgery can result in significant subsequent psychopathology. Psychological intervention with these families should focus on helping the parents establish adaptive responses to the infant prior to and following surgery. Effective coping may well require the ability to shift one's emotional set once the physical problem has been resolved. Support, information, and clear guidelines for parents are needed during this difficult transition.

References

Ainsworth, M.D.S. The development of mother-infant attachment. In B.E. Caldwell & H.N. Ricciuti (Eds.), *Review of child development research* (Vol. 3). Chicago: University of Chicago Press, 1975.

Aisenberg, R.B., Rosenthal, A., Wolff, P.H., & Nadas, A.S. Hypoxemia and auditory reaction time in congenital heart disease. *Perceptual and Motor Skills,* 1977, *45,* 595–600.

Aisenberg, R.B., Wolff, P.H., Rosenthal, A., & Nadas, A.S. Psychological impact of cardiac catheterization. *Pediatrics,* 1973, *51*(6), 1051–1059.

Bowlby, J. *Attachment: Attachment and loss* (Vol. 1). New York: Basic Books, 1969.

Cayler, G.G., Lynn, D.B., & Stein, E.M. Effect of cardiac 'nondisease' on intellectual and perceptual motor development. *British Heart Journal,* 1973, *35,* 543–547.

Danilowicz, D.A., & Gabriel, H.P. Postoperative reactions in children: "Normal" and abnormal responses after cardiac surgery. In S. Chess & A. Thomas (Eds.), *Annual progress in child psychiatry and child development.* New York: Brunner/ Mazel, 1972.

Finley, K.H., Buse, S.T., Popper, R.W., Honzik, M.P., Collart, D.S., & Riggs, N. Intellectual functioning of children with tetralogy of Fallot: Influence of open-heart surgery and earlier palliative operations. *The Journal of Pediatrics,* 1974, *85,* 318–323.

Fishman, C.A., & Fishman, D.B. Emotional, cognitive, and interpersonal confrontation among children with birth defects. *Child Psychiatry and Human Development,* 1971a, *2*(2), 92–101.

Fishman, C.A., & Fishman, D.B. Maternal correlates of self-esteem and overall adjustment in children with birth defects. *Child Psychiatry and Human Development,* 1971b, *1*(4), 255–265.

Frisancho, A.R., Thomas, R.B., & Baker, B.T. Growth patterns of a highland Peruvian population: A preliminary analysis. Department of Sociology and Anthropology, Pennsylvania State University, 1965. Cited in A. Rosenthal and A.R. Castaneda, Growth and development after cardiovascular surgery in infants and children. *Progress in Cardiovascular Diseases,* 1975, *18,* 27–37.

Garson, A., Jr., Benson, R.S., Ivler, L., & Patton, C. Parental reactions to children with congenital heart disease. *Child Psychiatry and Human Development,* 1978, *9*(2), 86–94.

Garson, A., Jr., Williams, R.B., Jr., & Reckless, J. Long-term follow-up of patients with tetralogy of Fallot: Physical health and psychopathology. *The Journal of Pediatrics,* 1974, *85,* 429–433.

Kupst, M.J., Blatterbauer, S., Westman, J., Schulman, J.L., & Paul, M.H. Helping parents cope with the diagnosis of congenital heart defect: An experimental study. *Pediatrics,* 1977, *59*(2), 266–272.

Kupst, M.J., Dresser, K., Schulman, J.L., & Paul, M.H. Improving physician-parent communication: Some lessons learned from parents concerned about their child's congenital heart defect. *Clinical Pediatrics*, 1976, *15*, 27–30.

Levy, R.J., Rosenthal, A., Castaneda, A.R., & Nadas, A.S. Growth after surgical repair of simple D-transposition of the great arteries. *The Annals of Thoracic Surgery*, 1978, *25*(3), 225–230.

Linde, L.M., Rasof, B., & Dunn, O.J. Mental development in congenital heart disease. *The Journal of Pediatrics*, 1967, *71*(2), 198–203.

Linde, L.M., Rasof, B., & Dunn, O.J. Longitudinal studies of intellectual and behavioral development in children with congenital heart disease. *Acta Paediatrica Scandinavica* 1970, *59*(2), 169–176.

MacVicar, M.G., & Archbold, P. A framework for family assessment in chronic illness. *Nursing Forum*, 1976, *15*(2), 180–194.

Melamed, B.G., & Siegel, L.G. *Behavioral medicine: Practical applications in health care*. New York: Springer Publishing Company, 1980.

Myers, R.E. Four patterns of perinatal brain damage and their conditions of occurrence in primates. *Advances in Neurology*, 1975, *10*, 223–234.

Nadas, A.S. *Pediatric cardiology* (2nd ed.). Philadelphia: Saunders, 1963.

Naeye, R.L. Organ and cellular development in congenital heart disease and in alimentary malnutrition. *The Journal of Pediatrics*, 1965, *67*(3), 447–458.

O'Dougherty, M., Wright, F.S., Garmezy, N., Loewenson, R.B., & Torres, F. Later competence and adaptation in infants who survive severe heart defects. *Child Development*, in press.

Petrillo, M., & Sanger, S. *Emotional care of hospitalized children: An environmental approach* (2nd ed.). Philadelphia: J.B. Lippincott Company, 1980.

Phornphutkul, C., Rosenthal, A., Nadas, A.S., & Berenberg, W. Cerebrovascular accidents in infants and children with cyanotic congenital heart disease. *American Journal of Cardiology*, 1973, *32*, 329–334.

Rosenthal, A. Visual simple reaction time in cyanotic heart disease. *American Journal of Diseases of Children*, 1967, *114*, 139–143.

Rosenthal, A., & Castaneda, A.R. Growth and development after cardiovascular surgery in infants and children. *Progress in Cardiovascular Diseases*, 1975, *18*(1), 27–37.

Silbert, A., Wolff, P.H., Mayer, B., Rosenthal, A., & Nadas, A.S. Cyanotic heart disease and psychological development. *Pediatrics*, 1969, *43*(2), 192–200.

Solnit, A.J., & Stark, M.H. Mourning and the birth of a defective child. *Psychoanalytic Study of the Child*, 1961, *16*, 523–537.

Sroufe, L.A. The coherence of individual development: Early care, attachment, and subsequent developmental issues. *American Psychologist*, 1979, *34*(10), 834–841.

Torres, F., Frank, G.S., Cohen, M.M., Lillehei, C.W., & Kaspar, N. Neurologic and electroencephalographic studies in open heart surgery: A preliminary report. *Neurology*, 1959, *9*(3), 174–183.

Travis, G. *Chronic illness in children: Its impact on child and family*. Stanford, California: Stanford University Press, 1976.

Tyler, H.R., & Clark, D.B. Incidence of neurological complications in congenital heart disease. *Archives of Neurology and Psychiatry*, 1957, *77*, 17–22.

Vanden Belt, R.J., Ronan, J.A., Jr., & Bedynek, J.L., Jr. *Cardiology: A clinical approach*. Chicago: Year Book Medical Publishers, Inc., 1979.

Volpe, J.J. Perinatal hypoxic-ischemic brain injury. *Pediatric Clinics of North America*, 1976, *23*(3), 383–397.

Wright, F.S., & O'Dougherty, M. Neurologic complications in children with congenital heart disease. Unpublished manuscript, University of Minnesota, 1979.

Zavanella, C., & Subramanian, S. Review: Surgery for transposition of the great arteries in the first year of life. *Annals of Surgery*, 1978, *187*(2), 143–150.

5 | The Endocrine System: Diabetes Mellitus

Diabetes mellitus is a metabolic disorder caused by a deficiency or lack of the pancreatic hormone, insulin. This deficiency disturbs energy metabolism and can lead to an aberration in the metabolism of fat, protein, and carbohydrates. The immediate consequence of this disruption in metabolism is increased glucose in the blood (hyperglycemia) and in the urine (glycosuria) (Sperling, 1982). Diabetes mellitus is the most common endocrine/metabolic disorder of childhood and has important consequences on physical, social, and emotional development.

There are two primary types of diabetes, insulin dependent and noninsulin dependent, both of unknown cause. (Since the latter form usually occurs later in adult life it will not be discussed here.) Type I is characterized as insulin dependent diabetes and can occur at any age. The usual age of onset is in childhood or at puberty, and it can result from a deficiency in, or a total lack of, insulin. Incidence and prevalence figures vary, and range from 1 in 500 children under 20 (Sperling, 1982) to 1 in 2500 under the age of 15 (Knowles, 1971). Sperling cites the annual incidence rate as 16 new cases per 100,000 children and reports that both incidence and prevalence rates in black Americans are one-third to one-half those found in Caucasian Americans. There does not appear to be a sex difference in incidence.

Etiology and Genetics

The term diabetes originated from the Greek word for "siphon," indicating "to go through," and was coined by Arataeus around 100 A.D. (Reed, 1954). He believed that it was a disorder associated with "a melting down of flesh and limbs into urine" (p. 419). In 1679 an English physician attributed the disease to strong wine, nervous system juice, and prolonged sorrow (Allan, 1953). The discovery in 1920 that total pancreatectomy in dogs resulted in diabetes, however, led to the landmark research by Banting and Best culminating in the discovery that insulin lowered blood glucose in both animals and man (Banting & Best, 1922).

In juvenile diabetes the insulin producing capacity of the pancreas is decreased because of a failure of the beta cells of the Islets of Langerhans, the site of insulin synthesis. In time, the pancreas is not able to produce any insulin at all. The specific mechanism of genetic transmission is unclear; it is primarily thought to be an autosomal recessive trait requiring both parents to share the propensity; however, a dominant disorder with incomplete penetrance or a multifactorial mode of inheritance is also postulated. The importance of exogeneous factors in precipitating the disorder has been particularly implicated in juvenile onset diabetes. Inflammation, viral infection, trauma, and emotional stress have all been postulated as precipitating factors, but to date, definitive evidence supporting any of these explanations is lacking (Garner & Thompson, 1978).

Clinical Diagnosis

An outline of the major medical symptoms, possible treatments, and psychological issues in diabetes is presented in Table 5-1. The major signs and symptoms can occur quickly and are the direct result of the insulin deficiency. If there is a delay in seeking medical treatment, the child may rapidly develop more intense symptoms, such as acidosis, dehydration, flushed cheeks, sunken eyes, and may progress into ketoacidotic coma (Garner & Thompson, 1978). At the time of initial diagnosis fasting blood glucose levels are elevated and glycosuria is evident. If diabetic ketoacidosis is present, the child will require emergency treatment. Untreated, ketoacidosis can lead to coma, vascular collapse, and death. Ketoacidosis can develop as a result of a variety of factors, including failure to diagnose diabetes mellitus, infection, nonadherence to diabetic management, as well as response to emotional stress. During these episodes the child may be unconscious or disoriented. Diagnosis should be established through determination of blood concentration of glucose, ketones in the blood and urine, and evaluation of acid-base status and electrolyte disturbances. Fluid and electrolyte therapy and insulin to restore and maintain adequate metabolism are the critical ingredients of medical management of the ketoacidosis (Sperling, 1982).

Clinical Management

Given the severity of the initial symptoms prior to diagnosis, most juvenile patients are initially treated in the hospital, both to alleviate the symptoms of hyperglycemia, glycosuria, and acidosis, as well as to determine the required balance of insulin, caloric intake, and exercise that will maintain a normal growth pattern for the child (Garner & Thompson, 1978). In the 4-8 weeks after initial diagnosis, Garner and Thompson indicate there is a tendency for a decreased requirement for insulin. They refer to this stage as the "honeymoon" period which is often accompanied by early false hopes of a cure or a diminished need for insulin injections. In order for the family to become accustomed to the therapeutic regimen, many

TABLE 5-1

Diabetes

Definition	Major Symptoms and Signs	Possible Medical Treatments	Psychologic Issues
Metabolic disease in which there is a lack of insulin or impairment in the insulin mechanism	*Early*	Insulin injections	Parent control struggle over insulin-food-exercise regimen
Genetic transmission (recessive; likely multifactorial)	intense thirst (polydypsia)	Diet restrictions	Adolescent rebellion
	frequent urination (polyuria)	Blood and urine testing	Pain of daily injections
	severe hunger (polyphagia)	Hospitalization for initiating treatment and acute episodes	Fear of coma or insulin shock
	weight loss		Anxiety over long-term complications
	fatigue		
	Progressive Illness		
	hyperglycemia		
	coma (ketoacidosis)		
	Long-term Complications		
	diseases of the small blood vessels of the eyes (retinopathy)		
	kidneys (nephropathy)		
	nerves (neuropathy)		

diabetologists continue to have the parents administer small insulin injections throughout this period. Typically, during the subsequent 6-24 months, the child's insulin requirements increase. Travis (1976) describes the subsequent impact on the family as they learn to cope with this condition:

> Understanding what the child and family are confronted with, and the effects on family life, requires some comprehension of the special treatment of emergency conditions and of the lifelong, everyday treatment: insulin injection, nutrition, control of energy expenditure, care during impending coma, care during insulin reaction (the functional opposite of coma), and skin care. (p. 346)

Each of these aspects will be outlined to provide the health professional with a preliminary overview of the stressful conditions the family may face and the type and extent of participation required of the parent and child to insure adequate management of the disease. The primary goal of medical management is to obtain an optimal balance between caloric intake, energy expenditure, and the dosage of insulin required. In a normal individual, sufficient insulin is secreted by the pancreas to convert the sugar consumed into energy and to store the excess in body fat or in the liver. Since the child with diabetes has no (or too little) insulin, he or she must receive injections of the proper dosage and at the correct time. Amount and type of food consumed, the child's health status, and type and amount of physical activity all dynamically change the balance among these factors and require appropriate adjustments and tailoring to the individual's changing experiences (Travis, 1976).

Hypoglycemic reactions (insulin reactions). A hypoglycemic reaction occurs when there is more insulin in the body than is needed to handle the food intake. Most diabetic children experience hypoglycemic episodes at some time during the course of their illness. The symptoms can occur very quickly, often in minutes, unlike ketoacidosis, which develops over hours or days. Some of the symptoms reflecting glucose deprivation to the brain include dizziness, hunger, confusion, and mood or personality changes. If food, such as a fast acting carbohydrate, is not ingested additional symptoms can occur, such as mental confusion, seizures, and coma. The latter two symptoms reflect the severity of the reaction and brain injury may result. Other symptoms, such as trembling, shaking, and tachycardia, are due to the increase in catacholamines. Education of the patient and family to recognize the early signs of hypoglycemic reactions is essential, and carbohydrate containing snacks, such as orange juice or a carbonated beverage containing sugar, should be taken. Parents, school nurses, and patients should also receive instruction in administering glucagon intramuscularly, a procedure particularly necessary if the patient is losing consciousness or vomiting.

There are a number of reasons for hypoglycemic reactions: incorrect insulin dosage, inadequate calorie intake, exercise, infection or illness, stress, or deliberate noncompliance with the treatment regimen. All these factors need to be examined carefully by those caring for the child. Since juvenile diabetes is particularly difficult to control, it has been characterized as "brittle," since often blood and urine sugar rise without an obvious or understandable reason. The interaction of stress, maturation, diet, insulin requirements, exercise, and rebellious acting out may contribute to the variability and occurrence not only of hypoglycemic reactions, but of ketoacidosis as well. It is also important to note that even careful adherence to diet, exercise, and insulin requirements may not insure adequate control in children with "brittle diabetes" (Garner & Thompson, 1978). The Somogyi effect, in which the child requires more insulin without decreasing the sugar in the urine, can occur. This excess of insulin results in hypoglycemia, quickly followed by hyperglycemia and ketonuria. Such instability in blood glucose and variable response to insulin adjustments require careful and constant monitoring, but even with vigilant attention to these factors, adequate control may not be achieved.

Insulin injections. Some children can obtain adequate management of their diabetes with a single daily insulin injection, although in children less than 5 years old and for adolescents during the pubertal growth spurt, Sperling (1982) has found that a twice daily injection regimen often permits better metabolic control. The data for this finding, however, remain somewhat controversial; and the child's acceptance of two injections a day also becomes an important factor to consider. If the child's diabetes is poorly controlled, as many as four injections may need to be given throughout the day. (Insulin usually comes in various concentrations, typically 40 units of insulin per ml (U40 red cap) and 80 units of insulin per ml (U80 green cap). There are also variations (fast, intermediate, long) in onset and duration of action for the different concentrations.)

In the beginning, the parents are taught the technique of insulin injection using a hypodermic syringe. The importance of rotating the injection site, arms, thighs, buttocks, and abdomen, is emphasized to help insure absorption of the insulin and to diminish the amount of tissue (lipodystrophic) changes, such as atrophy or hypertrophy. (The latter side effects can be unattractive and quite embarrassing to the child.) Depending on the cognitive or emotional maturity of the child, increasing responsibility for self-management is encouraged. The assumption of responsibility for self-monitoring is a gradual process shared by parent and child, typically with self-injections occurring by age 9 or 10, with total responsibility for urine testing and insulin adjustment occurring after 12 years of age.

Urine is tested for sugar content 4 times daily at set intervals, typically the second voiding of the day, before lunch and dinner, and in the evening. Two types of tests are performed. The first test for glycosuria, the 2 drop Clinetest, involves mixing two drops of urine, ten drops of water, plus a tablet for glucose (Clinetest). Urine tests should not always be negative; if they are, the child's blood sugar may be excessively low and a hypoglycemic reaction could occur. On the other hand, if the urine tests consistently show 4+ sugar in the urine, the amount of insulin is too low for the child's food intake. Establishing the appropriate insulin dosage and nutritional requirements can be a lengthy, frustrating, and difficult process, particularly if the child has "brittle" diabetes (described earlier). When 4+ reactions are obtained, an additional test must be performed to determine whether ketones (fat breakdown products) are present in the urine. In this test, urine is placed directly on an Acetest tablet. If ketones are detected, the child needs either more insulin or a change in diet in order to avoid possible coma (Travis, 1976). The most frequently omitted test is the one prior to lunch when the child is in school, since many children report that they are embarrassed to test there. A 24 hour urine collection test may also be performed and analyzed to determine whether any changes in the type and dose of insulin are required.

Unfortunately, recent studies (summarized in the Appendix, Table A-6) have indicated that urine glucose testing is not an adequate measure of metabolic control. There are often significant errors in the child's recording of this level; and use of multiple measures (e.g., fasting blood glucose, urine glucose, urine acetone, 24 hour excretion of glucose, and percent of urine specimens free of sugar) indicate that only a small percentage of diabetic children have consistently good diabetic control. Recently, blood glucose monitoring has been attempted at home with adolescent and adult patients (see the Appendix, Table A-6), using small portable machines such as the Autolet. This assessment technique has formerly been possible only at the physician's office. Now it may provide a more accurate pattern of blood glucose changes which will, it is hoped, allow for more appropriate adjustments in insulin and diet.

Diet. Food holds an important place in our (and in most other) cultures. It is one of the earliest and most direct forms of nurturance provided and becomes a focal point of social interaction within the family and with friends. The parents of a diabetic child are in the difficult position of forbidding their child to eat certain foods rather than encouraging and allowing gratification of oral desires. Often the diabetic regimen can be frustrating or appear punishing to a young child who does not understand the reasons for specific food restrictions. Since sweets are often given to reward good behavior or withheld to punish bad behavior, feelings of deprivation or persecution can develop when desserts, candy, or soft drinks are denied. The parent who must enforce these restrictions often feels conflict and anxiety over consistently following through (Garner & Thompson, 1978). The burden of having to eat the same food values at the same time each day can also be frustrating and upsetting for the child and may lead to resentment in the mother or caregiver who must prepare the food, since neither child nor parent can sleep late or skip a meal (Travis, 1976).

Decisions regarding the types and amounts of food to be eaten, the time at which food is required, and the relationship of food intake to needed insulin are complex issues that require the interdisciplinary cooperation of physicians, dieticians, nurses, laboratory technicians, and parents. Although some general principles can be outlined, the individual needs of each child and the social and ethnic background of the family must be considered before making recommendations. Since the dose of insulin is determined on the basis of specific caloric intake, a regular eating pattern is essential. Typically, the daily caloric intake is divided so that two-tenths is provided at breakfast, two-tenths at lunch, three-tenths at dinner, and one-tenth each for mid-morning, mid-afternoon, and evening snacks (Sperling, 1982). The American Diabetes Association has provided meal plans and methods of computing food exchanges that have been of great assistance to families. While foods containing refined sugars are contraindicated, occasional exceptions can be made on special occasions such as birthdays and holidays. If cakes, cookies, or candies are included on special occasions, the food exchange value and carbohydrate content must be calculated for the day's meal plans.

The majority of carbohydrate content should be derived from complex carbohydrates, such as starch, with intake of refined sugars avoided because the complex carbohydrates have a slower digestion absorption time, so that plasma glucose metabolizes slowly. In contrast, refined sugars are quickly absorbed, which can cause marked hyperglycemia or wide swings in metabolic control. Similarly, fat intake is adjusted so that the polyunsaturated/saturated ratio is increased. This is typically achieved by substituting margarine and vegetable oils in cooking and by using lean meats such as veal, chicken, turkey, or fish rather than fatty meats like beef, ham, or bacon. Cholesterol intake is also limited (Sperling, 1982). Special considerations and adjustments in diet are often necessary during the adolescent growth spurt or when vigorous exercise is undertaken. Finally, the benefits of lenient versus strict dietary management have been debated. An extreme of either pattern can lead to difficulty: the former can result in hyperglycemia and ketoacidosis, whereas the latter may provoke rebelliousness, noncompliance, and other behavior problems (Johnson, 1981; Garner & Thompson, 1978).

Exercise. Physical activity and exercise are important components of growth and development throughout childhood. Unfortunately, one potential complication in diabetes is a hypoglycemic reaction during or shortly after exercise. With experience, however, the physician, parent, and child can usually determine the optimal management approach. If no hypoglycemia occurs, alterations in diet and insulin need not be made; however, if exercise is frequently associated with hypoglycemia, and/or if exercise occurs at regularly scheduled times, the insulin dose may need to be reduced by about 10 percent and/or a ready source of glucose, such as orange juice, should be available. Hypoglycemic episodes can occur with exercise because the increased blood flow to the muscles with vigorous activity can cause an increased rate of absorption of insulin. Exercise improves glucose regulation and lipid metabolism by increasing insulin receptors and by raising cholesterol (Sperling, 1982). Although exercise restrictions are not recommended, the parents and child need help in determining appropriate adjustments in insulin or diet.

The Relationship between Diabetic Control and Long-Term Complications

With increasing duration of diabetes, a variety of diseases of the small blood vessels of the eyes, kidneys, muscles, nerves, and skin have been observed. Retinopathy (diseases of the eye) often occurs 10 years after the child's growth spurt and is found in 50 percent of child diabetic cases. Retinopathy can progress to blindness in about 5 percent of the cases. Other eye problems can also occur, including hemorrhages, aneurysms, cataracts, and neovascularization. The nervous system can be affected as well; electromyographic and electroencephalographic changes most often occur after 8-10 years of diabetes. Some investigators have found a high correlation between abnormal EEGs and the frequency with which the child has experienced coma or seizures related to diabetes. Diseases of the peripheral blood vessels in the extremities, particularly the legs, occur with symptoms such as numbness, pain, discomfort, impaired circulation, difficulty feeling pressure, pain, or heat, and slow healing of sores because of poor blood supply. Pressure sores and gangrene can also develop if special precautions are not taken. If these complications do arise, amputations may be required. Finally, diseases of the kidney (nephropathy) can develop a few years after problems in the retina. If renal problems become chronic or severe, they can become life threatening (Travis, 1976; Garner & Thompson, 1978).

There has been considerable controversy over whether patients with consistently good diabetic control (normal physiologic glucose levels) have decreased or delayed nephropathy and retinopathy. Studies are currently underway to evaluate this, and data have been obtained both supporting and refuting this relationship. The official position of the American Diabetes Association has been to strive for an optimal regulation of glucose levels in the hope of reducing microvascular complications (Cahill, Etzwiler, & Freinkel, 1976).

The Effect of Life Stress on the Onset and Course of Diabetes

Can particular stressful life events precipitate diabetes in a genetically susceptible individual? Early retrospective studies explored the frequency of early loss (through death, separation, or divorce) and other stress factors in the period preceding the onset of diabetes. While some studies did report a significantly higher percentage of loss prior to disease onset in a diabetic group as compared to a control group, such losses occurred at various time periods ranging from 1 month to 10 years prior to the onset of the diabetes. In Johnson's (1981) comprehensive review, she concludes that such lengthy intervals militate against considering such losses "precipitating" factors in the onset of diabetes.

Other studies have examined the impact of stress on the subsequent course of the disease. For example, Chase and Jackson (1981) examined the relationship between stressful life events using the Coddington Questionnaire (Coddington, 1972) and long-term and short-term sugar control in a group of diabetic children aged 6-18 years. Life stress scores related to poor diabetic control in the adolescent age group (15-18 years) only. Children who had one or more hospitalizations for the treatment of ketoacidosis during the previous 3 months demonstrated significantly higher stress scores than children who had not been hospitalized.

In order to understand how stressful life events might adversely influence diabetic control, some familiarity with the physiological effects of stress in a normal individual is needed. In general, stress results in the production of catecholamines and pituitary hormones (adrenocorticotropin hormone [ACTH] and growth hormone [GH]). Their release subsequently leads to a decrease in insulin production, accompanied by an increase in fatty acids in the blood. If this stress is severe or prolonged and insulin production remains diminished, blood glucose levels are increased so that the central nervous system and body tissues have an adequate energy supply. When the stress terminates, there is a decrease in the production of stress hormones, an increase in the production of insulin, and a return to normal blood glucose levels and low free fatty acids. The diabetic patient, however, is not able to counteract the effect of the stress hormones during the recovery period by producing insulin. Although insulin injections can be helpful in mediating the stress effects, the inability of the diabetic patient's system to respond to changing needs may result in problems maintaining adequate diabetic control during fluctuating or adverse life circumstances (Efendic, Cerasi, & Luft, 1974).

Individual differences in degree of physiological responsivity or type of physiologic reaction to stress may also play an important role in maintaining or disrupting diabetic control. In many studies, blood glucose levels have been quite variable in response to stress. Both elevated and decreased levels of glycosuria have also been found, depending on the age of the patients studied and the type of experimental stress. Based on these findings, Warnberg (1974) suggests that life stress may be associated with metabolic instability, highlighting the need to examine the individuality of physiologic stress reactions in diabetic children in addition to examining differences between diabetic and normal subjects.

The importance of such an individualized assessment of physiologic responsivity was highlighted in two recent biofeedback treatment studies (see the Appendix, Table A-6 for an outline of these treatment procedures). Frontalis EMG biofeedback was employed with two adult patients who had insulin dependent diabetes in order to determine if such biofeedback might allow for a decrease in insulin requirements. Both patients experienced severe insulin reactions during treatment due to the rapid decrease in insulin requirements obtained with this technique. Whether these findings will be replicated and whether such results would also be obtained with other relaxation procedures, such as hypnosis or Jacobsonian relaxation, need to be determined. These preliminary findings indicate the need for proceeding with extreme caution in using such techniques with diabetic patients, since effective use of the procedure may result in marked instability in diabetic control (Fowler, Budzynski, & VandenBergh, 1976; Seeburg & DeBoer, 1980).

Child Characteristics Relating to Diabetic Control

Early research in this area was strongly influenced by prevailing psychosomatic concepts relating specific personality conflicts to specific physiologic disorders. Alexander and French (1948) hypothesized that the basic conflict in diabetic patients might involve the wish that they would be cared for and the perceived expectation that they take care of others. As found in other disease areas, this hypothesis has not been confirmed, nor has a specific diabetic personality profile emerged (Garner & Thompson, 1978).

Although some children with diabetes have displayed serious psychiatric symptomatology (often those children with poor diabetic control), an increased incidence in psychiatric problems in diabetic children as a group, compared to control children, has not been well documented. Johnson's (1981) comprehensive review of 16 controlled studies assessing personality characteristics in diabetic children found surprisingly few differences between diabetic and control children. She concluded that:

> Further work in which children with diabetes are compared to "normal" controls on one or more personality measures does not seem to be warranted. . . . Perhaps a more fruitful approach would be to study the multivariate conditions (e.g., family characteristics, cultural factors, and the course of the disease) under which psychological disturbance or psychological health is associated with a chronic disease such as diabetes. (p. 278)

She identified five major methodological problems in these studies: 1) low reliability and validity of the tests employed to assess personality characteristics; 2) prior knowledge by the examiner of the child's diagnosis and/or whether the child's diabetes was well or poorly controlled; 3) varying subject selection procedures and assessments of metabolic control; 4) incomparability of assessment techniques between studies; and 5) inability to separate cause from effect in interpreting the findings of increased personality problems (Johnson, 1981).

Variations in Child and Family Patterns of Coping with Diabetes

There are a number of aspects of juvenile diabetes that make it particularly difficult to cope with. For example, in the case of "brittle" diabetes no matter how carefully and consistently the child and parents have regulated food intake, physical activity, and insulin dosage, problems in day-to-day management can still occur. When this is the result in spite of painstaking attention to the therapeutic regimen, the patient's and parents' motivation and willingness to comply can be markedly diminished. If noncompliance occurs in these cases, it is important to understand that it might be the treatment failing the family, rather than the family failing treatment. In addition, Garner and Thompson (1978) report that "during such periods, parents search anxiously for factors that may have contributed to the poor control and, in their haste and anxiety, may blame the child, the doctor, or one another unjustly" (p. 234). Particularly with juvenile onset diabetes, early age at onset is negatively related to adequacy of control (Koski, 1969). Such a relationship tends to work against continuing motivation. When adherence to the treatment program does not result in adequate control, the child and family's attitude can become "Why bother anymore?"

The major responsibility for daily supervision of the program rests with the parents. How effectively they are able to manage this disease is closely related to their preferred ways of dealing with stress, typical coping patterns, marital satisfaction, pre-existing relationships with the child, as well as the characteristic defense mechanisms they employ (denial, internalization, helplessness, aggression, acting out, projection) when the stress becomes overwhelming.

Koski (1969) and Koski and colleagues (1976) contributed greatly to our understanding of the defense mechanisms and coping patterns of parents of diabetic children. First, Koski explored the initial reactions of the parents to the diagnosis. The statements presented in Table 5-2 are reflective of the range of emotional reactions experienced by these parents.

The parents were divided into two groups on follow-up evaluation: those whose

TABLE 5-2

Initial Parental Reactions to the Diagnosis of Diabetes

Bewilderment and shock: "As if a blank wall had risen in front of me." or "As if everything had stopped."

Anxiety and fears: "I myself will be taken to a mental hospital." or "I am afraid of the insulin injection."

Depressive feelings: "We thought he might die in the hospital" or "We were quite down for a long time."

Guilt feelings:

Realistic: Mother's employment had prevented her from taking the child to the doctor earlier.

Unrealistic: "The child was breast fed for more than 1½ years; was it because of that he developed diabetes?" or "Perhaps I gave him too many sweets. I was never given sweets in my childhood, and I thought I would make it up to my children." or "What had I done to deserve this punishment?"

Aggression: "It would be better if the child were to die than remain sick."

Wishful thinking: "Perhaps it is a mistake." or "It can only be a temporary upset." or "There must be some place in the world where diabetic children are treated without insulin."

Adapted from M.-L. Koski. The coping processes in childhood diabetes. *Acta Paediatrica Scandinavica*, 1969, *198* (suppl.), pp. 27–28.

children had good control were compared to those whose children had poor control of their diabetes. The only initial reaction differentiating these groups was that insomnia and wishful thinking were most common in mothers of children with later good control. These mothers also initially expressed more emotion and more vivid immediate reactions than mothers of children in the poor control group, who tended to deny their feelings. The authors speculated that mothers of children in the good control group were able to work through and gain mastery over their initial feelings of anxiety and depression, whereas in the latter groups, the initial denial prevented working through these emotions.

On follow-up the families of children with good diabetic control were stable; the parents' attitude toward diabetic care was realistic and responsible; and there was appropriate boundary differentiation between the parents and child. In instances where only one parent was present, this parent displayed good ego strength. Children who had changed from good to poor control by the time of follow-up demonstrated an increased incidence in family disruption. Maladaptive coping patterns observed in parents of children with poor control included feelings of helplessness and loss of control over dietary management and injections, isolated or chaotic family life accompanied by denial of the illness, or an incorporation of the child into unresolved marital conflicts. Coping was also facilitated when the parents accepted the limitations and requirements necessitated by the illness, found the care of the child rewarding, and attempted to normalize the child's life in other respects (Koski, Ahlas, & Kumento, 1976).

Other adaptive or maladaptive responses associated with types of maternal attitudes and differential outcome and diabetic control were identified by Bruch (1949). These included: 1. a perfectionistic attitude (which resulted in good control of the diabetes, but behavioral and emotional problems in the child); 2. a masochistic, hostile, and rejecting attitude (which resulted in poor control of the diabetes and a pathologic mother-child interaction); and 3. a tolerant attitude that was associated with good control and normal personality development.

Careful exploration of the manner in which individual psychological reactions and pathologic parent-child relationships might influence diabetic control was undertaken by Minuchin and colleagues (1975; 1978). They hypothesized that psychological factors could influence diabetic control in two ways: 1. emotional problems may result in behavioral noncompliance (failure to follow diet, failure to test urine adequately, refusal of injections, etc.) which would then have a direct impact on metabolic control of the diabetes; or 2. emotional reactions might directly cause metabolic changes through psychophysiological mechanisms. Specific pathological family patterns typifying families having a member with a "psychosomatic" illness were identified. The most common characteristics included overprotectiveness, enmeshment, lack of role differentiation within the family, rigidity, inability to alter coping styles, and lack of conflict resolution. In this conceptual framework, family fighting is viewed as a triggering situation to which the child responds with emotional and physiological arousal. This is termed the "turn on" phase. The families' tendency to avoid the conflict or their inability to resolve this conflict results in the child's being unable physiologically to return to a normal baseline. This is termed the "turn off" phase (Minuchin, Rosman, & Baker, 1978). This model has been evaluated on a sample of diabetic patients and has shown some promise in differentiating subtypes of diabetic children (Baker, Minuchin, Milman, Liebman, & Todd, 1975). However, the small sample size, absence of appropriate control groups, as well as an inability to differentiate cause and effect, require futher investigation of the applicability of this model to families of diabetic children. Johnson (1981) speculated in her review of the area that a family pattern of conflict avoidance may actually develop in response to the child's heightened physiological reactivity rather than being a cause of this reactivity.

Children's Concepts of Diabetes

As indicated in Chapter 2, children's conception of body parts, body systems, and illness is often limited and may be quite distorted. In juvenile diabetes, the onset of the illness can be accompanied by severe and frightening symptoms, making the task of understanding what has happened all the more difficult. Garner and Thompson (1978) give us a striking example of the distortion and confusion that can arise during this time:

> One small diabetic girl . . . cried inconsolably during the first days of her initial hospitalization until it was discovered that she thought she was about to die. Sympathetic inquiry finally unearthed the fact that she had over-heard a remark that she had diabetes, which the child perceived as "die-abetes," and which she therefore took to mean that she was about to die "of betes." (p. 234)

Confusion is evident at older age levels as well. Rothenberg (1974) reports a case history of a fifteen year old, bright, adolescent boy from a stable middle-class family in which the maternal grandmother and great uncle had diabetes. When Tom's diabetes was first diagnosed, he received information from a variety of sources—his parents, his great uncle, as well as the medical house-staff. His answers to questions such as "What do you have?" or "How did you get it?" revealed the extent to which misinformation and confusion can create added stress. Tom responded that he thought diabetes was caused by a combination of "heredity and eating too many sweets" (p. 871). He also added that he thought if he would have played football in the previous fall, as he had done in previous years, he might have delayed the onset of his illness "because I would have burned up more sugar" (p. 871). Although he did understand the treatment regimen of self-administered insulin, diet, and urine checks, and knew that he would have this disease for the rest of his life, he had also heard from his great uncle that "he'd have to be especially careful as he grew older because he could get bad infections that could eventuate in his feet having to be amputated" (pp. 871–872). Thus, the diagnosis took on added meaning for him with ominous implications for his future. Careful discussion and clarification of these issues were required to reduce his anxiety and concern.

Kaufman and Hersher (1971) also provide clinical material that illustrates the impact diabetes can have on adolescents' understanding of the pathophysiological processes involved in diabetes, its effect on internal body organs, and subsequently its impact on body image. The patients had received instruction about diabetes from doctors and nurses and had also received programmed instruction on teaching machines. They were asked to draw pictures about their illness and were interviewed using Piaget's clinical method to elicit underlying beliefs and fantasies. The teenagers displayed factual information about their disease, as well as primitive and idiosyncratic fantasies, such as thinking that diabetes was due to a defective body with parts of the pancreas missing, blockages within the pancreas, or alterations in stomach size and function. One patient thought of her diabetes as resulting from an insatiable need for food and an inability of her stomach to stop expanding. This patient had begun overeating three years previously, when her mother, who was also diabetic, had her legs "removed" because of the illness. The patient explained "I feel comforted by eating as when mother was near. I get bored and lonely and nervous and I eat and eat and eat" (p. 125). Feelings of being defective, of having poisons inside the body, of being damaged, deprived, and helpless in the face of the disease were frequent. Although only five case studies are presented, the clinical material is rich and illustrative of the confusions and distortions that can have impact on the adolescent's self-esteem and body image.

Diabetic children have also been found to deny or underestimate the seriousness of their condition. Ratings by parents and children of degree of diabetic control do not always correlate well with objective clinical signs such as blood or urine sugar levels or instances of acidosis or coma (Garner & Thompson, 1978). The children also seem to prefer having their existing disease to another unknown problem such as constipation, pimples, or six toes (Davis, Shipp, & Pattishall, 1965). Taken together, the findings suggest that minimization of the disease may be a predominant way of coping. Whether such minimization also extends to poor treatment program compliance has not been systematically studied.

Other possible problems of particular concern to the adolescent female with diabetes are the low fertility rate among diabetic women, the increased incidence of termination of pregnancy by miscarriage or stillbirth, and the difficulty in maintaining diabetic control during pregnancy. There is always the hazard that the fetus could die in utero if the mother's diabetes goes out of control. In addition, menstruation can be accompanied by alterations in diabetic control; and the method of birth control selected often requires careful medical evaluation, since oral contraceptives are not always permitted. In addition, a young diabetic woman considering pregnancy must also weigh the possibilities that future complications of diabetes, such as blindness or serious kidney or heart disease, may substantially reduce her life expectancy (Travis, 1976).

Assessment of Knowledge and Skill in Managing Diabetes

What do diabetic children and their parents actually know about the disease? A number of studies have been carried out recently to determine the level of information in the areas of concepts of diabetes, insulin effects, level of control, symptoms, urine testing procedures, and nutritional requirements. These studies are summarized in the Appendix, Table A-6. Etzwiler (1962) developed an initial multiple choice questionnaire test that has been widely used. He found a significant difference in knowledge between elementary aged (6–11 years) and pubertal (12 years and older) children. The meaning and interpretations of urine testing for glycosuria were not understood until the child was over ten years of age. In a subsequent study by Collier and Etzwiler (1971), knowledge of diabetes was assessed in both parents and children. Areas of deficiency identified were failure to recognize symptoms associated with the development of acidosis, poor comprehension of dietary items and time needed for insulin actions, as well as poor comprehension of the difference between short- and long-acting forms of insulin, all critical areas of knowledge in appropriate control of this disease. Of interest was their finding that the children who had a family member with diabetes obtained *lower* knowledge scores than children without such family members. While the reasons for this were unclear, it is interesting to speculate on what may account for this finding. It may be that less education is given to these parents by health professionals who mistakenly assume a better understanding; or alternatively, the attitudes and beliefs of parents and children who have lived with the disease may be even more distorted, given the stress and long-term complications that can arise.

Other studies (also outlined in the Appendix, Table A-6) have assessed the accuracy of children's urine glucose testing. The results of these studies are startling and have critical implications for diabetes education and home management. First, skill at self-injection and urine testing was not significantly related to diabetes knowledge or problem solving (Johnson, Pollak, Silverstein, Rosenbloom, Spillar, McCallum, & Harkavy, 1982). Second, serious errors in urine testing are made by the majority of the diabetic children (Johnson et al., 1982; Epstein, Coburn, Becker, Drash, & Siminerio, 1980). Finally, nearly 40 percent of the children made errors in self-injection (Johnson et al., 1982). The most common error in urine testing was incorrect timing on a test of acetone, and the most common error on the self-injection test was bubbles in the syringe. Boys were more inaccurate than girls on both the urine test and the self-injection test. Information feedback was successful in increasing the percentage of correct glucose determinations, while extended practice with no feedback resulted in a deterioration in the children's performance (Epstein, Figueroa, Farkas, & Beck, 1981).

All these studies emphasize the importance of assessing the current level of the child's knowledge as well as skill in carrying out the required procedures. Although intensive teaching programs at the time of initial diagnosis are valuable, they need to be expanded and extended into a continuing supportive program of health education and care. In addition, Etzwiler has found that the medical personnel responsible for diabetes education are often poorly informed themselves and greatly in need of further education regarding diabetes management.

Implications for Intervention

The results of these studies suggest that total self-care may be forced upon the diabetic child before he or she has the cognitive maturity needed to understand the concepts or execute the procedures. Johnson et al. (1982) suggest that certain tasks may best be taught at different ages. They recommend emphasizing practical information about diet and insulin reactions in the 6–8 year old age group, with instruction in self-injection occurring by age 9. Given the poor skill level demonstrated by children on urine testing and injection, complete responsibility for these functions should not be undertaken until at least the age of 12, with more sophisticated instruction offered during adolescence. Further study is needed to determine optimal age periods for introducing more advanced information and skill instruction.

Greydanus and Hofmann (1979) stress the importance of dealing directly with the adolescent patient by beginning to have separate office visits so that the adolescent can be seen alone. This is often a period in which diabetic control is difficult because of rapid growth, menstruation, heightened stress, and other factors. In addition, the adolescent's need for control and mastery over life events and concern about his or her body are critical factors. These authors suggest that the physician should encourage age-appropriate self-management and be prepared for some experimentation or irregularity in compliance at this time. Avoiding power struggles in which control is a primary issue, as well as avoiding becoming a parent surrogate and fostering unhealthy dependence, is particularly important at this time. The physician's inability to respond to an adolescent's specific developmental needs may lead to acting out, evidenced in repeated acidotic or ketoacidotic episodes and hypoglycemic episodes. Greydanus and Hofmann (1979) comment that:

> Although such episodes are unquestionably unpleasant and maladaptive, the patient quickly gets well and forgets them, perceiving few long-term consequences. Substantial secondary gain may accrue through achieving a sense of control over parents and other adults. This may be far more preferable to the teenager than feelings of unjustified and enforced dependency. (pp. 1064–1065)

Group therapy approaches with adolescent patients, which often minimize the involvement of authority figures and utilize group leaders who are closer to the adolescent's age, have often been successful. Garner and Thompson (1978) report that medical specialists are best used as consultants in such groups, with the primary focus being on mutual sharing of problems, attitudes, and solutions with peers. In their experience with diabetic teenagers, discussion often includes not only details of diabetic management, but often addresses pressing issues such as anxieties over dating, marriage, parenthood, and employment opportunities. Young adults who have coped successfully with diabetes often express willingness to participate in an adolescent group and have served as helpful role models. Other successful approaches have been Minuchin's et al. (1978) structural family therapy for psychosomatic families in which the goals of treatment are to reduce the overprotectiveness of the parents and to increase individualization by emphasizing role differentiation within the family. In addition, tasks facilitating flexibility in handling problems and establishing a capacity to accept and deal effectively with conflict situations, rather than avoiding and denying conflicts, are emphasized.

The American Diabetes Association is also a very valuable resource for families. This association provides a number of meal plans and suggestions to parents for managing difficult problems; it also publishes an informational sheet for school personnel, as well as a journal dealing with new research and medical policies in diabetes management. Children with diabetes also often benefit from participation in diabetic camps organized around their unique medical needs. Such camps provide valuable instruction in how to manage diet, insulin injections, urine testing, and decision making for activities. Such camps also provide an opportunity to meet other children who are coping with this disease. Although some health care providers argue against special camps for a specific handicap group (believing that such separation may have undesirable consequences on the child's self-image and peer relationships), many diabetic children are unable to attend regular camps because of their medical condition. For these children, the advantages of attending a camp for children with diabetes often outweighs the disadvantages. Parents also often need an opportunity for relief from child-care responsibilities. The extended opportunity for educational instruction about their disease, as well as the emotional support available in such a setting, can often be tremendously valuable in facilitating these patients' adaptation to diabetes (Travis, 1976).

References

Alexander, F., & French, T.M. (Eds.). *Studies in psychosomatic medicine: An approach to the cause and treatment of vegetative disturbances.* New York: Ronald Press, 1948.

Allan, F.N. The writings of Thomas Willis, M.D.: Diabetes three hundred years ago. *Diabetes*, 1953, *2*(1), 74–77.

Baker, L., Minuchin, S., Milman, L., Liebman, R., & Todd, T. Psychosomatic aspects of juvenile diabetes mellitus: A progress report. *Modern Problems in Paediatrics*, 1975, *12*, 332–343.

Banting, F.G., & Best, C.H. The internal secretion of the pancreas. *The Journal of Laboratory and Clinical Medicine*, 1922, *7*(5), 251–266.

Bruch, H. Physiologic and psychologic interrelationships in diabetes in children. *Psychosomatic Medicine*, 1949, *11*, 200–210.

Cahill, G.F., Jr., Etzwiler, D.D., & Freinkel, N. "Control" and diabetes. *The New England Journal of Medicine*, 1976, *294*(18), 1004–1005.

Chase, H.P., & Jackson, G.G. Stress and sugar control in children with insulin-dependent diabetes mellitus. *The Journal of Pediatrics*, 1981, *98*(6), 1011–1013.

Coddington, R.D. The significance of life events as etiologic factors in the diseases of children. I. A survey of professional workers. *Journal of Psychosomatic Research*, 1972, *16*, 7–18.

Collier, B.N., Jr., & Etzwiler, D.D. Comparative study of diabetes knowledge among juvenile diabetics and their parents. *Diabetes*, 1971, *20*(1), 51–57.

Davis, D.M., Shipp, J.C., & Pattishall, E.G. Attitudes of diabetic boys and girls towards diabetes. *Diabetes*, 1965, *14*(2), 106–109.

Efendic, S., Cerasi, E., & Luft, R. Trauma: Hormonal factors with special reference to diabetes mellitus. *Acta Anaesthesiologica Scandinavica*, 1974, *55*(suppl.), 107–119.

Epstein, L.H., Coburn, P.C., Becker, D., Drash, A., & Siminerio, L. Measurement and modification of the accuracy of determinations of urine glucose concentration. *Diabetes Care*, 1980, *3*(4), 535–536.

Epstein, L.H., Figueroa, J., Farkas, G.M., & Beck, S. The short-term effects of feedback on accuracy of urine glucose determinations in insulin dependent diabetic children. *Behavior Therapy*, 1981, *12*, 560–564.

Etzwiler, D.D. What the juvenile diabetic knows about his disease. *Pediatrics*, 1962, *29*, 135–141.

Fowler, J.E., Budzynski, T.H., & VandenBergh, R.L. Effects of an EMG biofeedback relaxation program on the control of diabetes. *Biofeedback and Self-Regulation*, 1976, *1*(1), 105–112.

Garner, A.M., & Thompson, C.W. Juvenile diabetes. In P. Magrab (Ed.), *Psychological management of pediatric problems* (Vol. 1). Baltimore: University Park Press, 1978.

Greydanus, D.E., & Hofmann, A.D. Psychological factors in diabetes mellitus: A review of the literature with emphasis on adolescence. *American Journal of Diseases of Children*, 1979, *133*, 1061–1066.

Johnson, S.B. Psychosocial factors in juvenile diabetes: A review. In S. Chess & A. Thomas (Eds.), *Annual progress in child psychiatry and child development*. New York: Brunner/Mazel Inc., 1981.

Johnson, S.B., Pollak, R.T., Silverstein, J.H., Rosenbloom, A.L., Spillar, R., McCallum, M., & Harkavy, J. Cognitive and behavioral knowledge about insulin-dependent diabetes among children and parents. *Pediatrics*, 1982, *69*(6), 708–713.

Kaufman, R.V., & Hersher, B. Body image changes in teen-age diabetics. *Pediatrics*, 1971, *48*(1), 123–128.

Knowles, H.C., Jr., Diabetes mellitus in childhood and adolescence. *Medical Clinics of North America*, 1971, *55*(4), 975–987.

Koski, M.-L. The coping processes in childhood diabetes. *Acta Paediatrica Scandinavica*, 1969, *198*(suppl.), 7–56.

Koski, M.-L., Ahlas, A., & Kumento, A. A psychosomatic follow-up study of childhood diabetics. *Acta Paedopsychiatrica*, 1976, *42*(1), 12–26.

Minuchin, S., Rosman, B., & Baker, L. *Psychosomatic families: Anorexia nervosa in context*. Cambridge: Harvard University Press, 1978.

Reed, J.A. Arataeus, the Cappadocian: History enlightens the present. *Diabetes*, 1954, *3*(5), 419–421.

Rothenberg, M.B. The unholy trinity—activity, authority, and magic. *Clinical Pediatrics*, 1974, *13*(10), 870–873.

Seeburg, K.N., & DeBoer, K.F. Effects of EMG biofeedback on diabetes. *Biofeedback and Self-Regulation*, 1980, *5*(2), 289–293.

Sperling, M.A. Diabetes mellitus. In S.S. Gellis & B.M. Kagan (Eds.), *Current pediatric therapy 10*. Philadelphia: W.B. Saunders Co., 1982.

Travis, G. *Chronic illness in children: Its impact on child and family*. Stanford: Stanford University Press, 1976.

Warnberg, L. Psychological aspects of juvenile diabetes. *Journal of Pediatric Psychology*, 1974, *2*, 10–11.

|6| The Gastrointestinal System

Rumination

Differential Diagnosis

Rumination in infancy is a rare disorder characterized by regurgitation of food: the food is either rechewed and swallowed or spit out. It should be differentiated from vomiting (the forceful expulsion of food and gastric contents from the mouth), simple regurgitation (the nonforceful expulsion of food with no rechewing or re-swallowing), gastroesophageal reflex (GER), and esophagitis.

Spitting up (reflux) of a small amount of food is very common during infancy, par-ticularly when the baby is burped. This probably results from the poor tone of the lower esophageal sphincter in the newborn infant (Leape, 1982). With maturation, improved feeding techniques, dietary changes, and better posturing during feeding, 80-90 percent of infants with reflux outgrow it by 12-15 months of age (Leape, 1982). Other infants need further assistance in developing a competent antireflux mechanism. If the reflux is severe, the infant may lose a significant amount of food and malnutrition may result. Anorexia may also develop, particularly if there is dis-comfort because of frequent regurgitation.

Vomiting during infancy is a symptom that should not be treated without first determining the underlying cause. Projectile vomiting suggests that the infant may have pyloric stenosis, a condition requiring surgical correction. Other causes of vomiting are multiple and could include cow's milk intolerance, other allergies, drug withdrawal in neonates born to mothers who are addicts, central nervous system disease or infection, intestinal obstruction, various metabolic disorders, diseases, or other infections (Leape, 1982).

In contrast, rumination is often thought to be a voluntary, purposive, pleasurable act. Observations of infants who ruminate indicate that a series of abdominal con-tractions, tongue movements, and hand stimulation of chin, mouth, and throat areas precede the regurgitation (O'Neil, White, King, & Carek, 1979). It can also be a part of a symptom picture that includes other self-stimulatory behaviors such as rocking, head banging, and in the older child, masturbation. (See Table 6-1 for a complete listing of signs and symptoms.) The disorder also occurs in children who are mentally

113

TABLE 6-1

Rumination

Definition	Major Signs and Symptoms	Possible Medical Treatment	Psychologic Issues
A disorder characterized by regurgitation of food following which the food is either rechewed and swallowed or spit out	Straining of abdomen, chin and throat muscles Spitting up and reswallowing food Malnutrition Dehydration Growth failure Self-stimulatory behaviors Loss of enamel on teeth	Postural and dietary therapy: Upright positioning Thickening of feeding Reduced volume of feeding More frequent feeding Intravenous or naso-gastric drip feeding Cholinergic agents Bethanacol Metaclopramibe	Difficulty in mother-infant relationship Improper feeding techniques Family disruption and stress Social deprivation or neglect Maternal mental illness

retarded and has been observed more frequently in infants and children who live in institutions or in neglectful home environments (Whitehead & Schuster, 1981).

Etiology

Early etiologic hypotheses attributed rumination to the absence of a satisfying mother-infant relationship. As indicated above, some of these infants have been separated from their mothers or are living in an environment that provides little social and tactual contact. In other instances, the infant's mother may be emotionally immature, economically disadvantaged, or suffering from a serious mental illness such as schizophrenia or depression (Einhorn, 1972). When seen for evaluation of rumination, the infants may appear poorly cared for, unresponsive to their mothers or others in the environment, markedly withdrawn, and self-absorbed. Such infants are likely to be severely malnourished and may demonstrate serious growth failure as well. Rumination is thought to have developed as a self-stimulatory behavior in a baby who has received inadequate attention and caretaking.

Recent case studies have reported instances of rumination in which poor feeding techniques and inappropriate responses to the rumination when it occurs have resulted in maintaining the rumination response at a high level and jeopardizing the infant's nutritional status (Whitehead & Bosmajian, 1982). Improper feeding techniques are often associated with an inexperienced or overly anxious mother who feeds the baby excessively, causing overdistention of the stomach and regurgitation. When this occurs, the mother increases her responsiveness and attention toward the infant. In time, a pattern of contingent attention to the rumination develops and results in more frequent rumination. These infants may also be constitutionally predisposed to regurgitation because of their difficulty in establishing a competent antireflux mechanism or other difficulties in the feeding process or in digesting food.

Prognosis

Whitehead and Schuster (1981) report that, although rumination is a rare disorder which accounts for only 0.05-0.07 percent of all admissions to a pediatric hospital, when it does occur it can become life threatening. Mortality rates are quite high; approximately 15 percent of infants hospitalized for rumination die from malnutrition, aspiration, or other metabolic complications of the disease.

Psychological Intervention

The type of psychological treatment program employed differs according to the presumed etiology of the disease and the associated problems. When overfeeding and maternal inexperience are the primary factors in producing this behavior and if the child's rumination has not resulted in significant weight loss, parent guidance may be sufficient to alter the behavior. Modeling of appropriate feeding techniques (upright positioning, reduced volume of feeding, thickening of feeding, and feeding smaller amounts at more frequent intervals) and observation and instruction during feeding may suffice. For these infants, rumination may be a manifestation of gastroesophageal reflux or unusual gastric sensitivity in conjunction with inappropriate maternal behaviors during feeding. If the mother can be helped to alter her approaches to caring for this infant and not to feel as anxious or inadequate as a parent when difficulties arise, the cycle of poor feeding resulting in rumination may be broken (Flanagan, 1977).

If, however, the behavior is indicative of a disturbed parent-infant relationship in which neglect, social deprivation, or significant family stress and disruption are significant features, therapeutic efforts should be directed toward ameliorating the disturbed interaction. Whitehead and Bosmajian (1982) recommend a program in which the infant is held for 10-15 minutes before and after feeding. This approach was effective in eliminating or greatly reducing rumination in 16 of 19 case studies. The tactual contact provided appears to be critical, since toy play alone with the children during periods of no rumination did not suppress the behavior. Finally, the mother may also require psychiatric treatment, particularly if psychotic depression or schizophrenia prevent her from relating to the infant in an appropriate manner. If needed, antipsychotic medication may be utilized in conjunction with a therapeutic program focused on altering the negative mother-infant interaction. Provision of an adequate mother substitute may be needed initially. Such a person can provide a model for the parent, as skill in caring for the infant physically and emotionally is gradually developed.

In other instances an approach employing punishment or aversive conditioning may be employed. Examples of this technique are presented in Table A-7, in the Appendix. Electric shock has been employed in instances in which the infant's health is seriously jeopardized because of malnutrition resulting from rumination (Cunningham & Linscheid, 1976; Lang & Melamed, 1969). The shock employed typically produces a startle reaction but no crying. It is presented immediately when the infant ruminates and terminated when the rumination stops. With this technique, rumination is rapidly eliminated—typically within 5 to 10 training sessions. Follow-up evaluation of infants treated by this method indicate that weight gain is maintained and that the rumination does not recur. Attempts to use other aversive stimuli (e.g., lemon juice, Tabasco sauce), although somewhat successful in reducing the rumination, have not been as rapid or as consistently effective (see Table A-7, in the Appendix for further details). Finally, positive reinforcement programs combined with punishment procedures have achieved some success (Wright, Brown, & Andrews, 1978). Typically the parents or hospital staff are instructed to leave the room immediately (time out) when the infant ruminates and to return shortly thereafter (3-5 minutes) to wipe the infant's face. Positive attention and reinforcement is provided when the infant is not ruminating. Although this approach has been successful in eliminating rumination, a considerably longer treatment period is required. If the infant's condition is life threatening, electric shock may produce more rapid remission. Once this life endangering symptom has been removed, attention can be directed towards improving parenting skills and strengthening the mother-infant relationship.

Encopresis

Functional encopresis is a term that has been used to describe "any involuntary passage or seepage of feces into a child's clothing that occurs beyond the age of toilet training and is not caused by organic disease" (Wright, Schaefer, & Solomons, 1979, p. 274). When soiling occurs as a result of successive fecal retention and impaction, the term megacolon has been more commonly used. When soiling is not related to stool retention, the stool passed is typically soft, of regular consistency, and of normal size. In such instances, the fecal soiling is rarely the only difficulty present, but is rather one symptom of serious emotional disturbance or family problems. Table 6-2 summarizes the major signs and symptoms of the major subtypes of encopresis and constipation.

Subtypes of Encopresis

Organic. A number of neurological problems can cause encopresis; the presence or absence of these factors must be established prior to initiating treatment. In general, however, organic etiologies are rare. Wright et al. (1979) report that estimates of the ratio of psychogenic to organically based encopresis range from 65:35 and 95:5. The most common organic reason for encopresis is Hirschsprung's disease which is characterized by an absence of ganglion cells in one segment of the colon. In this disease, the dysfunctional segment is typically the rectosigmoid junction. This section of the bowel does not relax to allow passage of stool because the local ganglion plexus is absent. This disease is treated through surgical removal of the aganglionic section and reattachment of the healthy section of the colon to the rectum (see Table 6-2). Other neurologically based causes of encopresis include spinal cord injury or disorders of the motor area of the cerebrum. Finally, a bowel obstruction secondary to a variety of diseases can result in soiling or chronic fecal impaction.

Encopresis subsequent to fecal retention (constitutional constipation). In Levine's (1975) comprehensive study of 102 children with encopresis, he documented that 39 of these patients had been treated for constipation in infancy. Since this information was collected on a retrospective basis, it is impossible to determine whether constipation did in fact exist or whether the extent of this constipation was either

TABLE 6-2

Constipation and Encopresis

Disease	Definition	Major Symptoms and Signs	Possible Medical Treatment	Psychologic Issues
Anatomic Abnormality Hirschsprung's Disease	One segment of the bowel, the rectosigmoid junction, does not relax to allow passage of stool because the local ganglion plexus is absent	Early in life, diarrhea, constipation, or obstruction of the bowel Poor growth Poor appetite Sallow color Abdominal distention Soiling is rare	Rectal examination Barium enema Rectal biopsy Removal of the aganglionic segment	Parent education and support
A. CONSTITUTIONAL CONSTIPATION (Functional constipation with or without encopresis)	A. A tendency to infrequent bowel movements that is probably hereditary; "sluggish bowels"	A & B. Abdominal pain and distention Difficult and painful defecation (straining) Hard dry stool and overflow incontinence Fecal impaction	A & B. Explanation of bowel function Colon evacuation—impaction, digital removal enemas Effective stool softening: mineral oil, other laxatives, milk of magnesium, bulk--high fiber diet, increased water intake	A. Predisposition to respond to stress with bowel dysfunction Excessive fear, anxiety, inhibition Depression Poor bowel habits
B. PSYCHOGENIC ENCOPRESIS (Functional constipation with encopresis)	B. Normal stool elimination until beginning of toilet training, birth of sibling, or other stressful event; then involuntary passage of fecal material onto clothing or unacceptable place. Excessive parental concern or punitive coercive attempts to	Failure to detect the urge to defecate Staining or stool in underwear Secondary bladder dysfunction due to fecal impaction Possible laceration of the anus and fissure formation	Establish regular bowel patterns; set times for defecation Increase exercise	B. Poor toileting habits or coercive toilet training and predisposition to bowel dysfunction Emotional disturbance, negativism, manipulating obstructionism, insecurity, inhibition, noncompliance Expression of anger, resentment

induce elimination result in parent-child power struggle.

Parent-child interaction difficulties

C. POOR SOCIALIZATION (Encopresis, no constipation)

C. Little or no toileting instruction

C. Normal defecation in underwear

C. None

C. Parent training Possible developmental delay

under- or over-reported. Levine speculated that the invasive procedures often used in response to stool retention (e.g., enemas, suppositories, digital disimpaction) may also predispose the infant to later bowel dysfunction. Such an early manifestation of bowel difficulty, however, may also suggest genetic or constitutional predisposition to bowel dysfunction.

If significant stool impaction has occurred, the child's colon is quite full and distended, a condition referred to as megacolon. In this condition, the affected part of the colon does not have normal shape and muscle tone if it remains distended for a long period of time. The bowel loses the ability to respond with a defecation reflex when filled with normal amounts of fecal material. In such a situation, encopresis or soiling can occur by seepage of loose fecal material around the large impacted fecal mass. Defecation usually occurs very infrequently, is quite painful, and accompanied by a very large, hard stool which may need to be broken up prior to flushing (Wright et al., 1979). Such severe constipation was quite characteristic of the encopretic children in Levine's (1975) study. Of the 102 children in this study, 81 were found to have stool impaction accompanying the encopresis at the time of their examination. Because such a serious degree of impaction frequently accompanies encopresis, abdominal and rectal examination is indicated. In addition, X-ray examination may be needed to establish whether or not the colon has been completely evacuated prior to initiating treatment.

Nonretentive encopresis. In some children, there is no accompanying fecal impaction, and the stool passed is normal in size and consistency. Such fecal soiling may be a manifestation of a serious underlying emotional disturbance or may relate to faulty parental toilet training procedures, the presence of intellectual deficiency, or poor or inadequate toilet facilities at home or at school. In some children, the soiling can be a part of overall retardation of developmental function. Similarly, children with minimal cerebral dysfunction or those who are hyperactive and distractible may have encopresis as an associated symptom. In these instances the soiling may relate to poor planning, poor organization, and lack of attention to internal body cues (Bemporad, 1978).

Soiling in response to severe stress. Some shy, sensitive, anxious children respond to stressful or anxiety provoking situations with loss of bowel control. Freud and Burlingham (1943) noted an increase in such soiling among normal children in England during the World War II bombing raids. Clinical reports have documented that children also can respond to a variety of perceived stresses or threats, such as parent scoldings, attending school for the first time, taking an examination, or even pleasurable but exciting or overstimulating events, with bowel distress and loss of bowel control. This group of children might be more appropriately considered as part of the irritable bowel syndrome discussed in a subsequent section of this chapter.

Neurotic encopresis. Bemporad (1978) has identified a subgroup of encopretic children whose soiling he describes as neurotic in that the symptom "... has become a form of communication with an environment that is perceived as hostile and ungratifying" (p. 161). For these children soiling is often an integral part of a parent-child power struggle in which soiling represents a hostile assertion of the child's will. Bemporad relates a rather typical family structure and pattern of interaction in such cases. Typically, the encopretic child is described as angry, unhappy, oppositional, and often feels unloved, unwanted, and unable to express resentment. These children are reported to be difficult to engage in therapy, noncommunicative, and resistant to relinquishing their soiling. Psychological testing often indicates a predominance of aggressive fantasies and feelings of deprivation, inadequacy, and hopelessness over ever being able to communicate with their parents. There is often a high rate of divorce (50% of families studied by Bemporad), and in cases in which the parents have not divorced, the typical pattern reported is that the father is physically or emotionally absent from the home. Personality characteristics of the father have included depression, fear of social contact, and withdrawal from the children. Many of these encopretic boys maintained an idealized picture of their father and blamed themselves for the lack of their fathers' attention. In contrast, the mothers of neurotic encopretic children have been described as cold, critical, domineering, and intrusive. In their interactions with their encopretic children, vacillation between infantilizing, overprotectiveness, and rejection has been described. In therapy, Bemporad reports, these mothers initially present the facade of an efficient, unemotional, and capable adult; however, more prolonged contact often reveals great sadness and disappointment in their roles as wife and mother and a sense that their daily responsibilities are unfair burdens and sources of frustration. Bemporad (1978) provides some insight into the historical basis for such a disturbed mother-child pattern:

> If this description of the encopretic child's mother seems harsh and unfair, it should be tempered by an understanding of her situation. Her husband was either absent or unable to fulfill any emotional demands. The burdens of the household fell almost entirely on her. In addition, the neurotic encopretic child . . . eventually develops a personality that, quite frankly, is difficult to relate to in a warm manner. He becomes an angry, sullen oppositional child who silently harbors hostile desires or who has aggressive outbursts at the slightest provocation. . . . By the time such children are seen for therapy, an almost uniform relationship of hostile dependency exists, one in which the child resists separation from the mother or behaves in an infantile manner while trying to irritate her through soiling or passive-aggressive maneuvers. In return, the mother feels furious and defeated by a child who is a constant source of embarrassment. (p. 164)

The fact that the encopresis may become a hostile means of expressing anger towards a parent does not, however, explain why soiling was selected in the first place (Bemporad, 1978). There are many families characterized by an absent or distant father and an angry, critical, and insensitive mother in which the child also displays psychopathology, but does not soil. Constitutional and environmental factors, as well, might predispose children to encopresis. These might include: 1) traumatic bowel training; 2) neurologic immaturity; 3) a triggering stressful event such as a traumatic separation or loss of parent; and 4) a critical, perfectionistic, and demanding attitude of the mother toward developing bowel control (Bemporad, 1978; Levine, 1975).

Treatment of Nonneurotic Forms of Encopresis

Prior to initiating a therapeutic program, the child should receive a complete medical evaluation. Evidence of organic pathology, anatomic malfunctions, or neurological pathology should be sought. In addition, since many encopretics also have some degree of constipation, factors that contribute to such constipation should be explored. Such factors might include: 1) an early predisposition to constipation manifested in infancy or early childhood; 2) a dietary intake low in fiber and high in fats, carbohydrates, and sugars; 3) difficulty eliminating because of either very large or hard stools; 4) the presence of pain during elimination resulting in a phobic or avoidant response toward toileting; 5) the presence of extensive fecal impaction; 6) unclean or inadequate toilet facilities (toilet is too high for child so that appropriate leverage cannot be obtained; bathroom facilities are not private or are unclean). If a sufficient degree of constipation is evident on medical evaluation, consultation to determine which laxative and purgatives should be used, in what quantities, and for what period of time is needed.

Psychological evaluation. An initial interview with the parent and child is necessary to differentiate among the various subtypes of encopresis. If severe emotional disturbance in the child or pervasive and serious family psychopathology is evident in the interview or in subsequent testing, it may be necessary to address these problems before initiating treatment of the encopresis. However, Wright and Walker (1976) recommend that if only moderate behavioral difficulties are present, it is helpful to institute the program immediately, since improvement in overall adjustment is often seen following successful treatment of the encopresis. Psychometric testing is often an important component in making a differential diagnosis. Such testing can provide an index of general intellectual functioning when mental retardation is suspected and clarifies the degree and extent of emotional, learning, or behavioral difficulties. Family variables should also be assessed, particularly: 1) the degree of cohesiveness or conflict among family members; 2) the parents' motivation and ability to follow instructions and consistently maintain the treatment program; 3) the parents' understanding of the bowel factors that can be involved in encopresis and fecal retention; and 4) their willingness to institute a program that requires close monitoring of the child's bowel habits. The history of the parents' attempts to deal with the symptom (punishment, reward, use of laxatives, enemas, etc.), the effectiveness of such procedures, and the child's response to these procedures should be assessed prior to initiating treatment (Wright & Walker, 1976; Doleys, 1979).

Intervention techniques. There are six major treatment approaches to encopresis management: 1. pediatric management, which involves complete bowel catharsis followed by education in bowel function, use of laxatives, and bowel training; 2. pediatric management plus behavior therapy, which includes the above program plus a system of positive reinforcement of appropriate toileting and no soiling, punishment of soiling, or a combination of the two; 3. behavior therapy alone, which can include shaping of appropriate toileting behavior, as well as positive reinforcement or appropriate punishment following soiling; 4. biofeedback training, which typically includes providing feedback for the child's constriction of his external sphincter to progressively decreasing rectal distention volumes; 5. self-hypnosis (typically the child is taught self-hypnosis using the coin induction method accompanied by suggestions that he or she will be able to use this technique to control the anus muscles and allow him or her to solve the problem of constipation and soiling; and 6. individual or family therapy for the emotionally disturbed encopretic child. Each of these techniques will be described in some detail, using representative investigators in each area. Indications and contraindications for each of these treatment procedures follow. A summary of the major treatment outcome studies in this area is presented in Table A-7 in the Appendix.

Pediatric Management

Davidson, Kugler, and Bauer (1963) and Levine and Bakow (1976) provide the most comprehensive description of the pediatric management program. In this program, the first step in management involves a careful medical evaluation to define the pathogenesis of the encopresis, associated symptoms, and additional complications for each child. An X-ray film of the abdomen is performed to determine the degree of stool retention and to provide evidence for functional megacolon. Barium enemas and rectal biopsies are not typically performed, unless signs indicative of Hirschsprung's disease are evident. Once the diagnosis has been made, both the child and the parents receive information about the problem and supportive guidance. The families are given an opportunity to express their feelings about the encopresis, and the pediatrician attempts to alleviate guilt or concern that someone was "at fault" in causing the symptoms (Levine & Bakow, 1976). The physician then discusses normal intestinal functioning in language the child can understand, accompanied by pictures of a normal colon, showing the walls of muscle and the central lumen within the muscle through which the waste passes. A diagram showing an intestine blocked with large amounts of fecal material is then drawn, showing how the muscles become distended, thin, and weak. The physician then talks with the child about how such stretched, thin, and weak muscles do not allow normal bowel movements to occur and are not able to stop movements from occurring. It is explained to both parents and child that because of this lack of muscle control, it is not the child's fault he or she is having soiling accidents. It is also explained that a distended colon is less sensitive and does not offer the child warning about the need to have a bowel movement. Finally, it is suggested that because of the frequent soiling, the child may have become accustomed to fecal odor and, for this reason, is not aware he has soiled.

This approach emphasizes a positive, nonaccusatory style of interacting with both parents and child; and according to Levine and Bakow (1976), is greeted with relief and enthusiasm by most families. When the physician observes that the mother is overly involved, the child is encouraged to assume responsibility and the mother instructed to avoid contact with the child's anal and genital area. The children are encouraged to clean themselves after each accident, although the mother does continue to assume responsibility for washing soiled underwear. Critical and punitive remarks and comments, as well as punishment, are to be avoided at all times in this training program. The basic theme of the treatment for the child becomes the building up of the needed muscles for appropriate bowel function, and the training program is compared to a training program for athletes. With improved "muscle build-up," the child is told that he or she will have improved bowel control. The training program is related to concepts of autonomy, independence, effectiveness, control, and growing up.

There are three components to the treatment program. First, initial catharsis is undertaken in which enemas and laxatives are given until the bowel is thoroughly cleaned out. This is substantiated by an X-ray film demonstrating either complete bowel evacuation or indicating the need for further treatment. In cases of particularly severe constipation, with diffuse megacolon, or where there is a psychological or social reason for not giving the enemas at home, the child is admitted to the hospital for the initial bowel evacuation phase. Experience with this approach has revealed that when disimpaction is not complete prior to initiating treatment, there is a high relapse rate. Next, the child is placed on a maintenance program using light mineral oil at an initial dose of 30 cc. twice each day (for 7 year olds) with the dose raised rapidly if the child does not have a regular bowel movement at least once every two days. Vitamin supplements are provided. If signs of stool retention occur (large stools, less frequent defecation, stomach pain, soiling, or leakage of mineral oil), the child receives a supplemental oral laxative for one or two weeks. Suppositories and enemas are not used to avoid "anal assaults" on the child. Finally, the child is encouraged to establish a bowel rhythm by scheduling two regular bathroom visits (each at least 10 minutes in duration), regardless of whether bowel movements occur at this time, and receives a reward for each visit. Outcome for this treatment program is provided in Table A–7 in the Appendix.

Pediatric Management with Behavior Therapy

The treatment program developed by Wright (1973) and Wright and Walker (1976) combines both medical mangement and behavioral principles. (A complete description of this program is contained in the latter article.) The essential elements of this program include:

1. A thorough evacuation of the child's colon is accomplished through the use of enemas. This is typically done at home, but may be done by the physician if the home evacuation procedure is not completely successful.
2. The child is instructed to go to the bathroom immediately upon awakening in the morning. If the child is successful in producing stool, he is praised and given a small reward. Choice of rewards is made in advance and is determined after careful interview of both the parents and child. Rewards Wright and Walker have found successful include money, candy, small toys, praise, extra privileges, tickets to recreational events, and the allotment of a certain period of time (20–30 minutes) at the end of each day in which the parents interact with the child on a task, game, or experience of the child's choosing.
3. If the child does not produce a reasonable amount of stool (typically ¼–½ cup of stool), the parent inserts a glycerine suppository. The child then dresses, eats breakfast, and prepares for school. Prior to leaving for school the child again attempts to defecate in the bathroom. If the child is successful, he or she receives a smaller reward than the one given for defecating without a suppository.
4. If no defecation has occurred prior to leaving for school, the parent gives the child an enema to produce defecation. No reward is given if an enema is needed. If enemas and suppositories are frequently needed, consultation with the child's pediatrician is recommended. In addition, if the child has difficulty defecating on a regular basis on his own, dietary manipulation including fiber, fruit juices, and the use of stool softeners may be incorporated into the program.
5. At the end of the day the child's clothing is examined for evidence of soiling. If there is no soiling, he or she receives a reward; if soiling has occurred, a mild punishment is given. It is important that the punishment is something the child definitely wants to avoid. Punishments the authors have found effective are restriction of television viewing, loss of privileges, being grounded, loss of money, and having to do extra chores.
6. The program is carried out on a daily basis, and the importance of 100 percent consistency in following through on it is stressed to the parent and the child. The parents also keep a data-based notebook, including time the child woke up, what happened during the bathroom procedure, whether a reward was given, how the child reacted, and other details. They also record the result of the clothing inspection and the reward or punishment delivered. The report is then mailed to the office at the end of each week. Once the therapist receives the written report, phone contact is made with the family to deal with problems that have arisen or to answer questions and give support.
7. After two consecutive weeks in which no soiling has taken place, the program

is gradually phased out. If soiling occurs during the phaseout period, the parent moves back one step and starts the procedure again. This program typically alleviates the soiling problems within 15–20 weeks (See Table 1–7 in the Appendix)

Other Behavioral Approaches

A variety of other approaches incorporating behavioral management principles have been utilized. A brief summary of the various procedures employed is also included in Table A-7 in the Appendix. In general, the studies can be differentiated according to those which employ primarily positive reinforcement of appropriate toileting with no consequences for soiling, those which specifically punish soiling, and those which combine positive reinforcement and punishment.

Doleys and colleagues (1975, 1977, 1979) have developed a comprehensive program for encopresis that incorporates principles from Azrin and Foxx's (1974) toilet training program. In their approach, baseline information is collected by the parent on the following factors: time of each soiling accident; the number of attempts the child makes to defecate; the number and type of bowel movements; the extent of soiling accidents; and the child's response to such accidents when they occur. This information is used as a guide in establishing normal, more appropriate bowel habits. Complete records are also kept on the amount of laxatives taken during the baseline period. If the child has been exposed to punitive measures regarding toileting prior to initiating treatment, a program of positive reinforcement, desensitization, and relaxation may precede the initiation of the treatment for encopresis. General elements in the program include a combination of positive reinforcement and mild punishment.

In this program the parent engages in periodic pants checks or toileting checks. Initially, the parent may have to check the child's pants on an hourly basis if possible and to reinforce clean pants when obtained. This procedure is obviously more feasible with preschool or younger children. Gradually the interval between checks is increased. If soiling occurs, the parents initiate a "full cleanliness training procedure (FCT)." This involves expressing displeasure over soiling, having the child scrub his undergarments for 20 minutes, and having the child take a cool bath to clean himself for 20 minutes. If the child becomes disruptive or defiant during the FCT procedure, the amount of time is extended, and the child is not released from the task. The next part of the program consists of positive reinforcement for appropriate toileting and defecation. The child receives a predetermined number of tokens or points contingent upon each bowel movement in the toilet. These points can be exchanged for specific rewards. Details on outcome using this procedure are provided in Table A-7 in the Appendix.

The use of punishment in the treatment of encopresis has been questioned. Many feel that it aggravates an already strained parent-child relationship and, consequently, do not incorporate any form of punishment in the treatment procedures. Others have found that incorporating a mild punishment enhances treatment response and reduces the time needed to achieve no soiling. Doleys (1979) recommends the limited use of mild punishment only in conjunction with positive reinforcement. Azrin and Foxx emphasize that the FCT procedure can be carried out without increasing negative confrontations between parent and child. They suggest emphasizing to the child that the procedure allows him to take control of the toileting process and that performing these undesirable tasks should increase the child's motivation to avoid having to perform them. (Other punishments employed include reduction in earned time out or confinement to the bedroom following a soiling episode.)

Biofeedback Procedures

In 1974, Engel, Nikoomanesh, and Schuster published an article on the first attempt to employ operant conditioning with biofeedback in the treatment of fecal incontinence. In the Engel et al. (1974) study, five adults and one child were studied. All had a history of chronic, severe fecal incontinence; the adults had no history of fecal impaction, rather, the incontinence was related to organic deficit. The child had a history of fecal impaction and also myelomeningocele. The details of this and other biofeedback procedures are summarized in Table A-7 in the Appendix.

Although the specific biofeedback techniques employed differ, certain general principles are followed. First, the mechanics of defecation are explained in terms the child can understand and related both to muscle control and the ability to sense when stool is in the rectum. Initially, the child's rectal-anal reflexes are examined, often by inserting a small double balloon tied around a plastic tube into the child's anus at approximately the position of the internal and external sphincters. The balloon is then inflated with 20-30 cc. of air, and the responses of the internal and external sphincters recorded on an oscilloscope and chart recording. In normal children, the sudden inflation of the rectal balloon causes a reflex relaxation of the internal sphincter. If the child demonstrates a normal rectal-anal reflex, he or she is asked to duplicate that pattern on the oscilloscope; if no reflex or an abnormal reflex is obtained, the child is shown how to increase the pressure in the balloon by placing his hand on his abdomen and pressing down. The child is also encouraged to explore other ways in which he could duplicate this pressure response by using anus and buttocks muscles. Depending on the deficits detected in this evaluation procedure, biofeedback training is designed to enhance anal-rectal appreciation of volume distention and/or to increase the strength of the external sphincter contraction (Olness, McParland, & Piper, 1980; Whitehead & Schuster, 1981).

This technique has been particularly effective with children whose soiling is related to a physiological defect in the continence mechanism, often due to injury to muscles or nerves in this area (spinal cord injuries or injury during surgery), to birth defects involving these muscles and nerves (myelomeningocele), or to incontinence secondary to imperforate anus (Engel et al., 1974; Olness et al., 1980; Whitehead & Schuster, 1981). When this technique was employed with a more typical group of encopretic children (encopresis secondary to fecal retention), however, no greater success rate was achieved than that attained by conventional laxative therapy alone (Hardin, Kerzner, & McClung, 1982). Although biofeedback training did significantly improve rectal sensation in these children, this did not necessarily reduce the incidence of fecal soiling. Anal-rectal sensitivity was also significantly improved following enemas or spontaneous defecation. Continued stool retention was associated with progressive impairment in sensitivity. Additional studies exploring which type of patient responds best to which treatment modality appear to be needed.

Self-Hypnosis

Three preliminary reports on using self-hypnosis have been made. These are also outlined in Table A-7 in the Appendix. As indicated in the table, the number of subjects in each study is small. In this procedure, suggestions are typically made during the hypnotic session which focus on the children's ability to learn to control their bowels and which suggest they will be able to use their own powers to solve their problems of constipation (Olness, 1976). Hypnotic techniques may be a useful adjunct to treatment, particularly for children for whom power struggles with authority figures and control are major factors. As with biofeedback procedures, further research is needed to provide a means of identifying which children might benefit from this form of therapy.

Individual and Family Therapy

When disturbed family interaction patterns exist, Bemporad and others (Hoag, Baird, 1974; Norriss, Himeno, & Jacobs, 1971) strongly recommend family therapy. If the father can be encouraged to participate more actively in interacting with his child, in many cases the soiling is dramatically reduced. Bemporad (1978) offers two reasons to explain the dramatic change: 1) the greater participation of the father may reduce the mother's resentment and allow her to become a more sensitive and responsive parent; or 2) the father may provide emotional support in what had become a chronic mother-child power struggle.

Bemporad (1978) discourages the search in therapy for unconscious symbolic fantasies underlying soiling or interpretations of soiling as regression to an anal-libidinal organization. Rather, he views soiling as ". . . a semi-autonomous act that is elicited by certain environmental frustrations in susceptible children and afterwards serves both to arouse reactions in others and to express unacceptable feelings" (p. 167). In his experience, improvement in family relationships often results in a dramatic removal of the symptom. He considers the primary task of the therapist to be to identify the sources of discontent, resentment, and dissatisfaction in each of the family members and to alter interactions in these critical areas. Initially, both parents and child are so preoccupied with their own internal distress that it is very difficult for them to appreciate and respond in an empathic way to the needs and experiences of the other family members. Another obstacle in treatment is often that the parents prefer to focus on the encopretic symptom rather than on the complex family interactions that eventually lead to such symptom expression. In addition, he reports that it is often difficult to engage the neurotic encopretic child in treatment because of engrained personality characteristics, such as a tendency to be impulsive, explosive, or indirect in expressing anger. When encopresis persists in an older child, more intensive individual treatment may be indicated. If the symptom persists until adolescence, it is particularly difficult to treat. In these instances, separation from the family or intensive family therapy is often not successful in eliminating the soiling, and the symptom can become very resistant to treatment.

Summary

Children who have encopresis and a variety of associated behavioral (aggressiveness, hyperactivity, or depression and social withdrawal), learning (developmental delay, learning disabilities), or constitutional (severe constipation from infancy) problems are frequently treatment failures. Such children require a broad, interdisciplinary management program. Parental compliance in following recommendations, keeping appointments, and adhering to the treatment regimen is also a critical factor in successful intervention. Some families may become noncompliant only after the treatment program appears to be failing. In such instances, additional support and reassurance, evaluation of other possible intervention methods, and more frequent visits can be helpful in developing a more effective treatment plan (Levine & Bakow, 1976).

When treatment succeeds in reducing or eliminating soiling, many therapists have observed that the children show improvement in other areas of their lives as well. In particular, the children seem happier, more self-confident, perform better in school, and respond to discipline in a more positive manner. The impact on self-esteem, peer relationships, and family cohesiveness is also often enhanced once control over this socially embarrassing symptom has been achieved (Wright & Walker, 1976).

Peptic Ulcer

Definition

Ulcers in children are typically one of two types: primary or secondary. Secondary ulcers are acute stress ulcers, accounting for 80 percent of ulcers in infancy and less than 30 percent afterwards. In infants, these ulcers are secondary to sepsis, meningitis, respiratory distress syndrome, or central nervous system disease. In infancy, the disease is associated with a high mortality rate and is likely to involve fundamentally different causal factors from those for ulcers occurring later in childhood. In older children secondary ulcers are associated with immunosuppressive therapy (aspirin, corticosteroids, indomethacin), extensive burns, sepsis, or central nervous system disease (Kirschner, 1976; Medley, 1978). Primary ulcers are those whose cause is typically unknown and which arise in otherwise healthy (usually older) children. The ulcers are located in the duodenum almost 6 times more frequently than in the stomach; when primary ulcers do occur in a child under 6 years of age, the stomach, rather than the duodenum, is usually involved (Medley, 1978).

Incidence

Most studies report a slight (1.3-2.0:1) male predominance in childhood. Most literature on adults has reported a strong male predominance, with many research efforts conducted exclusively with males (Weiner, 1973); however, there appears to have been a shift in sex incidence ratios. Weiner (1973) reports that prior to the turn of the century women evidenced more peptic ulcer disease, and it was only after 1900 that males predominated. Two recent studies (Christodoulou, Gargoulas, Papaloukas, Marinopoulou, & Sideris, 1977; Prouty, 1970) reported a slight female preponderance. The social and cultural context possibly associated with differing incidences of this disease between the sexes has resulted in speculations regarding changing stressors in different historical periods and different defense mechanisms characteristically employed by each of the sexes. Recent studies also report a rise in overall incidence of ulcer disease in childhood. This may be the result of heightened physician awareness that such a disease can occur during childhood, improved diagnostic techniques, and changing environmental factors. Approximately 10 percent of the U.S. population will experience peptic ulcers at some time in their lives, and about 10,000 people die each year from peptic ulcers (Whitehead & Bosmajian, 1982).

Genetic Predisposition

A family history of peptic ulcer disease has been reported in 20-65 percent of the cases (Kirschner, 1976; Prouty, 1970). Prouty speculated that the familial predisposition to gastrointestinal disease may actually be even higher, since many of the family members reported nausea, vomiting, "nervous stomach," and other symptoms of stomach distress although they did not demonstrate ulcers. Twin studies show a 50 percent concordance rate for monozygotic (MZ) twins, compared to a 14 percent concordance rate for dizygotic (DZ) twins (Eberhard, 1968), thus providing evidence for a genetic predisposition. Comparisons between MZ and DZ twins are essential to differentiate intrauterine and early neonatal environmental conditions from genetic factors. Blood group 0 and failure to secrete the blood group antigens ABH into the saliva and gastric juice have also been found more frequently in individuals with duodenal ulcers (Kirschner, 1976; Weiner, 1973).

The long-term outcome for children with primary ulcers is not favorable. Once diagnosed, the problem is likely to persist. Fifty to seventy percent of children with peptic ulcers continued to have recurrent symptoms as adolescents or adults. Finally, reports of peak age periods for diagnosis and symptomatic difficulty vary. The disease appears to be most prevalent in children 12–18 years of age and least prevalent in the 2–6 year old age range (Kirschner, 1976).

Signs and Symptoms

The symptoms of peptic ulcer are multiple and often nonspecific. Since the psychologist is much more likely to be consulted when a diagnosis of primary ulcers is made for a child or adolescent, rather than an infant, the discussion will focus on the former group. (See Table 6–3 for a description of signs, symptoms, and medical treatment throughout childhood.) In children 2–7 years of age, atypical poorly localized abdominal pain and vomiting are the most common symptoms. Older children show a pattern similar to adults which includes epigastric or periumbilical pain which is sometimes relieved by food, vomiting, or antacids. Bleeding does not occur in all cases; in fact, one-third of the children with ulcers may be missed if the physician relies on bleeding (Kirschner, 1976) as a sole symptom. In younger children the pain is rarely related to eating, making the complaints of vague generalized abdominal pain that spontaneously remits difficult to differentiate from functional abdominal pain or gastroenteritis. Diagnostic procedures (such as radiologic examination and gastro-duodenal endoscopic evaluation) are important in establishing the differential diagnosis.

Medical Treatment

The primary medical treatment usually consists initially of antacid medication on an hourly basis. Diet restrictions are employed if needed with avoidance of gastric irritants (aspirin, cola, coffee, tea, alcohol). Finally surgical intervention such as a vagotomy or pylorplasty may be required if uncontrolled bleeding, perforation, pyloric obstruction, or intractable pain occur (Kottmeier, 1982).

Psychophysiologic Aspects

In 1952 Mirsky, Futterman, and Kaplan identified a physiologic condition, hypersecretion of pepsinogen (hydrochloric acid), they believed necessary for the development of duodenal ulcers. In the normal process of digestion, hydro-

TABLE 6-3

Peptic Ulcer

Definition	Major Symptoms and Signs	Possible Medical Treatment	Psychologic Issues
Primary: ulceration of the mucous membrane of the esophagus, stomach, or duodenum arising in an otherwise healthy patient	Neonate: sudden hemorrhage or perforation	Antacid medication	Identification of precipitating or exacerbating environmental or psychosocial stresses
	Infant: vomiting, failure to gain weight, colic	Regular antacids alternating with Amphojel if diarrhea becomes a problem	Dependency-independency conflict
Secondary: acute stress ulcers associated with extensive burns, sepsis, intracranial lesions, immunosuppressive therapy, meningitis, CNS disease	2–7 years: atypical poorly localized abdominal pain, vomiting, hemorrhage	Surgical treatment (vagotomy, pylorplasty) rarely done	Inadequate parental emotional support
	Older children: similar to adults, epigastric or periumbilical pain, onset 1–3 hours after meal, vomiting, hemorrhage	Avoidance of gastric irritants Cimetidine	Underlying anxiety

chloric acid interacts with other enzymes to break down food into its component parts. If an excessive amount of hydrochloric acid is secreted, Mirsky, et al. (1952) postulated that the mucous layer protecting the stomach wall would be gradually eroded, with small lesions in the lining of the stomach or duodenum resulting. The various factors (environmental and psychological) that might cause such increased gastric secretion have been the subject of numerous experiments with humans and animals.

The major findings from these early studies exploring the relationships between emotion and gastric motility and secretion have been summarized by Weiner (1973) as follows:

1. Gastric secretion increases in response to a stressful interview.
2. Men increase their gastric output when reading erotic literature.
3. Gastric secretion, motility, and vascularity are hypothesized to increase in response to feelings of anxiety, anger, resentment, humiliation, and hostility, whereas sadness, grief, apathy, or loneliness are thought to depress these activities (see Table 6-4).
4. Alternatively, the same emotion may typically produce a similar gastric response in the same individual, but different individuals may show a different response to the same emotion (some individuals consistently show an increase, others a decrease, and still others show little change at all in response to the same emotion).
5. Changes in acid secretion and in volume of fluid disappear with vagotomy, indicating that these changes are mediated by an intact vagus nerve.
6. Studies of patients with gastric fistulas have further documented the correlation between specific emotions and changes in gastric function in infancy.
7. Chronically high acid secretion may predispose an individual to develop an ulcer under stress (some individuals identified as hypersecretors developed duodenal ulcers when placed in a stressful environment (Army Basic Training), whereas none of the hyposecretors developed ulcers.

TABLE 6-4

**Hypothesized Relationships Between Emotional State
and Gastrointestinal Function**

Emotion	*GI Function*
Anxiety	
Anger	Hypermotility
Resentment	Hypervascularity
Frustrated need	Hypersecretion
for affection	
Depression	Hypomotility
Loneliness	Hypovascularity
Grief	Hyposecretion
Apathy	

From these studies emerged a diathesis-stress model for peptic ulcer: a physiologically susceptible person (e.g., a hypersecretor of gastric acid) and a personal, social, or physical environment that is noxious to the individual. This model, however, does not explain the development of peptic ulcers in children, since only low correlations between acid secretion and peptic ulcer disease have been found in pediatric populations. Acid hypersecretion is reported in only 10–30 percent of the children with diagnosed ulcers. Although children with Zollinger–Ellison Syndrome have demonstrated hypersecretion, hyperacidity, and a high fasting serum gastrin level, the evidence supporting acid hypersecretion as a factor in causing childhood duodenal ulcer is inconclusive. Other factors, such as decreased gastric resistance (Kirschner, 1976) or deficient secretion of mucus that protects the stomach (Whitehead & Bosmajian, 1982), may be related to ulceration as well.

Stress Induced Ulcers

Early classic experiments in the animal literature on "executive monkeys" (Brady, 1958) and "executive rats" (Weiss, 1971) indicated that stressful environmental factors could produce ulcers in animals. Factors considered critical in determining the stressfulness of situations producing ulceration included: 1) pressure to respond quickly and make decisions over extended periods; 2) uncertainty as to the effectiveness of the response; or 3) inability to make any response that changes the stressful situation. In addition, important individual differences in the animals have been identified that make them either resistant or vulnerable to developing ulceration (Weiner, 1973). The findings from the animal stress studies are, however, difficult to apply directly to humans, since most animal ulcers are gastric ulcers, whereas most human ulcers are duodenal. In addition, stress ulcers in animals do not appear to be caused by excess acid secretion, since acid secretion is typically inhibited by *acute* stress (Whitehead & Bosmajian, 1982).

Epidemiological studies have frequently demonstrated a relationship, however, between *chronic* stress and ulcers. People living in urban areas, those in occupations requiring constant "life and death" decisions (air traffic controllers, policemen), and those living during times of war show a higher prevalence of peptic ulcers (Whitehead & Schuster, 1981). How such stress interacts with individual differences in autonomic reactivity, genetic or constitutional vulnerability of a particular organ system, or early learning experiences remains to be studied.

Personality Factors

Intensive case studies of children with peptic ulcers who are receiving psychotherapy have revealed similar personality traits. These children are described as tense, anxious, compulsive, high-strung, and nervous. Their perfectionism, drive to excel, and extraordinary need for love and approval from parents and teachers place high performance demands upon them. When such a child experiences stress from family or school problems, he or she is likely to respond with strong emotion— and subsequent somatic complaints. Multiple stressful events have also been reported in the recent pasts of children with ulcers. These include loss of a parent or relative, birth of a sibling, physical or sexual abuse, and family disruption. Prouty (1970), however, cites school problems as most frequently associated with ulcer symptomatology. Such stresses, although possibly important in the exacerbation of the ulcers, occur so frequently in a normal population and are so nonspecific that it is doubtful they play a causal role in producing ulcers in a person who is not physiologically susceptible. Children who develop ulcers may display a physiological response to these stressful events different from that of normal children. Finally, the personality characteristics of children who have peptic ulcers but who are not receiving psychotherapy have not been examined.

Psychologic Intervention

Relaxation training, stress management, and assertiveness training have been employed with some success with adult peptic ulcer patients. These patients have been encouraged to moderate their life styles and to develop alternative ways of responding to stress. When the situation cannot be modified, attempting to find ways to alter the patient's reaction to the situation can help in coping with a difficult situation more effectively. Approaches that have been most successful have included changing the ulcer patient's response to stress. Techniques for reducing worries and concerns by developing effective problem-solving skills and assertiveness (Brooks & Richardson, 1980) and for learning to relax in stressful situations (Price & Wolf, 1981) are of particular benefit. Biofeedback has been employed with peptic ulcer patients, with some patients able to modify their rate of gastric acid secretion using this method. However, extensive training is needed, and the technique does not appear to offer a cost effective alternative to a combined medical and behavioral approach employing relaxation and stress management (Whitehead & Bosmajian, 1982). Table A-7 in the Appendix includes summaries of available behavioral treatment studies with peptic ulcer patients.

Ulcerative Colitis

Description

Ulcerative colitis is a serious, chronic, and (at times) remitting disease involving the mucosa and submucosa of the large and, occasionally, small bowel. Primary identifying signs include bloody diarrhea, ulceration of the bowel, and an absence of pathogenic microorganisms. Each of these characteristics is needed to differentiate this disorder from simple nervous diarrhea or the irritable bowel syndrome (in which pain and diarrhea are present, but not blood or ulceration) and from infectious diseases of the bowel in which microorganisms are present as causal factors. The onset of this disease is usually insidious, although approximately 10 percent of the children show an acute and life threatening onset. Table 6-5 lists the major signs and symptoms. Serious long-term complications, such as cancer or severe anemia are not uncommon; and surgery, such as an ileostomy or colectomy, may be needed, primarily when the diarrhea is intractable, if massive hemorrhage or rectal incontinence occurs, or if cancer is detected. Ulcerative colitis is one of a group of disorders entitled inflammatory bowel disease. It should be differentiated from granulomatous colitis, which affects the entire wall of the large intestine, and from regional enteritis, a disease primarily of the small intestine (Vandersall, 1978).

Prevalence

The prevalence of this disease is difficult to determine, since most epidemiological data have been derived from small, select samples. It occurs more frequently in adults, with children and adolescents constituting only a small percentage of hospital admissions for this disease. Age of onset can be infancy, but more typically after age 9. The increasing prevalence in Western countries is thought to be a function of better hospital diagnostic services. Mendeloff (1975) reports that approximately 200,000–400,000 people in the United States suffer from some form of inflammatory bowel disease.

Etiology

Ulcerative colitis is one of the classic psychosomatic diseases postulated by Alexander, French, and Pollock, (1968). They proposed that this disease was caused by disappointment in, resentment toward, and a sense of loss about a loved person, often a parent. These feelings of disappointment and resentment are not expressed directly by the child, but rather are expressed through a physical modality—the gastrointestinal tract. According to Alexander et al., the physiological changes which accompany chronic states of resentment and disappointment eventually result in altered functions within the gastrointestinal system. The hypothesized relationships between emotional states and physiological functioning of the gastrointestinal tract are presented in Table 6-4. Continuation of these emotional states were thought to result in explosive diarrhea and ulceration. Exacerbations of the illness were also hypothesized to be related to activation of these conflicts, accompanied by their physiological and emotional counterparts.

Comprehensive study of these patients, however, has not revealed a distinct

TABLE 6-5

Ulcerative Colitis

Definition	Major Symptoms and Signs	Possible Medical Treatment	Psychologic Issues
A chronic inflammatory disease of the large intestine, characterized by an ulceration of the mucosa of the colon	Watery offensive stools with mucus and pus Abdominal pain, tenderness Colic Intermittent and irregular fever Hemorrhage Perforation	Sulfasalazine (antibacterial) Corticosteroids, intravenous ACTH or hydrocortisone retention enemas, oral prednisone Iron supplement Symptomatic relief of cramping and diarrhea (antimotility agents) Surgery (ileostomy and colectomy) Dietary restrictions (uncommon)	Restrictive, overly dependent relationships within family Insecurity; distrustfulness Fear of loss of control Feelings of shame and inadequacy, inferiority Vulnerability to separation, loss Fear of abandonment Giving up—hopelessness "toilet bowl" bound

psychological conflict or a specific set of family interactions. Rather, a variety of psychological disturbances have been reported among adults and children with this disease; and these disturbances are thought to arise secondarily from living with a chronic, painful, and socially stigmatizing disease. Early studies found children with ulcerative colitis to be emotionally immature, passive, dependent, and characterized by ambivalence and destructive urges. These findings, however, were based on select groups of children with ulcerative colitis who were referred to psychiatrists because of significant emotional disturbance. In addition, when these patients received psychotherapy an improvement in emotional state, but not in bowel function, was noted (McDermott & Finch, 1967). The psychological characteristics of these children are now thought to be related to the stress of living with a life threatening and possibly disfiguring disease and to the failure to develop successful coping mechanisms. Psychological stress or emotional conflict may play a part in precipitating or exacerbating episodes of ulcerative colitis, but are no longer thought to be causative (Whitehead & Bosmajian, 1982).

These children often have a family history of bowel disease, suggesting the importance of genetic and/or constitutional predisposing factors in this disorder, but no specific biological indices corresponding to the hypersecretion of gastric acid characteristic of adult ulcer patients have yet been identified. Etiologic factors implicated in the occurrence of ulcerative colitis are possibly thought to be related to infective, biochemical, or immunologic factors.

Medical Treatment

Until the etiology of ulcerative colitis is discovered, medical treatments are directed at symptom alleviation and efforts to obtain remission. Dietary restrictions, symptomatic relief of diarrhea (by antimotility agents) and treatment of iron deficiency (if this has occurred because of blood loss or poor nutrition) are initial steps in treating the disease. Sulfasalazine may be employed or the patient may require oral corticosteroids, if there is no response to sulfasalazine. ACTH or hydrocortisone may be given intravenously in cases of severe, acute colitis. Finally, hydrocortisone retention enemas may be employed, particularly if the colitis is confined to the rectum (Caplan, 1982). See Table 6-5 for further reference.

Although the mortality rate of these children has been greatly reduced in the last decade, many of them ultimately require an ileostomy and a colectomy. Such surgery is indicated when there is poor response to medical treatment, severe side effects from the corticosteroids, development of toxic megacolon, severe growth failure, or an increased probability of adenocarcinoma (Caplan, 1982). Although this surgery can have a deleterious impact on the child's self-image and self-esteem, Caplan reports that children often adapt better to an ileostomy than adults. The surgery can also have very positive outcomes. Vandersall (1978) writes that "children whose growth is arrested by severe ulcerative colitis usually show significant growth spurts and maturation when their colons are removed. Furthermore, the threat of malignant change in the gut is diminished and rendered manageable by colectomy" (p. 150). The psychologist's or psychiatrist's role in the management of ulcerative colitis is important at various stages: in the initial evaluation; for provision of support throughout the illness; and for consultation regarding the child's ability to cope with an ileostomy or colectomy, if either is to be undertaken.

Psychological Treatment

Current psychological approaches to the child with ulcerative colitis recognize that this is a multidetermined disease of the bowel, with genetic and constitutional factors likely serving as predisposing factors. Emotional factors are now thought to become important during the course of the illness, but are not considered causal factors. It is essential for the therapist to form a close liaison with the gastroenterologist who is primarily responsible for the child's care. Vandersall (1978) provides good suggestions in this regard:

> Most ulcerative colitis patients, and their families, are closely tied to the gastroenterologist caring for them. . . . It is essential that the entering psychotherapist become identified with, or allied with, this powerful figure, or the therapist's efforts will be degraded, debunked, and soon discarded. Most gastroenterologists are eager to have a psychotherapist as an ally who can aid them with their most difficult problems. Their main concern about the therapist, in my experience, is that he be realistic and clear in his perception of the patient and the family and free of jargon and preconceived ideas about the psychopathology of this disorder. (p. 147)

It is essential for the therapist to recognize the chronic nature of inflammatory bowel disease and the burden such a chronic illness can place on the family. While not all children with ulcerative colitis need psychologic evaluation, such evaluation may be very helpful for those children and their families unable to cope with this chronic disease or when there are identified conflicts in interpersonal family relationships. Table 6-5 outlines a number of psychologic issues that can arise and require psychological intervention.

Many of these children experience painful feelings of shame and inadequacy because of their inability to control their bowel functioning and can develop phobic avoidance of public places and social events because of their fear of loss of control. Restricting relationships to within the family and developing excessively dependent, hostile, and demanding relationships with one parent figure can present serious problems in overall family functioning. Jackson and Yalom (1966) report on a sample of eight families, each of which had a child with ulcerative colitis. These families participated in a series of investigatory interviews in which marital and family interaction, child rearing practices, family members' health status (mental and physical), and extrafamilial relationships were explored in relationship to the onset of the ulcerative colitis. They found a striking degree of similarity between these families during the conjoint family sessions. Overall, they report that these families restricted interactions within the family group; communicated in a very indirect, tentative, vague manner; avoided outside social contacts; had other members with various gastrointestinal disturbances (peptic and gastric ulcers and mucous colitis); gynecological disturbances; or emotional problems (phobias, "nervous breakdown," depression, etc.). They also reported a high incidence of loss through death, desertion, or suicide of extended family members. Such families may benefit from family therapy focusing on altering maladaptive communication and restrictiveness and attempting to reduce the stress and isolation experienced by many of the family members.

To date, there have been very few reports of other successful therapeutic approaches. Mitchell (1978) and Susen (1978) each report a single case application of relaxation procedures to the treatment of spastic colitis and ulcerative colitis in adult patients (see Table A-7 in the Appendix). Both authors found that muscle relaxation training was helpful in diminishing colitis attacks and the pain associated with the attacks, as well as general tension and anxiety. This technique has not yet been reported with children who have colitis, but may well be applicable and beneficial. Finally, some patients and their parents may benefit from supportive therapy periodically during the course of medical treatment. Times that can be particularly difficult are when the medical regimen has not brought satisfactory symptom relief and surgery is considered. Counseling at this time to help the child and parents work through their fears and anxieties about ileostomy and colectomy can be quite helpful (Vandersall, 1978). Booklets published by the National Foundation for Ileitis and Colitis can facilitate discussions about the impact of these surgeries; whenever possible, meeting with a child who has successfully coped with this surgery can be of great assistance.

The Irritable Bowel Syndrome

Description

The irritable bowel syndrome consists of a variety of gastrointestinal symptoms without underlying pathology and with no known pathophysiology. Consequently, this syndrome is typically described in terms of the symptoms: constipation, diarrhea, pain, and flatulence (see Table 6-6 for further definition and description). Many different terms have been used to describe this syndrome, including nervous diarrhea, functional diarrhea, mucous colitis, spastic colon, and colonic enterospasms. Although none of the terms is completely satisfactory, irritable bowel syndrome (IBS) is now more commonly used to describe it, since many of the patients do not

TABLE 6-6

Irritable Bowel Syndrome

Definition	Major Symptoms and Signs	Possible Medical Treatment	Psychologic Issues
Functional bowel disorder characterized by alternating diarrhea and constipation.	*Spastic Colon:* Lower abdominal pain Cramps Constipation alternating with diarrhea or normal bowels	*Spastic Colon:* High fiber diet Stool softeners Increase water intake and exercise Anti-depressant medication (adolescents) Treatment of impaction (see constipation)	Depression, anxiety, or hysteria Holding back vs. letting go Guilt determined inhibition of action Emotional tension and anxiety prevalent Conflicts about giving and re-ceiving and control of aggression Response to life stress
Other terms used: Spastic colon Functional diarrhea Mucous colitis	*Functional Diarrhea:* Little or no abdominal pain Constant or intermittent diarrhea	*Functional Diarrhea:* Diet restrictions or prescriptions Antispasmodics and other medication for symp-tomatic relief of diarrhea and cramping	

consistently have spasms, inflammation, or diarrhea. The disorder frequently begins during late adolescence and has a chronic, relapsing, but not progressive course (Latimer, 1983). It is the most common disorder of the gastrointestinal tract in adults, with estimates that up to 15 percent of the population has symptoms similar to IBS (Alpers, 1983).

Many individuals directly experience the impact of stress on bowel function in acute or time-limited situations, although the physiological mechanisms by which acute or chronic stress affects the intestines are not well understood. Commonly, before examinations in school, before important athletic events, or before other exciting or challenging situations, many individuals experience what is called "nervous diarrhea." These brief episodes appear to occur in otherwise healthy people. To date there have been no studies that have documented the frequency of bowel disturbances (diarrhea, constipation, abdominal pain) in the normal population, any specific psychological characteristics among people who develop this temporary bowel reaction, and no long-term follow-up studies to determine whether those who develop acute gastrointestinal symptoms go on to develop chronic symptoms (Farrar, 1973).

Disturbed emotional states appear to precipitate sudden transient episodes of diarrhea. There have been some attempts to identify specific stress factors that play a part in the exacerbation or onset of bowel difficulties; however, the stress factors which have been implicated are very broad and appear to be those to which many members of society are exposed (job stress, school examinations, etc.). Certainly not everyone exposed to these stresses develops bowel difficulties.

Patients with persistent bowel problems have, however, been shown to have a significant increase in psychiatric disturbance, particularly hysteria and depression (Young, Alpers, Norland, & Woodruff, 1976). Similarly, a number of symptoms of altered affect are more common among IBS patients, including fatigue, depression, insomnia, crying, anorexia, suicidal impulses, anxiety, and higher urinary epinephrine levels. Engel and Salzman (1973) note, however, that such studies do not reveal why some depressed, anxious, or hysterical patients suffer from diarrhea intermittently and chronically, while others never experience bowel symptoms. They conclude that neither anxiety nor neuroticism is a sufficiently explicit construct to explain the symptom of diarrhea. Thus, the information to date indicates only that patients with chronic diarrhea have an increased incidence of emotional problems; they do not seem to have greater environmental stress. It may be that patients who develop irritable bowel syndrome may be constitutionally predisposed to develop gastrointestinal symptoms when exposed to a level of external stress that does not cause such gastrointestinal alterations in other individuals.

Triggering Factors

A number of factors have been implicated in the genesis of this syndrome (Thompson, 1979). These include:

Fiber deficiency. Since irritable bowel syndrome seems to be prevalent in Western civilization but rare in rural Africa, where a diet high in fiber is common, many have speculated that dietary fiber deficiency may be an important factor in the genesis of this disease. Bran and other high fiber diets have been incorporated as part of the treatment for constipation and diarrhea, and there is now some support for its efficacy in the treatment of IBS. When sufficient amounts of fiber are added to the daily diet, stool bulk is increased and slow and fast transit problems are corrected.

Food sensitivity. Although a genuine food allergy is difficult to prove as a causative factor in the irritable bowel syndrome, many individuals have symptom exacerbation related to a variety of foods, particularly fresh fruits, fried foods, milk, fish, and coffee. Since a carefully controlled elimination diet is quite cumbersome, most physicians recommend that the patient keep a behavioral record of foods eaten and subsequent symptoms in order to provide clues to possible bowel irritants.

Dysentery. An acute gastrointestinal infection or upset may precipitate more prolonged colon dysfunction. For example, travelers who experience gastrointestinal symptoms while in a foreign country ("tourista," "Montezuma's revenge," etc.) have reported that sometimes such disturbances persist upon their return home.

Antibiotics. Acute diarrhea, typically thought to be related to resultant altered gut flora, can occur during antibiotic treatment. Although the diarrhea usually subsides when the medication is withdrawn, in some individuals continued bowel irritability remains. Occasionally, a grave complication called necrotizing enterocolitis develops and requires medical intervention.

Laxative abuse. Excessive use of laxatives may contribute to irritable bowel problems (particularly in patients with bulimia or anorexia nervosa).

Underlying disease. Independent organic illness may coexist with irritable bowel syndrome. Such an illness may affect bowel function, or the medication used in treating the disease may affect bowel function. Other diseases in which diarrhea is part of the symptom picture include Celiac disease, tumors producing polypeptides which stimulate colon motility, inflammatory bowel disease, and others. The importance of a thorough medical evaluation of all patients who have bowel symptoms should not be underestimated.

Colon Reactivity

Individuals with irritable bowel syndrome (spastic type) may demonstrate exaggerated sigmoid motility in response to certain stressful situations. Stress interviews conducted with such patients have indicated that when the patients' emotional conflicts or concerns were discussed in an unsympathetic way, a variety of changes in bowel functioning oecurred. For example, patients feeling hostile, angry, or anxious in such interviews evidenced increased sigmoid tone and vascularity, while subjects experiencing hopelessness, inadequacy, self-reproach, or weeping demonstrated a decrease in sigmoid tone and vascularity (Almy, Hinkle, Berle, & Kern, 1949). Thompson (1979) speculates that a fighting attitude (anger, resentment, hostility) seems to stimulate gastrointestinal activity, while a flight or avoidance response is associated with hypomotility. These different responses are thought to be related to diarrhea and constipation respectively. However, despite these studies much of the evidence remains anecdotal, with no clear personality profile emerging for the irritable bowel patients.

Physiologic Mechanisms Implicated in the Irritable Bowel Syndrome

Constipation, particularly when characterized by small, hard stools, is thought to be due to sigmoid spasm, slow intestinal transit time, and increased absorption of stool water. In diarrhea, colon factors, such as increased secretion of water electrolytes and mucus into the lumen and alterations in motility have been implicated; small intestine factors, such as hypersecretion of water by the ileum which overloads the colon, disturbance in small intestine mobility, and possibly increased movement of fluids and electrolytes through hormonal or central nervous system influences are likely involved as well. Functional abdominal pain is thought to be due to excessive bowel contraction, a hypersensitivity to distention, or both. Finally, flatulence is thought to be related to disturbed motility and a slow transit time which favors bacterial fermentation in the intestine (Thompson, 1979). Table 6-7 presents an outline of the location of gastrointestinal (GI) disturbances and possible GI disorders. A recent review of specific abnormalities in GI neuromuscular mechanisms (Cohen, 1983) summarizes the evidence implicating hormonal and myoelectric (abnormal patterns of muscle contraction) factors as primary etiologic factors in IBS.

TABLE 6-7

Gastrointestinal Disorders

Location		
Upper GI Tract	Watery diarrhea	Lack of appetite
	Peptic ulcer	Anorexia
	Indigestion (reflux)	
	Nausea	
	Ulcerlike symptoms	
Lower GI Tract	Mucous diarrhea	Constipation
	Mucous colitis	Functional megacolon
	Ulcerative colitis	

Differential Diagnosis

Adequate history, physical examination, and rectal and sigmoidoscopic examination are often needed to rule out other underlying serious bowel diseases. Thompson (1979) has identified particular historic features he feels help distinguish between functional and organic types of diarrhea. Functional diarrhea is more likely to be associated with longstanding diarrhea, emotional instability under stress, and more often precipitated by or developed following gastroenteritis, bereavement, or excessive use of laxatives. It is most typically a periodic problem which alternates with constipation. The patient is typically well nourished and has hard stools, mucus, abdominal distention, pain relief with defecation, and pain prior to the onset of diarrhea. In contrast, the patient with organic diarrhea is more likely to have continuous watery stools; weight loss; nighttime diarrhea; an onset under 15 years of age or over 60; fever; blood and pus in stool; more than five stools per day; incontinence; and previous gastrointestinal surgery (Thompson, 1979). Patients with irritable bowel syndrome are also likely to have symptoms, (nausea, heartburn, dyspepsia, and anorexia) which suggest upper gastrointestinal dysfunction. Further, the patient may complain of gas, bad breath, nervousness, sweating, fatigue, irritability, palpitations, and other symptoms of anxiety. As indicated earlier, the irritable bowel patient may be depressed. Numerous somatic complaints, as well as symptoms of hysteria or anxiety, may be present and require comprehensive mental status examination. The syndrome is more commonly encountered during adolescence and adulthood (Latimer, 1983; Thompson, 1979).

Treatment

Depending on the symptom picture, various treatments have been recommended: some regulation of diet, particularly including more dietary fiber and other bulk agents; supportive therapy, including stress management training and relaxation when stress factors are present, but personal conflicts are not of a severe degree; psychiatric treatment, if serious personality disturbances or severe depression exists; and drug therapy, which might include the use of antispasmodics, and if needed, antidepressants, or antianxiety medication. Use of stool softeners and evacuants for the treatment of constipation has been described and discussed earlier in the section on encopresis and may be helpful for patients with irritable bowel syndrome when constipation rather than diarrhea is the primary problem. However, the tendency towards laxative abuse must be monitored closely, particularly for patients with dramatic weight loss. Most laxatives are contra-indicated (Alpers, 1983).

Although no psychological treatment outcome studies including children or adolescents with irritable bowel syndrome could be identified, three recent studies including adults are summarized in Table A-7, in the Appendix. The importance of depression, anxiety, hysteria, and other serious psychological problems in these patients is highlighted in these reports and each emphasizes the importance of a thorough diagnostic interview to identify all major problem areas prior to initiating a treatment program. The extent to which these problems also exist in the pediatric population (particularly in adolescence) has not yet been established and merits careful study.

References

Rumination

Cunningham, C.E., & Linscheid, T.R. Elimination of chronic infant ruminating by electric shock. *Behavior Therapy*, 1976, *7*, 231–234.

Einhorn, A.H. Rumination syndrome (merycism or merycasm). In H.L. Barnett (Ed.), *Pediatrics* (15th ed.). New York: Appleton-Century-Crofts, 1972.

Flanagan, C.H. Rumination in infancy—past and present. *Journal of Child Psychiatry and Psychology*, 1977, *16*, 140–149.

Lang, P.J., & Melamed, B.G. Avoidance conditioning therapy of an infant with chronic ruminative vomiting. *Journal of Abnormal Psychology*, 1969, *74*(1), 1–8.

Leape, L.L. Gastroesophageal reflux and hiatal hernia. In S.S. Gellis & B.M. Kagan (Eds.), *Current pediatric therapy 10*. Philadelphia: W.B. Saunders Co., 1982.

O'Neil, P.M., White, J.L., King, C.R., Jr., & Carek, D.J. Controlling childhood rumination through differential reinforcement of other behavior. *Behavior Modification*, 1979, *3*(3), 355–372.

Whitehead, W.E., & Bosmajian, L.S. Behavioral medicine approaches to gastrointestinal disorders. *Journal of Consulting and Clinical Psychology*, 1982, *50*(6), 972–983.

Whitehead, W.E., & Schuster, M.M. Behavioral approaches to the treatment of gastrointestinal motility disorders. *Medical Clinics of North America*, 1981, *65*(6), 1397–1411.

Wright, D.F., Brown, R.A., & Andrews, M.E. Remission of chronic ruminative vomiting through a reversal of social contingencies. *Behavior Research and Therapy*, 1978, *16*, 134–136.

Encopresis

Ashkenazi, Z. The treatment of encopresis using a discriminative stimulus and positive reinforcement. *Journal of Behavior Therapy and Experimental Psychiatry*, 1975, *6*, 155–157.

Azrin, N.H., & Foxx, R.M. *Toilet training in less than a day*. New York: Simon & Schuster, 1974.

Baird, M. Characteristic interaction patterns in families of encopretic children. *Bulletin of the Menninger Clinic*, 1974, *38*(2), 144–153.

Bemporad, J.R. Encopresis. In B.B. Wolman, J. Egan, & A.O. Ross (Eds.), *Handbook of treatment of mental disorders in childhood and adolescence*. Englewood Cliffs, New Jersey: Prentice-Hall Inc., 1978.

Davidson, M., Kugler, M.M., & Bauer, C.H. Diagnosis and management in children with severe and protracted constipation and obstipation. *The Journal of Pediatrics*, 1963, *62*(2), 261–275.

Doleys, D.M. Assessment and treatment of childhood encopresis. In A.J. Finch Jr. & P.C. Kendall (Eds.), *Clinical treatment and research in child psychopathology*. New York: Spectrum Publications, 1979.

Doleys, D.M., & Arnold, S. Treatment of childhood encopresis: Full cleanliness training. *Mental Retardation*, 1975, *13*(6), 14–16.

Doleys, D.M., McWhorter, A.Q., Williams, S.C., & Gentry, W.R. Encopresis: Its treatment and relation to nocturnal enuresis. *Behavior Therapy*, 1977, *8*, 77–82.

Engel, B.T., Nikoomanesh, P., & Schuster, M.M. Operant conditioning of recto-sphincteric responses in the treatment of fecal incontinence. *The New England Journal of Medicine*, 1974, *290*(12), 646–649.

Freud, A., & Burlingham, D.T. *War and children*. New York: Medical War Books, 1943.

Hardin, T.M., Kerzner, B., & McClung, H.J. The role of biofeedback training for the control of fecal soiling. Unpublished manuscript, Ohio State University, 1982.

Hoag, J.M., Norriss, N.G., Himeno, E.T., & Jacobs, J. The encopretic child and his family. *Journal of the American Academy of Child Psychiatry*, 1971, *10*, 242–256.

Levine, M.D. Children with encopresis: A descriptive analysis. *Pediatrics*, 1975, *56*(3), 412–416.

Levine, M.D., & Bakow, H. Children with encopresis: A study of treatment outcome. *Pediatrics*, 1976, *58*(6), 845–852.

Olness, K. Autohypnosis in functional megacolon in children. *The American Journal of Clinical Hypnosis*, 1976, *19*(1), 28–32.

Olness, K., McParland, F.A., & Piper, J. Biofeedback: A new modality in the management of children with fecal soiling. *The Journal of Pediatrics*, 1980, *96*(3), 505–509.

Whitehead, W.E., & Schuster, M.M. Behavioral approaches to the treatment of gastrointestinal motility disorders. *Medical Clinics of North America*, 1981, *65*(6), 1397–1411.

Wright, L. Handling the encopretic child. *Professional Psychology*, 1973, *4*, 137–144.

Wright, L., Schaefer, A.B., & Solomons, G. *Encyclopedia of pediatric psychology*. Baltimore: University Park Press, 1979.

Wright, L., & Walker, C.E. Behavioral treatment of encopresis. *Journal of Pediatric Psychology*, 1976, *4*, 35–37.

Peptic Ulcers

Brady, J.V. Ulcers in 'executive' monkeys. *Scientific American*, 1958, *199*, 95–100.

Brooks, G.R., & Richardson, F.C. Emotional skills training: A treatment program for duodenal ulcer. *Behavior Therapy*, 1980, *11*, 198–207.

Christodoulou, G.N., Gargoulas, A., Papaloukas, A., Marinopoulou, A., & Sideris, E. Primary peptic ulcer in childhood psychosocial, psychological and psychiatric aspects. *Acta Psychiatrica Scandinavica*, 1977, *56*, 215–222.

Eberhard, G. Peptic ulcer in twins: A study in personality, heredity, and environment. *Acta Psychiatrica Scandinavica*, 1968, *44*(suppl. 205), 7–118.

Kirschner, B.S. Peptic ulcer disease in children. *Comprehensive Therapy*, 1976, *2*(2), 53–60.

Kottmeier, P.K. Peptic ulcers. In S.S. Gellis & B.M. Kagan (Eds.), *Current pediatric therapy 10*. Philadelphia: W.B. Saunders Co., 1982.

Medley, E.S. Peptic ulcer disease in children: Report of a case and a problem-oriented review. *The Journal of Family Practice*, 1978, *7*(2), 281–284.

Mirsky, I.A., Futterman, P., & Kaplan, S. Blood plasma pepsinogen. II. The activity of the plasma from 'normal' subjects, patients with duodenal ulcer, and patients with pernicious anemia. *Journal of Laboratory and Clinical Medicine*, 1952, *40*, 188–199.

Price, K.P., & Wolf, L. Eight behavioral approaches to treating GI and alimentary tract disorders. *Behavioral Medicine*, 1981, *8*(3), 34–38.

Prouty, M. Juvenile ulcers. *American Family Physician*, 1970, *2*(3), 66–71.

Weiner, H. On the inter-relationship of emotional and physiological factors in peptic ulcer disease. In A.E. Lindner (Ed.), *Emotional factors in gastrointestinal illness*. Amsterdam: Excerpta Medica Foundation, 1973.

Weiss, J.M. Effects of punishing the coping response (conflict) on stress pathology in rats. *Journal of Comparative & Physiological Psychology*, 1971, *77*, 14–21.

Whitehead, W.E., & Bosmajian, L.S. Behavioral medicine approaches to gastrointestinal disorders. *Journal of Consulting and Clinical Psychology*, 1982, *50*(6), 972–983.

Whitehead, W.E., & Schuster, M.M. Behavioral approaches to the treatment of gastrointestinal motility disorders. *Medical Clinics of North America*, 1981, *65*(6), 1397–1411.

Ulcerative Colitis

Alexander, F., French, T.M., & Pollock, G.H. *Psychosomatic specificity: Experimental study and results* (Vol. 1). Chicago: University of Chicago Press, 1968.

Caplan, D.B. Ulcerative colitis. In S.S. Gellis & B.M. Kagan (Eds.), *Current pediatric therapy 10*. Philadelphia: W.B. Saunders Co., 1982.

Jackson, D.D., & Yalom, I. Family research on the problem of ulcerative colitis. *Archives of General Psychiatry*, 1966, *15*, 410–418.

McDermott, J.F., Jr., & Finch, S.M. Ulcerative colitis in children: Reassessment of a dilemma. *Journal of the American Academy of Child Psychiatry*, 1967, *6*(3), 512–525.

Mendeloff, A.L. The epidemiology of idiopathic inflammatory bowel disease. In J.B. Kirsner & R.G. Shorter (Eds.), *Inflammatory bowel disease*. Philadelphia: Lea & Febiger, 1975.

Mitchell, K.R. Self-management of spastic colitis. *Journal of Behavior Therapy and Experimental Psychiatry*, 1978, *9*, 269–272.

Susen, G.R. Conditioned relaxation in a case of ulcerative colitis. *Journal of Behavior Therapy and Experimental Psychiatry*, 1978, *9*, 283.

Vandersall, T.A. Ulcerative colitis. In B.B. Wolman, J. Egan, & A.O. Ross (Eds.), *Handbook of treatment of mental disorders in childhood and adolescence*. Englewood Cliffs, New Jersey: Prentice-Hall Inc., 1978.

Whitehead, W.E., & Bosmajian, L.S. Behavioral medicine approaches to gastro-intestinal disorders. *Journal of Consulting and Clinical Psychology*, 1982, *50*(6), 972–983.

Irritable Bowel Syndrome

Almy, T.P., Hinkle, L.E., Jr., Berle, B., & Kern, F., Jr. Alterations in colonic function in man under stress. III. Experimental production of sigmoid spasm in patients with spastic constipation. *Gastroenterology*, 1949, *12*(3), 437–449.

Alpers, D.H. Functional gastrointestinal disorders. *Hospital Practice*, 1983, *18*(4), 139–153.

Cohen, S. Neuromuscular disorders of the gastrointestinal tract. *Hospital Practice*, 1983, *18*(4), 121–131.

Engel, G.L., & Salzman, L.F. A double standard for psychosomatic papers? *The New England Journal of Medicine*, 1973, *288*(1), 44–46.

Farrar, J.T. Functional aspects of small bowel and colon motility: Diarrhea. In A.E. Lindner (Ed.), *Emotional factors in gastrointestinal illness*. Amsterdam: Excerpta Medica Foundation, 1973.

Latimer, P.R. Irritable bowel syndrome psychosomatic illness review: No. 7 in a series. *Psychosomatics*, 1983, *24*(3), 205–218.

Thompson, W.G. *The irritable gut: Functional disorders of the alimentary canal*. Baltimore: University Park Press, 1979.

Young, S.J., Alpers, D.H., Norland, C.C., & Woodruff, R.A., Jr. Psychiatric illness and the irritable bowel syndrome: Practical implications for the primary physician. *Gastroenterology*, 1976, *70*(2), 162–166.

7 | The Respiratory System: Asthma

Asthma is a respiratory disorder characterized by repeated attacks of difficulty in breathing. It is the most common chronic illness that occurs during childhood and accounts for approximately 25 percent of all days lost from school because of chronic illness (Travis, 1976). The joint committee of the American Thoracic Society and the American College of Chest Physicians has defined asthma as a disease characterized by "increased responsiveness of the airways to various stimuli and manifested by the slowing of forced expiration, which changes in severity either spontaneously or as a result of therapy" (O'Connell, Twiggs, & Sachs, 1982, p. 607). Asthma occurs more frequently in children with an inherited allergic predisposition, often in response to an allergic inhalent.

Early classification systems divided asthma into three major forms: extrinsic asthma, intrinsic asthma and mixed types. In extrinsic asthma the child manifests an allergic reaction to any of a variety of external substances. Identification of the specific substance precipitating the asthmatic attack is usually established by history, examination, skin testing, and evaluation of pulmonary function. Among the precipitating factors that have been identified are: 1) allergens (pollens, molds, animal danders, specific foods); 2) irritants (smoke, dust, various chemicals); or 3) drugs (aspirin or prescribed medications, etc.). In extrinsically triggered attacks the severity of symptoms depends on the concentration of the allergen in the environment and the child's allergic threshold. This threshold is determined by the amount of substance needed to cause symptoms in an individual, and this threshold varies from person to person. Intrinsic asthma can develop following an infection, usually viral in origin, in the respiratory tract. This terminology is also used to refer to asthma that develops in a person who does not have evidence of a specific sensitivity to any external agents. Other precipitating factors might include exercise (running), anxiety, or other forms of emotional stress (O'Connell et al., 1982). Since many children with asthma display intrinsic and extrinsic characteristics, the diagnosis "mixed type" became so frequently employed that it lost much of its usefulness in differential diagnosis (Creer, 1982).

Frequency and severity of asthmatic attacks are influenced by a variety of factors: weather changes, fatigue, illness, vigorous exercise, endocrine changes, emotional

150

tension, consumption of unusual foods, etc. The asthmatic attack may develop gradually or it may have an abrupt onset. Often the attacks occur when the child is supine, typically at night while sleeping. Signs of an impending asthmatic attack include chest congestion or tightness, shortness of breath, labored breathing, increased sputum production, a paroxysmal cough, or other allergic manifestations. Table 7-1 includes a list of the major signs and symptoms as well as possible medical treatments. The child and the parents must be taught to recognize and respond to these early signs of an asthmatic attack. If the physiological response to the allergen or infection is not reversed, the mucus produced may partially or completely occlude the airways. The air is, thus, trapped in the alveoli, leading to poor oxygen/carbon dioxide exchange and may eventuate in hypoxia and acidosis. Fright and vagal stimulation may further aggravate the bronchial spasms and increase the severity of the symptoms. Continued obstruction of the airways, acidosis, and fatigue can result in a life-threatening medical emergency called status asthmaticus, a more or less continuous asthmatic state that may last for hours or days and is unresponsive to acute medical management. Status asthmaticus may result in respiratory failure, cardiac arhythmias, and if unabated, may eventuate in cardiac arrest, irreversible brain damage, or death (Frey, Hunsberger, & Tackett, 1981).

Incidence and Prevalence

The incidence of chronic asthma in the United States ranges from 2 to 5 percent depending upon the method of estimation used (Wright, Schaefer, & Solomons, 1979). Approximately 5 to 15 percent of all pediatric patients under the age of 12 suffer from asthma (American Lung Association, 1975). This condition usually occurs during childhood and adolescence, and boys below the age of 5 years are affected more frequently than girls, ratios ranging from 1.5-2:1. During the elementary school aged years, the sex ratio is approximately equal, while in adolescence girls predominate (Creer, Renne, & Chai, 1982). In many childhood onset cases the patient is symptom free 20 years after onset of the disease. Thus, unlike many of the other chronic conditions, which either continue or become worse with time, in many cases (estimates range from 26-78 percent) childhood asthma is successfully treated and its symptoms diminish with age (Creer, 1979, 1982). Asthma is also more common among upper- and middle-class families in urban areas and among whites. Finally, although many children may experience status asthmaticus, the fatality rate from asthma during the 20 years following symptom onset is reported at less than 1 percent (Ellis, 1979; Wright et al., 1979).

Etiology

A variety of etiologies have been proposed for asthma, among them infection, allergy, disorders of the central nervous system or the autoimmune system, and

TABLE 7-1

Asthma

Definition	Major Symptoms and Signs	Possible Medical Treatment	Psychologic Issues
Respiratory disorder characterized by intermittent, variable, and reversible attacks of difficulty in breathing	Wheezing, labored breathing, irritative tight cough	Bronchodilators	Fear of dying by suffocation
	Allergic manifestations (eczema, rhinitis, sneezing)	Mist inhalation	Fear of abandonment
	Occasional pre-attack behavioral changes	Allergy shots for hyper-sensitivity	Maladaptive use of wheezing to express conflicts
Often genetic predisposition to allergy	Increased sputum production	Antibiotics for infection	Family disruption (sleep interruption, dietary and housekeeping problems, relocation)
	Exercise intolerance	Repeated hospitalizations	Physical and social restrictions
		Corticosteroids	Growth retardation secondary to steroids
		Beta-agonists	

psychogenic factors. Unfortunately, professionals have often been in opposing etiologic camps; some strongly advocate physical causes and others focus primarily on the psychologic aspects of this disease. However, both medical and psychological explanations have often focused on factors that may be associated with an exacerbation of asthmatic symptoms, but are not truly causative factors. Bronheim (1978) writes that:

> There seem to be physiological differences in asthmatics that cause them to react to a variety of stimuli with bronchoconstriction. The various agents that trigger attacks in the asthmatic do not affect non asthmatics. The difference seems to be in the fact that asthmatics have a chronic increase in bronchial lability, even when symptom free. (p. 311)

Nevertheless, the exact physiologic dysfunction in individuals with asthma has not been determined. Current hypotheses include a dysfunction in sympathetic-parasympathetic interaction, an abnormal immune response to allergens, a deficiency in beta adrenergic receptors, or diminished adrenal medullary function (Bronheim, 1978; Wright et al., 1979). A variety of factors (allergic, viral, psychogenic) are thought to trigger asthmatic attacks in a physiologically susceptible individual. (The importance of each of these precipitating factors will be considered in a subsequent section.)

Finally, allergic potential is thought to be inherited, with symptom expression dependent upon exposure to allergens in the environment. Typically, the stronger the inherited predisposition, the earlier the child develops symptoms of either allergy or asthma. When eczema, rhinitis, and wheezing, or difficulty breathing occur during infancy or early childhood, the child often develops a severe form of asthma that is very difficult to treat. These children are thought to have a more serious disease because of a stronger inherited predisposition which acts as a more critical factor than either length or degree of exposure to environmental allergens. Other children do not develop asthma until middle childhood or adolescence. These children often have specific allergic sensitivities to pollens or other inhalants and show a more positive response to immunization, desensitization, or hyposensitization therapy. However, over half of the children with asthma develop symptoms before age five, placing them in the group that is difficult to treat (Travis, 1976).

Medical Treatment

As indicated above, in asthma there is a hyperresponsiveness of the trachea, bronchi, and bronchioles to a variety of stimuli. In the physiological response to these stimuli there is extensive narrowing of the airway causing impairment in the air exchange (Alexander, 1980). This narrowing can be caused by swelling of the mucous membranes, edema, spasm of the bronchiol smooth muscles, or an increased production of mucus which can partially or completely occlude the airways. These factors can act singly or in combination to produce an asthmatic attack. Acute episodes can be relieved by a variety of pharmacologic agents which may be inhaled, administered in an aerosol spray, taken orally, or injected. Theophylline products cause smooth muscle relaxation and bronchodilation by inhibiting diasterase. The major goal when using this medication is to provide the maximal bronchodilation and maximal air flow without producing toxic side effects. The side effects observed with this medication are dose related and include nausea, vomiting, headaches, and anorexia. Beta-agonists are also employed either orally or through inhalation. Historically, ephedrine was most widely used but because of the central nervous system and cardiac side effects it has been supplanted by more selective beta-agonist agents such as metaproterenol, terbutaline, isoetharine, salbutamol, and epinephrine (O'Connell et al., 1982).

It is important for the physician to instruct the child and parents in the proper use of the dose inhalant or the aerosol spray so that misapplication can be corrected early. If the child does not show a satisfactory response to the inhalation of these agents he or she can also receive a subcutaneous injection. If the child receives an injection, supplemental oxygen may be required and should be available. These beta-agonists are very useful in treating children with chronic or acute asthma and may be added to the maintenance therapy with theophylline. The primary side effect of this medication is tremor; it is dose related.

The most powerful drugs for controlling asthma are the corticosteroids. Although these agents are very effective, the considerable side effects associated with them limit the extent to which they can be used. These agents should be employed only as long as is necessary to control the acute asthmatic attacks. Side effects include growth failure; personality changes; adverse reactions in a variety of areas, including the musculoskeletal, gastrointestinal, dermatologic, neurologic, endocrine, ophthalmic, and metabolic systems. Prolonged use of corticosteroids must be monitored by the child's physician (O'Connell et al., 1982). In most instances asthma can be managed at home through daily administration of theophylline medication, at times in conjunction with a beta-agonist. When the child's asthma is severe, the parents may also be instructed to administer epinephrine by injection at home and to use a home aerosol unit. If the child does not respond positively to either of these interventions, the parents must take the child to an emergency room for evaluation (O'Connell et al., 1982).

Medical treatment in asthma secondary to infection. A viral or bacterial infection can precipitate an asthmatic attack. While antibiotic medication may be helpful in treating the bacterial infection, it is often of little use in managing the asthma. Typically, theophylline and, if necessary, corticosteroids are employed for 5 to 7 days in an attempt to reduce the bronchial inflammation, edema, mucous production, and bronchospasms.

Treatment of allergen induced asthma. When specific environmental allergens are thought to trigger or exacerbate asthmatic attacks, the child typically undergoes evaluation to determine the specific allergens as well as seasonal, climatic, and other factors precipitating symptoms. The mother is often asked to keep an accurate record of the child's food intake, activities, exercise, exposure to various animals, grasses, plants, etc., as well as of climatic factors like wind, humidity, and temperature. The process of identifying the specific allergen can be very tiresome and frustrating. The child undergoes allergy skin testing in which various antigens are injected into the cutaneous layer of the skin by the scratch or prick method. The antigens tested often depend on the child's age, the area of the country in which he or she lives, and information obtained from history, physical examination, and parents' observations (Frey et al., 1981).

If specific allergens can be identified, a home management program in conjunction with hyposensitization therapy is initiated. Hyposensitization shots are typically employed when the child has a history of a seasonal allergy which correlates with allergenic exposure and positive skin tests. In this form of therapy, purified allergenic extracts are injected in increasingly large doses to decrease the body's reaction to the antigen (Travis, 1976). This treatment provides seasonal relief, but does not produce an immunity to these substances as a vaccination does in other maladies. The injections are available only for inhalants such as pollens, danders, molds, etc. and are not available for foods or for poisonous substances, such as chemical sprays and pesticides. Typically, the series of injections takes from four to five months to complete and consists of weekly injections.

There has been considerable controversy over the effectiveness of the hyposensitization therapy. In 1966, Fontana, Holt, and Mainland reported that: "No justification was found for promising any greater benefit to children treated with allergens than they would obtain from placebo injection" (p. 985). However, there has been considerable improvement in isolating and purifying various substances such as ragweed, mold, grasses, and trees. If the antigen can be identified accurately and the correct dosage and timing of injection occur, treatment is often more successful. Travis cautions, however, that prolonged hyposensitization treatment should not be taken for granted, particularly since many children appear to outgrow their asthma. Periodic discontinuation may be indicated to determine whether prolonged treatment is needed. O'Connell et al. (1982) relate treatment failures to an improper allergen selection, an inappropriate dosage, a poor host response, or the unavailability of the purified allergen concentrate. They suggest that negative indicators for hyposensitization therapy might include factors such as a very short pollen season, allergic symptoms that are mild and easily controlled with bronchodilators, or poor parent compliance in bringing the child for weekly injection.

In addition to hyposensitization therapy, if a specific allergen can be identified, the patient and the family are instructed in possible ways to avoid or diminish exposure to the allergen. If a specific food allergy is identified, that food sometimes can be eliminated from the child's diet. Unfortunately, some of the foods most commonly reacted to are milk, eggs, grains, legumes, citrus fruits, beef, pork, shellfish, chocolate, nuts, and cinnamon. As a quick perusal of this list indicates, it would be quite difficult to eliminate all products that incorporate some of these ingredients and still provide adequate nutrition for a growing child. The parents often need careful instruction by a dietician who can provide a food chart that specifies the ingredients in various prepared food products, as well as necessary nutritional and dietary information. While artificial substitutes for milk have been developed for infants with a milk allergy, it is extremely difficult to prepare a diet that completely eliminates milk, eggs, and wheat.

Allergic substances which can be inhaled by the child such as the pollens, grasses, molds, animal danders, and chemicals can present serious problems for the entire family. The child who is sensitive to dust and mold may require an environment outside the family's financial means. For example, mold is frequently found in old houses with damp basements or aging wall paper, but the family may be unable to redecorate, reconstruct, or afford housing in more recently constructed dwellings. Similarly, specific requirements for eliminating dust and molds from the house can entail extensive housekeeping which working parents may not be able to perform. Children with sensitivities to dust benefit from sleeping in a dustproof bedroom, devoid of carpets and drapes, kept clean by daily mopping. Special mattresses, pillows, blankets, spreads, and if possible, air conditioning should be installed to purify the air in the child's room. Children with asthma are often especially sensitive to cigarette smoke, which can place restrictions on other family members' habits and practices at home. If the home is located near an industrial area in which fumes, chemicals, or other pollutants permeate the air, the child's family may be forced to seek other housing. Similarly, if the child is allergic to animal dander and does not receive adequate desensitization from shots, the family may be encouraged by the medical staff to give away the family pet. While it is obviously important to attempt to weigh the child's allergic sensitivity with the emotional attachment to the pet, in some cases it is simply not possible to keep the animal in the home. Travis (1976) describes poignantly the resentment that can occur between siblings when a decision is made to remove the pet from the home. She reports, "One mother of a quarreling household told of a family conference she called in desperation, hoping differences could be negotiated. Instead, a sibling said, 'Can't we get rid of Jimmy instead of Pal? I like Pal lots better.' " (p. 181) The child's extreme allergic sensitivity can also limit outings the family can enjoy together or may curtail visiting the homes of friends and relatives in which animals, chemical irritants, molds, or other allergenic factors are present. Finally, the extensive financial costs inherent in treating these repeated episodes can also create hardship and additional stress within the family (Travis, 1976).

Classification of Subtypes of Asthma

Earlier studies attempted to differentiate between allergic-type asthma and psychogenic asthma. Allergic asthma was thought to be caused by factors extrinsic to the child, to have an earlier age at onset, to occur in a family with a history of allergy, and to respond positively to allergy tests. This type of asthma has also been characterized as steroid dependent because it is very difficult to treat and often requires that the child be maintained on corticosteroid medication. Psychogenic asthma has been called intrinsic asthma and is thought to be precipitated by psychological stress or disturbed interpersonal interactions. This form of asthma often can respond quite quickly to medical intervention or separation from the psychopathological environment (Wright et al., 1979). The repeated observation that some children with asthma show a dramatic improvement when removed from their homes led Peshkin (1968) to recommend a "parentectomy" as the treatment for asthma in some children. However, removing the children from their homes confounded two important factors: 1) the presence of specific allergens in the home environment; and 2) removal from conflictual or anxiety provoking interactions with parents and siblings.

Purcell and colleagues (Purcell, Brady, Chai, Muser, Molk, Gordon, & Means, 1969), in a landmark study, explored the effect of both allergic and environmental factors by moving the families of the asthmatic child to a hotel. The asthmatic children remained in their own home environment under the care of a health professional. Only children whose asthma appeared to be influenced by psychological factors were included in the study. The authors demonstrated a small but statistically significant improvement on a number of asthma measures, thus, confirming the role of general family stress in the manifestation of asthma for this subgroup of asthmatic children.

Alexander (1980), however, argues against classifying asthmatic children along an emotional-organic continuum. He suggests that psychological factors may be implicated for many asthmatic patients some of the time, on certain occasions, or under certain circumstances. Severity of the asthmatic condition may also influence the extent to which psychological factors become secondarily involved. Bierman and Pearlman's (1980) classification system for rating asthma severity based on frequency of asthmatic attacks, functional impairment, activity restriction because of the asthma, and type, dosage, and frequency of medication is a very useful guide to assessing the severity of physical stress that the asthma presents.

The importance of evaluating the severity of the child's asthma with respect to the extent of psychological symptom expression is highlighted in Pless and Pinkerton's (1975) interactive model, illustrated in Figure 7-1. In this model increasing psychological disturbance is expected to accompany more severe forms of asthma; however, when a significant discrepancy is observed between either physiological severity or symptomatic complaints, the possibility of significant psychological overlay should be considered. Two markedly maladaptive patterns are readily apparent in Figure 7-1. In the first instance, the pathophysiological involvement is minimal, but there is substantial symptom expression. Children who respond in this manner are characterized as overly accepting of their illness, needlessly restricting their activities, and displaying tendencies toward neurosis and unnecessary invalidism. In the opposite case, however, in which the degree of

Figure 7-1 *Variations in Physiologic Dysfunction and Symptom Expression**

PHYSIOLOGIC DYSFUNCTION

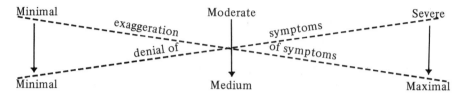

SYMPTOM EXPRESSION

*Based on a diagram in I.B. Pless and P. Pinkerton. *Chronic childhood disorders –Promoting patterns of adjustment*, London: Henry Kimpton Publishers, 1975.

pathophysiological involvement is severe but the child expresses minimal symptomatic expression, Pless and Pinkerton suggest that dangerous denial of the illness may be operating. This may lead to a hazardous neglect of symptoms and failure to respond with appropriate medications when needed. Both these groups display poor adjustment to their disease, but require very different intervention strategies. The latter group, characterized as "counter-neurotic, super-stable, non-complaining stoics" (p. 150), may actually be more at risk than the group displaying an exaggerated symptom response, since they may deny and fail to treat legitimate and life threatening symptoms (Pless & Pinkerton, 1975). In other instances, the child who has a very early onset of asthma with severe symptoms and a poor response to treatment may develop considerable psychopathology. The parents of this child may become more and more anxious and protective as the child's illness progresses and fails to respond to typical medical intervention. In addition, these children and their families often experience many frightening asthmatic episodes in which the child's life can be threatened or his or her health compromised (Egan, 1978). The passive, overdependent, hypersensitive, and neurotic characteristics ascribed to some asthmatic children may well develop in response to the severity of their disease (Alexander, 1980; Creer, 1978).

Psychosocial Impact

The psychosocial factors implicated in childhood asthma share many similarities with those found in several other chronic diseases. Early studies in this area explored the extent to which a common or typical personality profile could be identified in asthmatic patients and the degree to which a specific emotional concern might precipitate the onset of asthmatic symptoms. Alexander and French (1948) postulated that asthmatic children were anxious and insecure in their relationship with their mothers, who were either unable or unwilling to meet the children's dependency needs. Since these dependency needs were not met, the possibility of separation produced intense anxiety and emotion. The asthmatic attack itself was conceptualized as a repressed cry for the mother when separation occurred or was threatened. In this formulation, the more typical responses to separation (crying or protest) were not displayed because the child sensed that such a direct expression of dependency might be intolerable to the mother.

Case reports often provided some support for this formulation. The mothers of these children were often reported to be narcissistic, to consciously or unconsciously perceive the child as a burden, and to display outright rejection of the child or indirectly express such rejection by placing excessively high standards for performance upon the child with little provision of emotional support and guidance (Bronheim, 1978; Travis, 1976). While these case reports do provide extensive clinical information about the types of problems and difficulties that can arise in the parent-child interaction, they remain anecdotal and do not differentiate cause and effect. Other attempts to classify the types of mother-child interactions characteristic of large groups of asthmatic children have met with similar interpretive difficulties as well as limitations in relying on retrospective recordings. The extraordinarily high percentage of mothers classified as "rejecting" (98% in Miller and Baruch's study, 1948) is disconcerting, particularly since specific criteria for rating a mother as rejecting were not described.

A recent developmental investigation by Gauthier and colleagues (Gauthier, Fortin, Drapeau, Breton, Gosselin, Quintal, Weisnagel, & Lamarre, 1978; Gauthier, Fortin, Drapeau, Breton, Gosselin, Quintal, Weisnagel, Tetreault, & Pinard, 1977) examined parent-child relationships in young asthmatic children (14–30 months) and reassessed these children and their mothers when the children were 4–6 years of age. Strivings for autonomy, self-assertive abilities, signs of oppositional behavior or excessive passivity, and security in leaving mother were explored through comprehensive interviews, ratings, home observations, and structured play situations. Rather than finding a high incidence of psychopathology among these children, the majority of the children at both age levels were well adjusted and developing appropriately in social and emotional areas. High allergic potential was, however, associated with an increase in psychological disturbance. Their findings suggest that many children with asthma have a positive relationship with their mothers; psychopathologic outcome was characteristic of only a subgroup and was related to multiple maternal, familial, child and disease characteristics.

The tendency to "blame the mother" for the child's physical illness may relate more to social and cultural factors than to valid etiologic factors. The greater tendency of women in this culture to accept blame and the failure to comprehensively study the role of the father in producing or exacerbating symptoms may account for the predominant theoretical belief that maternal rejection is an etiologic factor in the development of childhood psychopathology (Mackler, 1976).

Similar attempts have been made to identify a personality type specific to asthmatic children. This group of children has been described as anxious, tense, inhibited, immature, dependent, shy, intelligent, perfectionistic, and ambitious (Bronheim, 1978). When the personality characteristics of children with asthma are compared to both normal controls, sibling controls, and a group of children with different chronic illnesses, however, little evidence for specificity according to disease has been obtained. In the Graham, Rutter, Yule, and Pless (1967) comprehensive comparative survey, asthmatic children were of a higher social class than the other groups and also performed better on tests of intelligence and achievement. However, while asthmatic children did not have an increased incidence of psychiatric illness, the mean number of behavioral symptoms recorded by the asthmatic children's parents was significantly greater than those of the control children. The asthmatic children did *not* differ in number of behavioral symptoms from children with other chronic physical handicaps. Based on these and similar findings (Neuhaus, 1958), it is now generally agreed that there is *no* specific personality profile unique to asthmatic patients, but rather that difficulties which develop are manifestations of unsuccessful coping with a chronic illness.

Emotional Precipitants of Asthma Attacks

Emotional factors have been thought to play a role in precipitating asthmatic attacks from a very early period. Hippocrates is reported to have cautioned an individual with asthma to "guard himself against his own anger" lest an asthmatic attack be precipitated (Cohen, 1971, p. 534). Clinical observation and patient or parent report of symptom onset have also implicated emotional stress and other psychological factors. Various efforts to precipitate asthmatic attacks in a laboratory have been attempted, including showing the patient a disturbing film, playing a tape recording of the mother's voice, engaging the patient in stressful conversations, or supplying hypnotic suggestions of various stressful experiences. While these techniques have been capable of producing changes in respiratory patterns and impairment in air flow rates, they have not actually precipitated an asthmatic attack. In addition, the effects obtained have been modest and did not occur in all individuals (Alexander, 1980).

The possibility that a bronchospasm or an asthma attack could become a conditioned response after sufficient pairings between the allergic substance and the response has also received attention. One early report by Sir James MacKenzie in 1886 dramatically illustrated this possibility. MacKenzie described a woman who was allergic to roses and subsequently developed wheezing when shown a paper rose under glass; however, there have been no convincing laboratory demonstrations of "conditioned asthma." Alexander (1980) attributes this to the long delay or trace conditioning evident in natural conditioning trials for asthma and also the numerous instances in which extinction trials occur in a natural setting. The finding that an asthmatic attack per se is unlikely to become a conditioned response does not, however, diminish the importance of conditioned anxiety reactions that might develop in response to asthmatic attacks or the power of suggestion in triggering asthmatic reactions.

Other evidence of the role of psychological factors in triggering asthmatic-like attacks has been provided in a classic experiment involving the role of suggestion and placebo effects in influencing pulmonary function (Luparello, Lyons, Bleecker, & McFadden, 1968). In this experiment, asthmatic patients were told that the aerosolized saline solution they were inhaling was an allergen or irritant to which they were known to be sensitive. During this procedure they subsequently developed increased airway resistance and, in some cases, asthmatic attacks. When they were then treated with a saline placebo solution, but told that the substance was a bronchodilator, the symptoms subsided. Luparello et al. (1968) reported that one of these asthmatic subjects even experienced hayfever symptoms, when he was told the inhalant was ragweed, and asthma alone, when told the inhalant was dust. This experiment provided compelling data supporting the role of psychological factors in triggering asthmatic attacks and highlighted the importance of exploring psychological interventions with asthmatic patients.

It still remains difficult, however, to specify the relationship between emotional reactions and asthma. Creer et al. (1982) conclude:

> There appears to be very little direct evidence that emotions *per se* trigger asthma attacks. There is some support, however, for the notion that emotions can produce responses which precipitate asthma attacks, either through mechanical means or motor activity. (p. 32)

For example, motor responses which often accompany emotional states, such as shouting, screaming, gasping in surprise, crying, coughing, etc., may trigger a reflex bronchospasm by stimulating vagal fibers. Similarly, the increased motor activity and agitation that often accompany strong emotional reactions may play a precipitating role (Alexander, 1980; Creer et al., 1982). The complex relationship between these emotional reactions and subsequent physiologic reaction is poorly understood.

Psychological Interventions

Psychological interventions in asthma have been directed toward a variety of different problems. Some interventions are specifically designed to improve pulmonary function during bronchospasm or asthmatic attacks; others are directed toward instructing the children in the proper use of the intermittent positive pressure breathing apparatus (IPPB) and in the use of other inhalation methods. Psychological interventions have also been directed toward reducing the anxiety and fear that can accompany the asthmatic attack and toward altering the environmental response to the child's symptoms to prevent reinforcing the symptoms by providing increased attention or by allowing avoidance of unpleasant activities if symptoms occur. Some behavioral interventions have been directed solely toward the child, while others have incorporated the school, family, or group milieus. A summary of the major treatment outcome studies is provided in the Appendix, Table A-8.

Psychological interventions have addressed a variety of asthma related problems. The foremost areas of concern for the pediatric and clinical psychologist have included: 1) the provision of information about asthma and self-management procedures in a manner appropriate to the child's level of cognitive and socio-emotional maturity; 2) the development of patient and parent skill in identifying early signs of an impending attack so intervention can be initiated at an early stage; 3) attempts to provide the child with self-control strategies (relaxation, biofeedback, systematic desensitization) for dealing with the anxiety and panic that can accompany asthmatic attacks; 4) appropriate use of the apparatus for administering medication during asthmatic attacks; and 5) the development of behavioral interventions designed to reduce emotional, social, and intellectual problems that can arise secondarily from asthma. The goal, in part, of each of these interventions is to reduce the disability (physical and psychological) that can be associated with recurring asthma attacks.

When evaluating the effectiveness of psychological interventions, it is important to include a variety of outcome measures of improvement. Medical assessments that should be made pre- and postintervention include: 1) the amount and type of medication used; 2) frequency of attacks; 3) number of hospitalizations; 4) duration of attacks; 5) clinical rating of the severity of asthma; 6) specific tests of pulmonary function; and 7) exercise tests documenting impairment in lung function after a set period of exercise. Alexander (1980) emphasizes the importance of including reliable pulmonary measures when discussing treatment outcome. When outcome is assessed only by patient self-report, an accurate index of true improvement in pulmonary function is often not obtained. Patients both over- and under-report episodes of breathing difficulty. Not all patients are able to identify asthmatic symptoms accurately and may report no subjective experience of breathing difficulty during an assessment period in which tests of pulmonary function indicate significant respiratory obstruction (Creer et al., 1982). In addition, a no treatment control group is needed to compare psychotherapeutic effects to effects related to spontaneous remission (Creer, 1982).

Self-control techniques. Techniques employed in an effort to facilitate the child's coping with asthma have included systematic desensitization, relaxation, hypnosis, and biofeedback. Key experimental treatment articles are briefly summarized in the Appendix, Table A-8.

Systematic Desensitization with Relaxation

One of the first behavioral techniques employed with asthmatic children was systematic desensitization with reciprocal inhibition. In this procedure the children are first instructed in Jacobson's method of progressive relaxation. Next, a hierarchy of situations related to asthma is created ranging from the least to the most disturbing to the child. The child is then instructed to relax and begin to visualize each of the scenes, beginning with the scene that arouses the least anxiety. Each scene in the hierarchy is visualized while the child continues to relax. This procedure continues until the child is able to imagine each of the scenes without experiencing anxiety. Creer (1979) and Creer et al. (1982) present an example of such a hierarchy obtained during work with a child who frequently panicked during asthma attacks. The hiearchy for this child is presented for illustrative purposes in Table 7-2.

This therapy has been effective in reducing the anxiety that can accompany attacks (see the Appendix, Table A-8). For some children, such therapy reduced their anxiety sufficiently to allow a reduction in their maintenance medications (Miklich, Renne, Creer, Alexander, Chai, Davis, Hoffman, & Danker-Brown, 1977); however, systematic desensitization with reciprocal inhibition has been only minimally effective in improving pulmonary function (see summaries in the Appendix,

TABLE 7-2

**An Anxiety Hierarchy Obtained for Treating Asthma
Panic Attacks by Systematic Desensitization**

a. "I got asthma while I was asleep. It was really a bad attack."
b. "I guess that I got out of bed, but I don't remember much about it. I can remember going out into the hall, but that's it. My parents said that my head hit their door when I passed out."
c. "The next thing I remember, we were racing down the street in the car. I can remember seeing some of the lights flashing off the windows of the stores we passed; everything was kinda hazy."
d. "I remember coming to in the emergency room of the hospital. My dad was running around trying to get someone to help me. Then I passed out again."
e. "I remember coming to on the stretcher. The people in the emergency room were taking me down the hall as fast as they could."
f. "They gave me oxygen. It seemed to help a lot. I also got my first IV about then."
g. "It wasn't until I was in a room under an oxygen tent that I really started to see what was happening. My parents and the doctor were there."
h. "My mother was crying, everyone looked scared. It was then that I really got scared."

From Thomas L. Creer, *Asthma Therapy: A Behavioral Health Care System for Respiratory Disorders*, pp. 178–179. Copyright 1979 by Springer Publishing Company, Inc., New York. Used by permission.

Table A-8). Thus, this technique may be most appropriately used as an intervention strategy to diminish the fear and panic that can occur when thinking about or experiencing an asthmatic attack. It should not be inferred that such therapy is able to alter the actual pulmonary response in asthmatic children (Alexander, 1980).

Relaxation and Hypnotherapy

Some children treated with this procedure indicated that relaxation alone, without systematic desensitization, seemed beneficial. Subsequently, various combinations of these approaches have been attempted with differing groups of asthmatic patients (see the Appendix, Table A-8). While patients whose asthma seems to be triggered by emotional factors appear to respond best to relaxation and hypnotic procedures, children with allergic and infective types of asthma have also benefited. Typically, patients who have a shorter duration of asthma and milder attacks obtain the most improvement using this technique. Unfortunately, although relaxation training has been effective in increasing air flow rate, the average increase in pulmonary function is only about 11 percent. Such a small increase in pulmonary function is not enough to produce clinical improvement in symptoms during an asthmatic attack. To obtain clinical benefit, pulmonary function needs to be improved by about 25 percent (Alexander, 1980). Consequently, this technique seems best utilized as a strategy for coping with anxiety associated with attacks. While respiratory efficiency may be enhanced during relaxation, the improvement is typically not sufficient to abort the occurrence of an asthmatic attack.

Biofeedback

Table A-8 in the Appendix also outlines the major treatment studies employing biofeedback conditioning. Often combinations of systematic relaxation therapy, with or without frontalis EMG biofeedback, have been attempted. As has been documented in the other areas, the use of EMG feedback with relaxation or EMG biofeedback alone typically does not bring about an improvement in pulmonary function sufficient to reduce asthmatic symptoms. Studies including both an attention placebo control group and using sophisticated measurements of pulmonary function have yielded disappointing results in the amount of pulmonary function improvement obtained. As has been found with relaxation procedures, this technique also appears to be most useful in reducing mild symptoms and in enhancing the patient's confidence that he or she can cope effectively with the onset of symptoms.

Instructing asthmatic children in the use of the IPPB apparatus. Careful instruction and intermittent checking of the children's use of the various inhalation procedures are an important aspect in insuring that the child receives the optimal benefit from medication during acute episodes. Only one study could be found that systematically evaluated the effect of instruction in the proper use of the IPPB apparatus. In this study (Renne & Creer, 1976) four children, aged 7-12, were taught proper inhalation procedures, facial posturing, and the diaphragmatic breathing necessary to use this equipment appropriately. The children received positive reinforcement for using the apparatus correctly and for reductions in their asthmatic attacks while hospitalized. These children demonstrated an increase in the effective use of the apparatus from 41 percent prior to training to 82 percent following training. At six month follow-up, 75 percent of the subjects were continuing to use the apparatus correctly. The project has important implications for developing effective health care programs for patient education. Creer et al. (1982) emphasize the need for including the patient in decision making processes involving self-care as well as providing strategies for self-monitoring and self-instruction in the identification and treatment of asthmatic attacks.

Reduction of associated psychosocial problems. Children with prolonged and severe asthma problems frequently develop a variety of other psychosocial difficulties. Primary among these are poor peer relationships, poor school performance because of frequent absences, inefficient work habits or underachievement, and a tendency for prolonged hospital stays in order to avoid unpleasant school, peer, or family situations. Creer and colleagues (Creer, 1970; Creer & Miklich, 1970; Creer, Weinberg, & Molk, 1974; Creer & Yoches, 1971) provide numerous illustrations of behavioral therapy approaches to reduce the hospital stays of asthmatic children and to improve peer relationships and school performance (see the Appendix, Table A-8). These investigators have employed a variety of techniques, all incorporating time out from positive reinforcement while in the hospital (e.g., placing the child in a hospital room by himself, allowing no visitors other than medical personnel and nursing, allowing only books related to schoolwork into the child's room, allowing the child to leave his or her room only to go to the restroom, reducing social contact by having all meals in the room, and not allowing the patient to visit other patients in the hospital.) These procedures resulted in a significant reduction in the duration of hospital stays and an increase in the duration of time between hospitalizations. In another innovative program for children who were over-users of the hospital, the children were allowed to use the recreational facilities of the hospital only during their outpatient clinic visits when they were free of symptoms (Hochstadt, Shepard, & Lulla, 1980). Each of these approaches prompted significant behavioral changes in children who had previously relied on their illness as a primary way of coping with difficulties in their lives.

Other approaches have included role playing and videotaping of appropriate behaviors, as well as inappropriate behaviors. In this approach the child is then asked to view and model the appropriate responses. Response cost techniques have also been employed to increase the proportion of attentive behaviors during schoolwork. These techniques have been quite successful in bringing the asthmatic child up to a satifactory achievement level and in facilitating more effective ways of coping with the disease. (For further illustration see Table A-8, in the Appendix.)

References

Alexander, A.B. The treatment of psychosomatic disorders: Bronchial asthma in children. In B.B. Lahey & A.E. Kazdin (Eds.), *Advances in clinical child psychology* (Vol. 3). New York: Plenum Press, 1980.

Alexander, F., & French, T.M. (Eds.). *Studies in psychosomatic medicine: An approach to the cause and treatment of vegetative disturbances.* New York: Ronald Press, 1948.

American Lung Association. *Introduction to lung diseases* (6th ed.). New York: American Lung Association, 1975.

Bierman, C.W., & Pearlman, D.S. (Eds.). *Allergic diseases of infancy, childhood and adolescence.* Philadelphia: W.B. Saunders Co., 1980.

Bronheim, S.P. Pulmonary disorders asthma and cystic fibrosis. In P.R. Magrab (Ed.), *Psychological management of pediatric problems: Early life conditions and chronic diseases* (Vol. 1). Baltimore: University Park Press, 1978.

Cohen, S.I. Psychological factors in asthma: A review of their aetiological and therapeutic significance. *Postgraduate Medical Journal*, 1971, *47*, 533–540.

Creer, T.L. The use of a time-out from positive reinforcement procedure with asthmatic children. *Journal of Psychosomatic Research*, 1970, *14*, 117–120.

Creer, T.L. Asthma: Psychological aspects and management. In E. Middleton Jr., C.E. Reed, & E.F. Ellis (Eds.), *Allergy: Principles and practice* (Vol. 2). St. Louis: C.V. Mosby, 1978.

Creer, T.L. *Asthma therapy: A behavioral health care system for respiratory disorders.* New York: Springer Pub., 1979.

Creer, T.L. Asthma. *Journal of Consulting and Clinical Psychology*, 1982, *50*(6), 912–921.

Creer, T.L., & Miklich, D.R. The application of a self-modeling procedure to modify inappropriate behavior: A preliminary report. *Behaviour Research and Therapy*, 1970, *8*, 91–92.

Creer, T.L., Renne, C.M., & Chai, H. The application of behavioral techniques to childhood asthma. In D.C. Russo & J.W. Varni (Eds.), *Behavioral pediatrics. Research and practice.* New York: Plenum Press, 1982.

Creer, T.L., Weinberg, E., & Molk, L. Managing a hospital behavior problem: Malingering. *Journal of Behavior Therapy and Experimental Psychiatry*, 1974, *5*, 259–262.

Creer, T.L., & Yoches, C. The modification of an inappropriate behavioral pattern in asthmatic children. *Journal of Chronic Diseases*, 1971, *24*, 507–513.

Egan, J. Asthma: Psychological treatment. In B.B. Wolman, J. Egan, & A.O. Ross (Eds.), *Handbook of treatment of mental disorders in childhood and adolescence.* Englewood Cliffs, New Jersey: Prentice-Hall, 1978.

Ellis, E.F. Allergic disorders. In W.E. Nelson, V.C. Vaughan, R.J. McKay Jr., & R.E. Behrman (Eds.), *Nelson textbook of pediatrics* (11th ed.). Philadelphia: W.B. Saunders Co., 1979.

Fontana, V.J., Holt, L.E., Jr., & Mainland, D. Effectiveness of hyposensitization therapy in ragweed hay-fever in children. *The Journal of the American Medical Association*, 1966, *195*(12), 985–992.

Frey, M.L., Hunsberger, M., & Tackett, J.J. Potential stresses during preschool years: Irreversible alterations in health status. In J.J. Tackett & M. Hunsberger (Eds.), *Family-centered care of children and adolescents: Nursing concepts in child health*. Philadelphia: W.B. Saunders Co., 1981.

Gauthier, Y., Fortin, C., Drapeau, P., Breton, J.-J., Gosselin, J., Quintal, L., Weisnagel, J., & Lamarre, A. Follow-up study of 35 asthmatic preschool children. *Journal of the American Academy of Child Psychiatry*, 1978, *17*, 679–694.

Gauthier, Y., Fortin, C., Drapeau, P., Breton, J.-J., Gosselin, J., Quintal, L., Weisnagel, J., Tetreault, L., & Pinard, G. The mother-child relationship and the development of autonomy and self-assertion in young (14–30 months) asthmatic children. *Journal of the American Academy of Child Psychiatry*, 1977, *16*, 109–131.

Graham, P.J., Rutter, M.L., Yule, W., & Pless, I.B. Childhood asthma: A psychosomatic disorder? Some epidemiological considerations. *British Journal of Preventive and Social Medicine*, 1967, *21*, 78–85.

Hochstadt, N.J., Shepard, J., & Lulla, S.H. Reducing hospitalizations of children with asthma. *The Journal of Pediatrics*, 1980, *97*(6), 1012–1015.

Luparello, T., Lyons, H.A., Bleecker, E.R., & McFadden, E.R., Jr. Influences of suggestion on airway reactivity in asthmatic subjects. *Psychosomatic Medicine*, 1968, *30*(6), 819–825.

Mackler, B. Essay: The mother blamers. *The Clinical Psychologist*, 1976, *30*, 9–11.

MacKenzie, J.N. The production of "rose asthma" by an artificial rose. *American Journal of the Medical Sciences*, 1886, *91*, 45–57.

Miklich, D.R., Renne, C.M., Creer, T.L., Alexander, A.B., Chai, H., Davis, M.H., Hoffman, A., & Danker-Brown, P. The clinical utility of behavior therapy as an adjunctive treatment for asthma. *Journal of Allergy and Clinical Immunology*, 1977, *60*(5), 285–294.

Miller, H., & Baruch, D.W. Psychosomatic studies of children with allergic manifestations: I. Maternal rejection: A study of sixty-three cases. *Psychosomatic Medicine*, 1948, *10*(5), 275–278.

Neuhaus, E.C. A personality study of asthmatic and cardiac children. *Psychosomatic Medicine*, 1958, *20*(3), 181–186.

O'Connell, E.J., Twiggs, J.T., & Sachs, M.I. Asthma. In S.S. Gellis & B.M. Kagan (Eds.), *Current pediatric therapy 10*. Philadelphia: W.B. Saunders Co., 1982.

Peshkin, M.M. Analysis of the role of residential asthma centers for children with intractable asthma. *The Journal of Asthma Research*, 1968, *6*(2), 59–92.

Pless, I.B., & Pinkerton, P. *Chronic childhood disorder—Promoting patterns of adjustment*. London: Henry Kimpton Publishers, 1975.

Purcell, K., Brady, K., Chai, H., Muser, J., Molk, L., Gordon, N., & Means, J. The effect on asthma in children of experimental separation from the family. *Psychosomatic Medicine*, 1969, *31*(2), 144–164.

Renne, C.M., & Creer, T.L. Training children with asthma to use inhalation therapy equipment. *Journal of Applied Behavior Analysis,* 1976, *9*(1), 1–11.

Travis, G. *Chronic illness in children: Its impact on child and family.* Stanford, California: Stanford University Press, 1976.

Wright, L., Schaefer, A.B., & Solomons, G. *Encyclopedia of pediatric psychology.* Baltimore: University Park Press, 1979.

8 | The Immunologic System: Juvenile Rheumatoid Arthritis

Juvenile rheumatoid arthritis (JRA) is a disease that affects the joints, connective tissue, and viscera. It demonstrates wide variation in symptomatology and an unpredictable course. Exact figures on the incidence and prevalence of this disease are not available because of the lack of uniform diagnostic criteria, but estimates have ranged from 3-9/100,000 new cases of JRA per year (Sullivan, Cassidy, & Petty, 1975). Petty (1979), reviewing published studies, estimated at least 40,000 children in the United States to have JRA. Table 8-1 presents the major signs and symptoms of this disease, medical treatment, and psychologic issues.

Clinical Description

Three major types of JRA have been described: systemic (Still's disease); pan-articular; and polyarticular JRA. These subgroups differ not only in their clinical manifestations, but also in their sex distribution, typical age of onset, prognosis for joint disability, types of additional complications, and serologic findings (Schaller & Wedgwood, 1972).

Systemic JRA, which encompasses between 13-26 percent of all cases, usually affects children five years of age or younger, and boys more frequently than girls. Schaller and Wedgwood (1972), however, found that this type of JRA occurs in older children as well. The child is very ill during the acute phase, having high intermittent fevers and a rheumatoid rash. Arthritic symptoms may be present at the illness onset or develop within six months. Other physical and medical problems can include morning stiffness, enlarged liver, lymph nodes, and spleen, and mild pericarditis with no difficulty breathing. This group includes the majority of children who are at risk for serious and, at times, life threatening complications (Baum & Gutowska, 1977; Bernstein, 1977). Although the child may have recurring rheumatoid rash and fever for six to nine months, complete remissions are common and accompanied by a good prognosis. However, joint deformity, growth disturbances and chronic polyarthritis may ensue (Hartson, 1981).

169

TABLE 8-1

Juvenile Rheumatoid Arthritis

Definition	Major Symptoms and Signs	Possible Medical Treatments	Psychologic Issues
An inflammatory process affecting the joints	*Early* Pain Swelling and tenderness Stiffness in the involved joints Difficulty sleeping due to pain *Long-term* Weakness (muscle atrophy) Crippling and joint deformities Fragile bones (osteoporosis) Ocular and cardiac difficulty	Aspirin Physical therapy Steroids Ophthalmologic treatment Gold therapy (injection) when aspirin and steroids are ineffective Orthopedic intervention—splints and surgery	Pain (feelings of maltreatment, punishment, persecution) Activity limitation Extent of deformity and crippling Depression Mood alteration (from docility to rage)

The panarticular type occurs in about 40 percent of children with JRA, with girls affected more frequently than boys. Peak onset occurs from 1-4 years of age, but can occur anytime from 6 months to 15 years of age (Hartson, 1981). Typically, one to four joints are involved (the knee is more frequently affected than the ankle and hip) and additional joint involvement occurs insidiously. Weight bearing joints show swelling and decreased motion and the child often experiences pain. Children with this form of JRA generally have normal growth and development, although they may exhibit mild signs of low grade fever or malaise. The most serious complication is iridocyclitis (an inflammation of the iris and ciliary body of the eye) and glaucoma. Such eye disease, which can lead to permanent visual loss if not detected early, has been reported in 25 percent of the patients with panarticular JRA (Schaller & Wedgwood, 1972).

Polyarticular JRA occurs in approximately 40 percent of all patients (Schaller & Wedgwood, 1972; Sullivan et al., 1975), with girls affected twice as often as boys. Age at onset has two peaks—one at 1-2 years of age and another at 8-10 years of age. Five or more joints are involved, often symmetrically, and include large joints (knees, wrists, ankles) as well as small finger joints. Swelling, tenderness, and stiffness of the joints are common, and the children may have a low-grade fever, weight loss, some malaise and anorexia. While 40 percent of the children may have enlarged lymph nodes (lymphadenopathy), few demonstrate enlarged spleen (splenomegaly) or liver (hepatomegaly). Although some of the children will have no exacerbations, 30 percent will have the disease 15 years after diagnosis and may have joint deformity or growth disturbances (Hartson, 1981).

The cause of the disease is still unknown, although factors postulated as causes of JRA include viral illness or infection, immunological abnormalities or deficiencies, trauma, and emotional disturbance (Wright, Schaefer, & Solomons, 1979). Boone, Baldwin, and Levine (1974) report a slight tendency of JRA to run in families.

Medical Treatment

The goal of medical treatment in JRA is to relieve the pain and inflammation, provide restorative physical therapy, and to facilitate the child's quick return to his or her normal activities without toxic side effects from the medications (Hollister, 1982). (Table 8-1 lists the possible medical treatments in JRA.)

Aspirin is the most basic component of treatment and is used both for pain and for reduction of inflammation. Since aspirin is such a commonly used medication for pain, parents need special instruction to understand the importance of continuing this medication to counteract the inflammatory process in JRA. A medical explanation of the active ingredient in aspirin (acetylsalicylic acid) and how it works may prevent the premature discontinuation of aspirin once the child's pain subsides (Travis, 1976). Aspirin is effective in reducing symptoms in 75 percent of all JRA patients (Hollister, 1982). Side effects can include gastric irritation, easy bruising, or aspirin toxicity manifested by ringing of the ears (tinnitus), fever, shortness of breath, lethargy, and vomiting.

When aspirin therapy alone is not effective, gold therapy may be administered through intramuscular injection; however, the additional cost and risk of side effects limit its use. Similarly, steroids may be employed, particularly in emergency situations (pericarditis, chronic iridocyclitis, etc.) although the serious side effects discourage its use (Hollister, 1982).

Prevention of serious long-term complications of this disease, such as chronic iridocyclitis, is attempted by including routine examinations by an ophthalmologist to detect early asymptomatic signs. Orthopedic surgery is employed when medications and physical therapy have failed to prevent continued joint deformity. Artificial joint replacement has been employed successfully, and braces, splints or other corrective devices may also be utilized.

Physical therapy forms an integral part of the child's treatment. Range of motion exercises should be performed to maintain or regain motion in affected joints and to build muscle strength. Warm baths prior to physical therapy or hot paraffin treatments can help to relieve stiffness and pain. Consultation with a physical therapist to learn proper positioning for sleep, watching TV, or sitting for prolonged periods is very helpful in preventing deformity. Resting night splints may be provided to relieve the contractures in wrists and knees and to provide support to prevent further deformity. Ordinarily the exercises are performed at home, once or twice daily. Professional physical therapy may supplement the treatment regimen as needed.

Psychological Issues

Impact of the disease. Coping with juvenile rheumatoid arthritis is particularly difficult because of the unpredictable course of the disease, with its peaks and valleys of flare-ups and remissions. During acute illness the child is handicapped by a reduction of resources in three critical areas (Wiener, 1975): first, the disease causes a reduction of *mobility* because of the incapacitating effect of pain or the fact that the child's weight-bearing joints may be so inflamed and/or deformed that walking is difficult if not impossible; second, there may be a reduction of *skill* attributable to increased pain and loss of dexterity and strength; and third, the child may experience a reduction of *energy*, possibly caused by the metabolic effect of the disease and by pain which drains energy and results in fatigue. A complex set of behavioral adjustments must consequently be made by patients with arthritis. Wiener (1975) describes many of the coping skills that must be acquired: hoping for illness remission, covering up of disability to some extent, pacing oneself, justifying inaction, learning to tolerate uncertainty, renormalizing one's life during periods of remission, eliciting appropriate help without becoming overly dependent or unduly self-sufficient, and balancing activity and treatment options. Further description of the use of such coping mechanisms in children at various developmental stages would be very helpful in providing needed guidelines for parents and children living with JRA.

Psychological precipitants of disease onset. Rheumatoid arthritis (the adult form) is considered one of the "core" psychosomatic diseases described by Alexander, French, and Pollock (1968). Other diseases typically included in this category are asthma, neurodermatitis, peptic ulcer, ulcerative colitis, and essential hypertension. Originally, these diseases were classified as "psychosomatic" by clinicians because they believed particular psychological characteristics and specific conflicts were symbolically expressed through specific diseases. Later, psychological factors were thought to play an important role in causing, precipitating, or exacerbating the illness.

Meyerowitz (1971) suggested three psychological hypotheses relevant to rheumatoid disease that could also be applied to the other psychosomatic illnesses: 1) a *specificity* hypothesis which assumed that identifiable psychological characteristics were present premorbidly; 2) a *disease-onset* hypothesis which implied a significant association between certain types of life experiences and/or psychological states and the onset of rheumatoid disease; and 3) a *disease course* hypothesis which suggested that specific psychological responses influenced the course of rheumatoid disease.

Early clinical case reports and impressionistic studies based on several case histories revealed that such individuals manifested conflicts and/or difficulties in expressing anger, aggression and wish for autonomy (i.e., these patients are typically reported to constrain or repress their hostility), and ambivalence toward parental figures. These descriptions are based on psychotherapeutic experience with arthritic patients who have been referred for treatment, however, and undoubtedly represent a biased sample. Conflicts in similar areas are also frequently found in many clinical populations and are hardly typical of, or specific to, individuals with arthritis.

Later efforts to identify neurotic patterns in patients with arthritis met with mixed success. In a comprehensive study of patients with early rheumatoid disease, Crown and Crown (1973) found that these patients did not differ from the normal population but were strikingly different from a neurotic population. They concluded that the personality descriptions of patients with a chronic form of rheumatoid disease were not characteristic of those in the early stages of the disease. Their findings raised the interesting possibility that the negative or maladaptive personality characteristics observed in chronic rheumatoid patients may represent a secondary response to the illness.

Alexander et al. (1968) postulated that the timing of the onset of rheumatoid symptoms in a vulnerable individual might be determined by a concurrent experience of psychological stress. This stress event was hypothesized to deplete the individual's coping capacities and to intensify pre-existing conflicts. Unfortunately, no patients have been followed longitudinally to explore this hypothesis. The data available were collected after illness onset and are only partially supportive of the hypothesis (Hoffman, 1974). Approximately half of the patients in one investigation, for example, reported a major stressful event prior to symptom appearance, but one-third reported no precipitating event prior to disease onset (Rimón, 1969). This investigation did, however, show a relationship between recovery from depression and rheumatological improvement in patients. Wolff (1971–72) found that psychological factors and responses to pain assessed preoperatively did predict postoperative rehabilitation. Supporting evidence was also obtained by Moldofsky and Chester (1970) who found that pain-mood relationships did differentiate patients' response to rheumatoid symptoms and rehabilitation. Such findings highlight the importance of individual variation in persons with arthritis and indicate the need for further efforts to identify those individuals who may need help in coping with disease onset, progression, or management.

Relationship between severity of JRA symptoms and psychological adjustment. As has been shown in other investigations of children with chronic illness, children with JRA have a higher rate of psychosocial disturbance than do healthy children (McAnarney, Pless, Satterwhite, & Friedman, 1974). The parents of children with arthropathies rated their children as having more abnormal behavioral symptoms and indicated more concern about their school adjustment than did parents of healthy children. School records indicated that twice as many children with JRA were referred to the school psychologist and nearly three times as many children evidenced low achievement scores despite intellectual ability comparable to the normal control group. Teacher ratings of school adjustment based on personality descriptions and academic achievement indicated that one-third of the JRA children had poor adjustment ratings compared to 9 percent of the control children. Tests of self-concept and personality verified these difficulties and indicated that more children with arthritis viewed themselves as "different," "inferior," and "less worthy," compared to their healthy peers.

When, however, the severity of disability (severe, moderate, mild, or no activity limitations) accompanying the child's JRA is examined with respect to psychosocial adjustment, an inverse relationship has been obtained (McAnarney et al., 1974). Contrary to expectation, children with no disability exhibited more psychosocial difficulties than did those with disability. Examining additional factors, such as the duration of the child's illness, extent of family disruption, or extent of mother's schooling, could not account for the findings. The findings suggest that the attitudes and behavior of family and peers may be a key determinant of adjustment, particularly for individuals whose disability is not severe.

An inverse relationship between disability and the extent of psychological difficulties has been found among other disease and handicapped groups as well. For example, difficulties in psychological adjustment have been more frequent among those who are partially blind rather than blind, those who are partially deaf rather than deaf, and those whose seizures are controlled rather than among those experiencing frequent seizures. McAnarney et al. (1974) speculate that when a chronic illness or handicap is accompanied by a severe disability, the patient and family are usually forced to accept the reality of the disability earlier and more completely. Such confrontation and acceptance may also facilitate the development of successful compensatory mechanisms. The nondisabled child diagnosed as having a chronic disorder likely undergoes many conflicting and confusing experiences. They write:

> . . . the nondisabled child is unlikely to be regarded by others as "sick" even though he is constantly reminded (through the treatment prescribed and the frequent visits to hospital) that he is not in perfect health. Nonetheless, he is expected to behave and perform in the same way as his healthy peers. The discrepancy may be great, however, between the way he feels and what he can actually do or what he is permitted to do by parents who, on the one hand, wish to deny his illness but who, on the other, remain anxious and uncertain about his future. (McAnarney et al., 1974, p. 527)

These findings highlight again the great difficulty in coping successfully with an "invisible defect." Such patients often do not receive the social support and consideration given to those more noticeably handicapped, and yet, they are also unable to integrate themselves successfully into the mainstream.

The Experience of Pain

One factor that distinguishes JRA from other chronic childhood diseases is the continuation of pain for many months, and for some children, many years. Although in many other diseases or in the treatment of these diseases, children experience pain (open heart surgery, pain from insulin injections, bleeding into the joints in hemophilia, etc.), in JRA pain is a continual factor during the acute phases of the illness when the joints are inflamed and tender and during physical therapy when these joints must be exercised to the limits of pain tolerance. Travis (1976) describes the level of trust that must be established between the physical therapist, the mother, and the child if the exercises are to be beneficial: "the forceful therapist, accustomed to stretching spastic muscles, or the therapist who cannot resist pushing just a little beyond the point where the child has called a halt, loses the child's confidence. If he resists, the exercises hurt worse, and 'bulldozing ahead' becomes a battle, not treatment" (Travis, 1976, p. 333). Both the therapist and the mother, who must repeat these exercises at home, must be able to deal successfully with their own emotions about "inflicting pain" on the child.

How the children cope with pain and what effect it may have on their emotional development is poorly understood. Perception and understanding of pain varies as a function of the child's developmental level, as well as prior experiences with pain.

In two excellent reviews of the area of child pain, Gross and Gardner (1980) and Gildea and Quirk (1977) summarize the major developmental changes from infancy through childhood as follows:

Infancy. During the first few months of life the infant's perception of pain closely relates to cortical development. Since myelinization is not complete until two to three weeks after birth for many infants (but not necessarily all), it is difficult to assess if pain is perceived. For example, on the first day of birth a large amount of electrical stimulation is needed to evoke a pain response. By the third month of life only half the prior amount of electrical stimulation is needed before a pain response occurs. Similarly, within the first few weeks of life the infant typically responds with a gross reflexive movement, involving much of the body, in response to pain. By the second or third month voluntary movements in response to pain are more frequent and the infant demonstrates the ability to localize pain by withdrawing the limb or area affected.

Toddler period. The language of the toddler is still quite rudimentary and, consequently, the primary means of communicating about pain continue to be non-verbal. Physical signs that the child may be experiencing pain include clenching the teeth, shutting the lips tightly, rocking, rubbing a body part, opening the eyes widely, or a changing behavior—often becoming agitated or aggressive.

Preschool age. Although significant cognitive advances are evident at this time (see Chapter 2), the preschool aged child has a limited capacity for rational thinking. Ideas expressed by these children are often concrete, egocentric, and magical. Pain may be perceived as a punishment for wrongdoing, or the person associated with the pain (parent, nurse, doctor, technician) may be viewed by the child as deliberately hurtful, persecutory, hostile, and harmful. Children in this age group do not understand temporal relationships very well and, consequently, are not necessarily comforted by reassurances that their pain will soon cease—they are hurting now and they fear it will be endless (McCaffery, 1979). Their concrete observation of other children crying during examination by the doctor or during physical therapy can lead to the conclusion that these procedures will hurt them too. Finally, the preschool aged child still has limited verbal abilities, making it difficult to describe pain and pain symptoms.

School age. By school age the child can understand more about the possible reason for pain. While the preschool aged child is primarily concerned about damage or injury to the body's surface (cuts, bruises, bleeding) because these are external, concrete, and visible, the school aged child demonstrates a greater awareness of the serious implications of pain originating from the inside of the body. As described in Chapter 2, the school aged child's understanding of illness is much more internal, and this carries with it a variety of additional concerns. School aged children often react to pain with anxiety and fear of bodily harm or death. They also worry about losing control. Boys and girls are reported to respond differently to questions about how they handled pain. Whereas girls typically report they felt "nervous" or "afraid," boys reported feeling "brave" (Gross & Gardner, 1980).

A variety of factors can make pain worse, foremost among them anxiety and apprehension, one's personal experience with and memory of pain, whether there will be relief from the pain, cultural and sexual factors facilitating or inhibiting the expression of pain, depression, and fear of the secondary consequences of illness (loss of physical vigor and energy, restriction of activities, isolation from friends, etc.). Beales (1979) describes how negative emotional reactions can contribute to increasing the pain perceived. He describes two components to pain—the sensation of pain and negative affect regarding pain. Each of these responses involves different areas of the brain. Consequently, he postulates that pain may be relieved by altering either of these factors, inhibiting the pain sensation or reducing the extent to which the sensation is experienced as unpleasant. In his work with children who had JRA he found that older children reported only slightly more pain sensation from their joints, but considerably more negative affect. These older children felt much more frustrated in achieving their goals than did the younger children. Some younger children denied pain completely, claiming that the sensation they experienced was not unpleasant. Beales's work is significant in highlighting the important role personal evaluation plays in perceiving pain. He postulates that the unpleasantness of a sensation is, in part, dependent upon the extent to which the sensation indicates undesirable consequences. He proposes that psychological interventions can play an important role in reducing the negative affect component of pain by reducing the unpleasant consequences often associated with the disease.

Psychological Treatment Considerations

When a patient with JRA evidences considerable difficulty in coping with pain, psychological intervention may provide additional coping strategies and complement the medical regimen. First, it is important to discover the meaning the disease has for the child and his or her parents. If the parents are highly anxious and/or feeling out of control, helpless, and unable to cope with the demands presented by the illness, their fears and anxieties may be contributing to the child's distress. Supportive counseling for the parents and collaboration with the child's health care team is often needed to facilitate the parents' understanding of the illness and enhance their skill in managing the treatment regimen (Gildea & Quirk, 1977).

Various self-control skills (relaxation, self-hypnosis) can also be quite effective for children whose chronic anxiety and tension heighten their experience of pain. These procedures allow the child to take some personal responsibility for reducing pain and can foster heightened self-esteem and feelings of internal control. Relaxation programs incorporating progressive relaxation, autogenic training, deep breathing exercises, and meditation have yielded success in ameliorating pain caused by a variety of conditions (Aronoff, Kamen, & Evans, 1981). It is extremely important to tailor the specific program to the child. Children differ in the types of techniques they feel comfortable in trying. While some might find the relaxation procedures helpful, others may derive more benefit from distraction or hypnotic techniques. Gross and Gardner (1980) emphasize that "the therapist must take care to use only those methods which are acceptable to particular children at particular times" (p. 138). In addition, specialized training in these approaches is needed to provide a foundation for applying the techniques to a pediatric population with various medical problems.

The symbolic meaning of pain for the child should also be explored. The child may actually be expressing anger at being deprived of certain activities (competitive sports, bike riding, jumping rope, etc.) or fear that he or she will be rejected by family or friends. Frequent complaints about pain may also represent an unhealthy use of this symptom to gain attention, sympathy, or special favors. In evaluating the possibility of secondary gain, the clinician needs to evaluate whether the parents' response to the child's distress is inappropriately overprotective or infantalizing (Gross & Gardner, 1980). If so, the parents and child may need to participate in a behavior management program in which inappropriate responses to pain are extinguished and positive activities and responses that can be strengthened identified. For example, if the child is reporting pain as a means of obtaining affection and social attention, alternative ways of gratifying these needs may result both in a diminution of the expression of pain and an increase in more adaptive behaviors (social interaction with parents or siblings in card playing or board games, cooking, crafts, listening to records, etc.). Identifying feasible positive activities for the child that include opportunity for social interaction may also alleviate the depression and isolation children with JRA often experience. Success in these areas may reduce the stress of this physical illness by reducing some of the adverse consequences of the disease. Such intervention is often particularly needed when arthritis begins in adolescence. At this stage in development, feelings of being different, unable to compete, and "defective" physically can be particularly difficult to bear. The adolescent's self-preoccupation and increased awareness of and sensitivity to a variety of stimuli may also add to the degree of pain they experience (Travis, 1976). While depression and withdrawal are quite appropriate responses during the active phase of the illness, if such responses persist psychotherapy may be indicated.

References

Alexander, F., French, T.M., & Pollock, G.H. *Psychosomatic specificity: Experimental study and results* (Vol. 1). Chicago: University of Chicago Press, 1968.

Aronoff, G.M., Kamen, R., & Evans, W.O. The relaxation response: A behavioral answer for chronic pain patients. *Behavioral Medicine*, 1981, *8*(7), 20–25.

Baum, J., & Gutowska, G. Death in juvenile rheumatoid arthritis. *Arthritis & Rheumatism*, 1977, *20*(Suppl.), 253–255.

Beales, J.G. Pain in children with cancer. *Advances in Pain Research and Therapy*, 1979, *2*, 89–98.

Bernstein, B. Death in juvenile rheumatoid arthritis. *Arthritis and Rheumatism*, 1977, *20*(Suppl.), 256–257.

Boone, J.E., Baldwin, J., & Levine, C. Juvenile rheumatoid arthritis. *The Pediatric Clinics of North America*, 1974, *21*(4), 885–915.

Crown, S., & Crown, J.M. Personality in early rheumatoid disease. *Journal of Psychosomatic Research*, 1973, *17*, 189–196.

Gildea, J.H., & Quirk, T.R. Assessing the pain experience in children. *Nursing Clinics of North America*, 1977, *12*(4), 631–637.

Gross, S.C., & Gardner, G.G. Child pain: Treatment approaches. In W.L. Smith, H. Merskey, & S.C. Gross (Eds.), *Pain: Meaning and management*. New York: Spectrum Publications, 1980.

Hartson, A. Juvenile rheumatoid arthritis. In J.J. Tackett & M. Hunsberger (Eds.), *Family-centered care of children and adolescents: Nursing concepts in child health*. Philadelphia: W.B. Saunders Co., 1981.

Hoffman, A.L. Psychological factors associated with rheumatoid arthritis: Review of the literature. *Nursing Research*, 1974, *23*(3), 218–234.

Hollister, J.R. Connective tissue: Collagen vascular disease. In S.S. Gellis & B.M. Kagan (Eds.), *Current pediatric therapy 10*. Philadelphia: W.B. Saunders Co., 1982.

McAnarney, E.R., Pless, I.B., Satterwhite, B., & Friedman, S.B. Psychological problems of children with chronic juvenile arthritis. *Pediatrics*, 1974, *53*(4), 523–528.

McCaffery, M. *Nursing management of the patient with pain* (2nd ed.). Philadelphia: J.B. Lippincott Co., 1979.

Meyerowitz, S. The continuing investigation of psychosocial variables in rheumatoid arthritis. In A.G.S. Hill (Ed.), *Modern trends in rheumatology* (Vol. 2). New York: Appleton-Century-Crofts, 1971.

Moldofsky, H., & Chester, W.J. Pain and mood patterns in patients with rheumatoid arthritis. *Psychosomatic Medicine*, 1970, *32*, 309–318.

Petty, R.E. Epidemiology of juvenile rheumatoid arthritis. In J.J. Miller, III (Ed.), *Juvenile rheumatoid arthritis*. Littleton, Massachusetts: PSG Publishing Co., 1979.

Rimón, R. A psychosomatic approach to rheumatoid arthritis. A clinical study of 100 female patients *Acta Rheumatologica Scandinavica*, 1969, *13*(Suppl.), 11–154.

Schaller, J., & Wedgwood, R.J. Juvenile rheumatoid arthritis: A review. *Pediatrics*, 1972, *50*(6), 940–953.

Sullivan, D.B., Cassidy, J.T., & Petty, R.E. Pathogenic implications of age of onset in juvenile rheumatoid arthritis. *Arthritis and Rheumatism*, 1975, *18*(3), 251–255.

Travis, G. *Chronic illness in children: Its impact on child and family*. Stanford, California: Stanford University Press, 1976.

Wiener, C.L. The burden of rheumatoid arthritis: Tolerating the uncertainty. *Social Science and Medicine*, 1975, *9*(2), 97–104.

Wolff, B.B. Current psychosocial concepts in rheumatoid arthritis. *Bulletin on the Rheumatic Diseases*, 1971–72, *22*, 656–661.

Wright, L., Schaefer, A.B., & Solomons, G. *Encyclopedia of pediatric psychology*. Baltimore: University Park Press, 1979.

9 | Genetic (X Linked) Disorders

Hemophilia

Clinical Description

Hemophilia is an X-linked recessive disorder of the blood-clotting mechanism that results from a deficiency in one of two clotting factors, factor VIII or IX. Normal blood clotting occurs by a series of enzymatic steps involving inactive plasma factors. In patients with hemophilia, since one of the factors is reduced or missing, blood clotting is delayed when bleeding occurs either internally or externally (Markova, MacDonald, & Forbes, 1980). Severity of the disease is typically determined by the level of the deficient factor in the blood: severe (less than 1% of factor VIII or IX present); moderate (1-5% of the factor present); and mild (5-50% of the factor present) (Thurber, 1981). The carrier is usually the mother who has a defective gene on one of her X chromosomes. There is a 50 percent chance that any of her sons will have the disease and a 50 percent chance that any of her daughters will be carriers. A hemophiliac father will not have hemophiliac sons, but all his daughters will be carriers. Clear evidence of a family history of hemophilia is found in the majority of cases, but in about 15-20 percent of families there is no clear evidence of a family history. In these cases the disease is presumed to be due to mutation (Markova et al., 1980).

There are two types of hemophilia. Classic hemophilia (Hemophilia A) results from factor VIII deficiency and accounts for 80 percent of all hereditary clotting diseases. Christmas disease (Hemophilia B) is clinically indistinguishable from Hemophilia A except that in this disease factor IX is deficient. Fifteen percent of all cases are of this type. Significant symptoms are not usually present until the infant begins to crawl. Then parents may notice excessive bruising, hematoma formation, spontaneous bleeding, or bleeding into joint cavities such as the knees, elbow, or ankles. Such bleeding may lead to hemarthrosis which is characterized by severe pain, swelling of the joints, and limitation of movement or contracture. Diagnosis of this illness is usually made during emergency treatment for bleeding. Parents typically report a history of bleeding episodes and prolonged blood-clotting time. Factor assays are employed to determine which factor is deficient (Thurber, 1981). Although there is no cure for hemophilia, the bleeding can now be controlled through replacement of the deficient factor (through a transfusion of fresh frozen plasma or plasma concentrate) or through local control (e.g., topical application of adrenalin, direct pressure, immobilization, elevation of the bleeding body part, ice packs, or packing the wound with fibrin foam or gelfoam). Prevention of disability and deformity due to joint damage from repeated hemarthrosis are essential and yet pose many difficult parenting decisions. Parents are advised not to give the child aspirin or any other medication which might affect platelet function. Factor concentrates may also be administered prior to dental or surgical procedures to prevent hemorrhage. Physical activity must be curtailed, a restriction which can be very frustrating for the child. Repeated hospitalization and long periods of bed rest pose additional restrictions and limitations with which both parent and child must cope (See Table 9-1).

There are a variety of physical sequelae to the bleeding episodes, depending on where the bleeding occurs. Although many hemophilia patients and their parents are fearful of excessive bleeding if they are injured externally, spontaneous internal bleeding is more frequent, dangerous, and painful (Salk, Hilgartner, & Granich, 1972). Only a small percentage of the bleeding episodes is caused by external trauma (e.g., injury or surgery) and these instances often occur in the patients who are mildly affected (Biggs & MacFarlane, 1966; Salk et al., 1972). Spontaneous hemorrhaging can occur in any organ or tissue of the body. Some of the most disabling sites include: 1. bleeding into the joints (hemarthrosis), which is quite painful and if untreated can result in severe joint deformity called arthropathy; 2. hemorrhaging into the eye, which can result in blindness; 3. hemorrhaging into the brain, which can cause brain injury and possible intellectual impairment; and 4. hemorrhaging from the kidney, which can result in hematuria and possible urinary obstruction (Wright, Schaefer, & Solomons, 1979).

Frequency of bleeding has been related to the child's developmental stage and emotional factors. Once the infant begins walking there appears to be an increase in the number of hemorrhages. The peak period has been reported to be between the ages of 5 and 7 years. After this the hemorrhaging stabilizes at a fairly constant rate that remains higher than the rate before age 5, but lower than during the 5-7 year range (Olch, 1971). Adolescence is often accompanied by a decreased frequency of hemorrhaging, possibly due to muscular skeletal changes and to hormonal influences. Finally, various authors report that particular emotions such as anger, excitement over particular events (such as going on a holiday, to camp, or special occasions) (Mattsson & Gross, 1966a, 1966b), or grief following the death of a hemophiliac sibling, at the anniversary of such a death, or when the child attains the age at which the sibling died, seem to be associated with bleeding episodes (Spencer, 1971).

TABLE 9-1

Hemophilia

Definition	Major Symptoms and Signs	Possible Medical Treatment	Psychologic Issues
Hemorrhagic disease resulting from absence or reduction of a specific blood coagulation factor	*Early* Spontaneous, excessive bleeding, internally or externally *Long-term* Contractures of major joints from prolonged bleeding into the joints (hemarthrosis) Possible intracranial or ocular hemorrhage	Transfusion Cryoprecipitate injections Hospitalization Physical therapy	Fear of death from bleeding Inevitable overprotection Life and death consequences of normal activities Maternal guilt and paternal rejection or distancing Complicated extended family relationship due to genetic transmission Pain and immobilization Passivity vs. dangerous risk taking

Medical Treatment

Until recently hemophiliacs often did not survive to adulthood. Now improved treatment of the bleeding episodes, as well as development of an antihemophiliac factor (AHF, Factor VIII) freeze-dried concentrate which can be infused by patients outside the hospital, has radically changed the care and treatment of hemophiliac patients. The psychological and developmental experiences of living with hemophilia, as well as the familial responses and interactions that can occur once a genetically transmitted X-linked disorder has been diagnosed, can, however, be crucial factors in determining adaptive or maladaptive coping with this illness.

In addition, recent reports have indicated that hemophiliac children are at increased risk for acquired immunodeficiency syndrome (AIDS), characterized by a defect in cell mediated immunity and a marked susceptibility to infections or malignant neoplasms. Although a causative agent has not been identified, the possibility of transmission by an infectious agent through blood products is currently under study. Use of the Factor VIII concentrate may, thus, represent a serious risk to the hemophiliac patient since the antihemophiliac factor is derived from pooled blood samples (e.g. plasma from multiple donors). Another risk factor for these patients is potential virus-induced liver disease (hepatitis) (Desforges, 1983; Ragni, Lewis, Spero, & Bontempo, 1983).

Child and Parent Coping Styles

Mattsson and Gross (1966a, 1966b), in their descriptive study of the adaptational behavior of young hemophiliacs and their parents, explored the families' understanding of hemophilia, the clinical course and the child's reactions, and the coping strategies employed in dealing with this serious and chronic illness. They studied 35 hemophiliac boys (representing 22 families) over a 2 year period and found that 27 of these boys (77%) demonstrated satisfactory to optimum adaptation to their illness. These boys were functioning effectively at home, at school, and with their peers and displayed few or no activity limitations other than those imposed by their disease. Eight (23%) of the boys were considered poorly adjusted; within this group five (14%) displayed "daredevil" high-risk-taking behavior, whereas three (8%) boys were characterized by extreme passivity and dependence.

Mattsson and Gross (1966a) outlined the common coping and defense mechanisms of these two groups and related these to parental management. In summary, the mechanisms of hemophiliacs who had adapted well or poorly were as follows:

Well adapted hemophiliacs:

1. Displayed withdrawal during serious and painful hemorrhagic episodes, but resumed their typical verbal and emotional interactions with parents and staff when the physical emergency subsided;

2. Displayed a tendency to deny or minimize the previous pain, fear, and current discomfort, to isolate their distressing feelings, and to focus their attention on the discharge date;

3. Demonstrated a strong dislike for immobilization and inactivity and evidenced distress when restrained in bed;

4. Expressed emotion during episodes of bleeding but remained cooperative with treatment (e.g., restricted anger, frustration, and sadness, although at times resentful feelings were projected onto parents and staff);

5. Denied the possibility of premature death and anticipated and hoped for a rapid recovery. (Younger children in this group were more reliable in reporting injuries, more accepting of necessary physical restrictions, and cooperative with treatment. Older children, 7–8 years and above demonstrated a more intellectual approach to the illness and identified with hospital staff.);

6. Accepted compensatory activities such as reading, building models, playing table games, etc.

7. Participated in approved physical activities (bicycling, swimming, fishing, golf, etc.).

8. Used fantasy as a means of vicarious enjoyment of prohibited hazardous sports such as horseback riding, ice hockey, car racing.

9. Displayed school achievement commensurate with their ability and few discipline problems.

Poorly adapted hemophiliacs:
Passive Dependent Types

1. Demonstrated reluctance to participate in any physical activities because of fear of trauma;

2. Frequently stayed in bed watching television or reading even during symptom-free periods;

3. Passively accepted treatment procedures and remained irritable and depressed long after hemorrhagic episode had subsided;

4. Displayed very close emotional ties to their mothers who were quite worried and overprotective.

Rebellious Risk Takers

1. Displayed active and daring risk-taking behavior in which injury and trauma resulted from carelessness and the pursuit of dangerous activities;

2. Evidenced recurrent anger, frustration, and depression about the chronic nature of the illness and lack of curative treatment;

3. Used marked denial and counterphobic behavior as defense mechanisms to master their fear and anxiety;

4. Demonstrated poor academic achievement and often became school dropouts;

5. Rebelled against maternal oversolicitousness and overprotective attitudes and behavior.

Parental characteristics associated with poor adaptation:

1. Mother unable to deal with her guilt over having a child with a serious illness or over her own carrier status.
2. Mother views herself as the only protector of the child; the father plays little or no role in the care and rearing of the child. He may divorce the mother or abandon the family.
3. The parents had received little guidance. They feel isolated, afraid, and question their ability to raise the child.
4. An overprotective attitude is coupled with a strong resentment of the situation.
5. Five of the eight mothers had experienced the death of their own children or siblings from hemophilia or another congenital illness.
6. They evidenced rigid precautions and activity limitations.
7. Reaction formation is excessive among these parents and results in excessive protectiveness, a martyr-like attitude, and expressed bitterness and resentfulness.

Parental characteristics associated with good adaptation:

1. Effective coping with anxiety, sadness and guilt following diagnosis.
2. Use of denial of the dangers of the illness within optimum limits.
3. Cooperation with medical care and raising the child with realistic restrictions.
4. Mother able to explain nature of illness to child and siblings at an early age and did not try to deny her genetic role.
5. Fathers active in caring for their ill son, provided a good masculine model, and tried to relieve the mother's guilt by stressing their mutual responsibilities for having a hemophiliac son and for raising him.
6. Use of "control through thinking" and isolation of painful affects as ways to handle emergencies and to protect the child and family from unbearable anxiety and despair.
7. Modulated use of reaction formation which allowed devoting energy to caring for child and for seeing illness as a challenge (Mattsson & Gross, 1966a).

Given the many special needs that the hemophiliac child presents, the extent to which the parents' child-rearing practices and ability to work together in caring for the child is adversely affected assumes primary importance in clinical intervention with these families. Important comparative information on these issues has been compiled by Markova et al. (1980). These investigators contrasted the child-rearing practices of parents who had a child with hemophilia with those of parents who had healthy children. Differences within the families of hemophiliac children were also examined according to the degree of severity of the condition (mild, moderate, severe). All families had young children, ranging in age from 3-5 years.

The parents of normal and hemophiliac children differed on several variables. In the hemophiliac families the father took more care of the boy when he was a baby, currently spends more time with the boy, helps the mother more in caring for the other children, and sees his role in the family as more similar to the mother's role (e.g., care and protection of the child, rather than as heading the household). Mothers of hemophiliac boys had more definite views about child rearing than mothers of healthy boys. When asked about the child's future, the hemophiliac child was more likely to be perceived by the mother as continuing to be dependent in 15 years time. Both parents of hemophiliac children viewed themselves as having stricter standards than other parents they knew and as training the hemophiliac child in more responsibilities. Most mothers of hemophiliac boys, in contrast to mothers of healthy boys, did not allow their child to play with metal toys, were more concerned if their sons were playing out of their sight, and worried more about the physical dangers of crowds and playgrounds at school. A high proportion of the mothers with a hemophiliac child worked. Financial necessity created by the cost of treatment, hospitalization, protective clothing, and special needs likely dictated this.

When comparisons were made within the hemophiliac group, highly significant relationships were found between the severity of the hemophilia and child-rearing practices. The more severe the condition the less the parents agreed about child rearing, the less the father participated in infant care, and the less the parents were able to look ahead and plan for their child. Similarly, if the condition was more severe, the mother had fewer ideas on child rearing, attended more to the baby's crying, gave the child fewer household tasks, and spent more time playing with the child. None of the parents of boys with severe hemophilia made any plans for their future. Finally, the more severe the hemophilia the less social contact the parents had. This was due, in part, to their fear of leaving the child with someone not prepared to cope with severe bleeding.

Of the eight couples who had relatives with hemophilia, only three had discussed the possibility of having a child with hemophilia prior to conception and made a joint decision to have the child. In each of these three cases, both parents subsequently felt responsible for raising the child. Similarly, in the eight families with no genetic history of hemophilia, the mother received reasonable support from her husband following the diagnosis. In three of the five families in which there was a positive family history of hemophilia, but where the parents did not discuss the possibility that the mother was a carrier, the mother received less support from the father. However, in two of these cases the child was severely affected, and in one case, moderately affected, making it difficult to determine if the lack of support was due to the severity of the disorder or the fact that no joint decision had been made following discussion of the risks.

Although the number of families studied is small and the findings need replication in other centers or with a larger sample, the results highlight the complex interaction between severity of illness and coping ability. Parents whose child had mild hemophilia (compared to parents with a severely affected child and parents of healthy boys) were more cooperative and involved, had better formulated views concerning child rearing, and were more able to encourage independent behavior in their child. The authors suggest that:

> If the haemophilia is mild, the family, in some respects, profits from the situation: there is a degree of uncertainty, worry and emotional strain, but it usually mobilises all the emotional strength of the parents, motivates them to take precautions and to become aware of certain dangers for the child, and result in greater parental co-operation and more attention to child-rearing. Faced with the problems of bringing up a mildly affected haemophiliac child, parents may have to think out their responsibilities and roles to a greater extent than parents who have a child with no medical problem (Markova et al., 1980, p. 160).

When the child is severely affected, however, the strain on the parents is excessive; and they are often unable to cope with the constant risk of bleeding and the life-threatening nature of the condition. In addition, there are few available guidelines for these parents on how much to restrict the child, since many of the bleedings appear spontaneously or cannot be connected to specific events. Such parents, particularly mothers because of their carrier status, are also likely to experience considerable guilt and are in need of a great deal of support, reassurance, and counseling (Markova et al., 1980).

Child personality characteristics. Although earlier reports had documented a higher frequency of psychiatric disorders in hemophiliac boys and disturbed parent-child interactions in hemophiliac families, improved antihemophilia therapy has diminished the extent of psychological disability. One recent investigation (Steinhausen, 1976) found no differences between 50 hemophiliac boys and 50 matched controls in the frequency of neurotic disorders or of maternal overprotectiveness. Any attempt to characterize the personality profile of hemophiliac patients must take into account the severity of the illness and the presence of disability. Steinhausen (1976) found that serious emotional problems arose in severe cases of hemophilia or when late or insufficient treatment of bleeding led to severe physical handicap. Mother-son interaction also became more impaired when these factors were present. The hemophiliac child also demonstrated lower extraversion and higher neuroticism (on personality testing) as his physical handicap increased.

Psychological Intervention

Multiple factors, in both physical and psychosocial areas, must be considered in evaluating the child's and family's adaptation to the disease. Agle and Mattsson (1976) suggest a systems model of childhood hemophilia as a guide to providing comprehensive care. This model explores biological (severity of AHF deficiency; autonomic and central nervous system stress mediating mechanisms) psychological (coping and defending techniques) and environmental (family acceptance and stability, peer relationships, community support, financial aid) factors in relationship to subsequent adaptation. Hemorrhagic episodes, other physical complications, and the development of behavior problems are viewed within this entire biopsychosocial matrix.

The assessment of whether a family can appropriately manage home care of hemophilia requires sensitivity to these multiple factors. While for some families the availability of AHF concentrate for home transfusions normalizes the child's activities, improves school attendance, and decreases time in the hospital, in other children school performance, absenteeism, and the parent-child relationship do not improve despite improvement in the child's physical health (Agle, 1975; Fajardo, 1973; Lazerson, 1972).

When there is such lack of improvement in adapting to the illness, the primary health team may find it necessary to suggest psychological intervention for the child and parents. If repeated risk taking, marked anxiety about bleeding, unrealistic passive dependence, depression, school failure, or excessive use of AHF concentrate is evident, the child and family may need additional psychological assistance (Agle & Mattsson, 1976). In the parents, unresolved and persistent guilt, excessive overprotection and restriction, inadequate discipline, rejection, or neglect may be present and require intervention. Table A-9 in the Appendix summarizes several clinical studies that have attempted to deal with many of these difficulties in adjustment.

Parent support groups have been particularly valuable in helping parents cope with and adapt to the stress of raising a child with hemophilia. Such groups have both been able to increase the parents' confidence and competence in handling episodes of severe bleeding, as well as resolving feelings of overwhelming guilt, blame, and depression.

Other interventions have been directed toward facilitating the hemophiliac child's sense of self-control in managing bleeding episodes, reducing tension and anxiety during bleeding episodes, and alleviating worry and apprehension about possible future bleeding episodes. Both group and individual hypnotherapy has been attempted with evidence of success, as indicated by significant decreases in need for blood transfusions and reduced number of hospitalizations (see Table A-9 in the Appendix). When persistent behavioral problems interfere with adequate home-care management, parent guidance incorporating behavioral management techniques also has been quite successful in enhancing appropriate and diminishing inappropriate behavior. Finally, if severe emotional disturbance is evident or if the child's emotional state is having a marked impact on his use of the AHF concentrate, comprehensive psychiatric intervention may be required.

Muscular Dystrophy

There are three main types of muscular dystrophy: 1) pseudohypertrophic muscular dystrophy (Duchenne, Aran-Duchenne dystrophy); 2) facio-scapulo-humeral dystrophy (Landouzy-Dejerine dystrophy); and 3) limb-girdle dystrophy (Erb dystrophy or Leyden-Moebius dystrophy). Of these three, Duchenne's muscular dystrophy is by far the most common type (Wright, Schaefer, & Solomons, 1979) and will be summarized to illustrate key issues and psychologic concerns. Moosa (1974) has provided an excellent review discussing the different types of dystrophy and their differential diagnoses. (Each of these major types is described briefly in Table 9-2.)

Clinical Description

Duchenne muscular dystrophy (DMD) is an inherited, fatal muscle disease characterized by progressive muscle degeneration and weakness. It is transmitted as an X-linked recessive disorder in which males are primarily affected (1 in every 3,000 live births [Wright et al., 1979]). The age at onset is usually between 2-6 years. Prevalence is reported at approximately 200,000 in the United States (Travis, 1976). Death often occurs following cardiac complications, lung infection, or respiratory failure between the ages of 15-25 years. Typically, the child requires almost total care for 6 to 8 years.

Early symptoms include bilateral weakness of the pelvic girdle, later progressing to the shoulder girdle. The child is clumsy, falls frequently, has a waddling gait, and difficulty climbing stairs, riding a tricycle, and rising from a prone position to a standing position. Many children are able to walk until about 12 years of age, but as the disease progresses there is muscle atrophy, pseudohypertrophy of the calves, contractures, and joint deformity. Eventually the child is not able to walk unassisted and must use braces, and finally a wheelchair. The course is determined by the rate of muscle deterioration. In the final stages of the disease the diaphragm, the heart, and the respiratory muscles become involved. The major signs and symptoms, as well as possible medical treatments, are presented in Table 9-3.

Impact on the Family

The anguish parents feel at the initial diagnosis of muscular dystrophy is considerable. Reactions differ depending on whether there is a history of muscular dystrophy in the mother's family, among her relatives, or whether this is the first diagnosis of muscular dystrophy. When such a history does exist, the mother has often been fearful and anxious throughout her pregnancy. Her subsequent guilt and self-blame upon hearing the diagnosis can precipitate serious depressive reactions. How the father responds to the knowledge of the mother's carrier status, as well as his own realization that half of his male offspring could have muscular dystrophy and half of his female offspring carriers, can greatly accentuate or ameliorate the mother's grief and despair. In cases in which there is no prior history of muscular dystrophy or no known history, the shock at hearing the diagnosis is

TABLE 9-2
The Primary Myopathies of Muscular Dystrophy
Primary Myopathies — Muscular Dystrophy

Major Types	*Alternate Names*	*Types of Inheritance*	*Clinical Onset*	*Initial Symptoms*	*Progression*	*Treatment*
Pseudo-hypertrophic	Duchenne	Sex-linked recessive, transmitted through unaffected females. There is a 50% probability that male offspring will be afflicted, and a 50% probability that female offspring will be carriers.	Early childhood	Swayback, a waddling gait, and difficulty in rising from the floor and climbing stairs, due to pelvic girdle muscle weakness. Fat deposits replace wasting muscle tissue in the calves.	Rapid, ultimately involving all the voluntary muscles. Death usually occurs within 10–15 years of clinical onset.	None. Physical therapy may delay atrophy of disuse of healthy muscles and antibiotics control secondary illnesses, but neither halts the dystrophic process.
Facioscapulo-humeral	Landouzy-Dejerine	Autosomal dominant, transmitted by either parent to children of both sexes, with a 50% probability of incidence.	Early adolescence, occasionally in the twenties.	Lack of facial mobility, difficulty in raising arms over head, forward slope of shoulders, due to initial weakness of face and shoulder girdle muscles.	Very slow, often with intervals in which the disease marks time. Average life span rarely shortened, despite considerable disability.	None. Physical therapy may delay atrophy of disuse of healthy muscles and antibiotics control secondary illnesses, but neither halts the dystrophic process.
Limb-girdle	Includes Juvenile Dystrophy of Erb	Autosomal recessive, transmitted to children of both sexes *only* when both parents carry the defective gene. 25% may then be disabled, and up to 50% carriers.	Any time from the 1st to the 3rd decade of life.	Usually weakness of the proximal muscles of both the pelvic and the shoulder girdles.	Variable, sometimes slow and sometimes fairly rapid. Disability may remain slight and some patients live to old age.	None. Physical therapy may delay atrophy of disuse of healthy muscles and antibiotics control secondary illnesses, but neither halts the dystrophic process.
Muscular dystrophy of late onset		Not known to be hereditary. Affects both sexes.	4th or 5th decade of of life.	Weakness of the proximal muscles of the pelvic girdle.	Variable.	None. Physical therapy may delay atrophy of disuse of healthy muscles and antibiotics control secondary illnesses, but neither halts the dystrophic process.
Myositis Polymyositis		None	Any time of life.	Proximal muscle weakness not connected with any identifiable systemic disorder.	Variable, may be mild and chronic, severe and chronic, or rapidly fatal. Occasional periods of remission.	Corticosteroid therapy brings marked improvement in many cases.
Dermato-myositis		None	Any time of life.	Similar to polymyositis symptoms, with the addition of a reddish skin eruption on face and upper trunk.	Similar to polymyositis.	Corticosteroid therapy brings marked improvement in many cases.

From J.J.M. Tackett and M. Hunsberger (Eds.), *Family-Centered Care of Children and Adolescents: Nursing Concepts in Child Health*, Philadelphia, W.B. Saunders Company, 1981, p. 1322. Adapted from the chart of Differential Diagnostic Characteristics of the Primary Diseases Affecting the Neuromuscular Unit. Made available through the Muscular Dystrophy Association. Reprinted with permission.

TABLE 9-3

Duchenne Muscular Dystrophy

Definition	Major Symptoms and Signs	Possible Medical Treatment	Psychologic Issues
A neuromuscular disorder in which striated muscle progressively deteriorates	*Early*	Physical therapy	Anguish and guilt over the diagnosis
	Waddling gait	Caloric restricted diet	Repression, anxiety and other emotional reactions to knowledge of early crippling and death
	Toe walking	Surgery for contractures	
	Frequent easy falling	Correction of spinal deformity	
	Difficulty climbing stairs	Antibiotics	
	Swayback (lordotic)	Postural drainage exercises	Learning problems
	Weakness	Orthopedic prostheses and motorized equipment	Chronic physical and mental exhaustion
	Later		Progressive helplessness and dependency because of loss of strength
	Generalized weakness		
	Loss of ambulation		Isolation, taunts, and physical abuse by peers
	Weight gain		Sacrifices required by other family members
	Respiratory infection and respiratory failure		Great difficulty in managing anger and aggressive feelings
	Brittle bones (osteoporosis)		Need for respite for parents and siblings

considerable. Although many parents are aware that something is wrong because of the child's clumsiness and incoordination, they typically suspect cerebral palsy or mental retardation, not muscular dystrophy. The information that their child has this crippling and fatal disease, so widely publicized in muscular dystrophy telethons, can be overwhelming for them.

It is particularly important during the initial diagnostic period for a psychologist or social worker to help the family cope with the overwhelming grief and sadness that can arise. At this time, the basis for a continuing, supportive therapeutic relationship can be established between the parents and health professionals. Initial reactions often follow the pattern described by Kübler-Ross (1969) for patients who learn they have a terminal illness. Genetic counseling of the parents, as well as marital and contraceptive counseling, is often indicated. The impact on other siblings in the family must be considered as well. Daughters are often particularly distressed and concerned over their possible carrier status. Since Duchenne muscular dystrophy, like hemophilia, is inherited as an X-linked recessive condition, similar patterns of marital reactions are often observed and may require similar psychotherapeutic interventions (see section on hemophilia).

The full impact on the family is not realized, however, until the child is 8-12 years of age. It is at this time the awful physical burden of this disease becomes apparent. As the child loses ambulatory abilities and becomes either wheelchair dependent or bedridden, the demands for physical care as well as the psychosocial implications increase dramatically. These have been well described by Travis (1976):

> . . . The child more nearly resembles a quadriplegic than a paraplegic, because of weakness in the shoulders and upper arms. The disease itself is painless. It has no remissions and allows no letup like arthritis. There are no good periods in which the family and child can regroup their psychic forces and renew their hopes. The rate of progression is generally predictable (though with a wide variation among some individuals). In most cases one can foresee what is going to happen and plan accordingly. Muscular dystrophy is an upside-down disorder, developmentally. Normal children grow stronger and more independent. Children with Duchenne's grow weaker and more dependent. (p. 404)

Psychological Assessment Issues

Intellectual functioning. In addition to deterioration of muscle, the central nervous system may be impaired as well. Recent studies concur that intellectual impairment is associated with DMD (Dubowitz, 1978; Prosser, Murphy, & Thompson, 1969). Typically, reviews find that the mean IQ of DMD children is approximately 85, one standard deviation below that of the normal population. The range of IQ scores resembles that of the normal distribution curve; and about 30 percent of these children would be considered mentally retarded, having an IQ score below

75. This compares to approximately 5 percent of the normal population so classified (Dubowitz, 1978).

The precise nature of the central nervous system involvement, however, is unclear, since there are no consistently identified abnormalities in the central nervous system. When neurologic abnormalities have been identified, they have not correlated with the incidence of mental retardation (Dubowitz, 1978). In addition, no single pattern of intellectual deficit has been noted. Varying patterns of intellectual impairment, not completely explained on the basis of age or degree of physical disability, have been obtained. For some children, verbal ability is impaired early on whereas nonverbal abilities are initially normal. Other children display early deficits in both verbal and nonverbal areas (Marsh & Munsat, 1974; Karagan & Zellweger, 1978).

The most likely current hypothesis to explain the intellectual impairment associated with DMD is that the Duchenne gene exhibits pleiotrophic effects that influence not only the skeletal muscle tissue, but also the myocardium and the central nervous system (Dubowitz, 1978). In time a biochemical factor connected with the disease itself may be identified that could affect the brain's development. However, the effects of depression, anxiety, and low motivation, which undoubtedly accompany this crippling, progressive, and fatal disease, must also be considered as further possible suppressors of optimal intellectual functioning. Before more definitive conclusions can be drawn about the nature of intellectual impairment in DMD, longitudinal studies are needed to answer critical questions of the static or progressive nature of the cognitive impairment. The use of comparable psychometric instruments and the comparison of various age and stage groups would facilitate our understanding of this disease. This information is important since cognitive abilities play such an important role in the development of competence and coping skills.

Personal and social adjustment. Clinical studies of children with DMD have found no specific personality configuration or distinct psychopathological entities characteristic of DMD children (Mearig, 1973). The severe forms of psychiatric illness are also no more frequent than in the general population, although there is a high frequency of minor to moderate psychological problems. These problems are most often neurotic or personality disordered in nature, rather than psychotic. Studies of the emotional adjustment of DMD children, however, have often yielded widely discrepant viewpoints, with observations ranging from extraordinary adjustment to marked immaturity and serious interpersonal problems. Individual variations in personality development, family and home environment, the social milieu, and the availability of other support systems undoubtedly account for this, but precise delineation of any or all of these factors has not yet been attempted.

Of interest is the repeated observation that the pattern of reaction in children with DMD often differs from the reactions of children with other crippling conditions (Sherwin & McCully, 1961; Mearig, 1973). The findings reported have also not been necessarily typical or characteristic of children with chronic or fatal diseases. The tragic aspects of this disease, combining chronic, progressive crippling with a fatal outcome, present relatively unique adaptive problems for these children. Sherwin and McCully (1961) note that nondystrophic, disabled children often show limited drive toward or interest in motor activities, focusing instead on more passive verbal pursuits such as reading. In contrast, they found that DMD children did not tend to compensate for their physical deficit by concentration on verbal activities. As described in the previous section, the early verbal disability of some of these children and near normal early nonverbal skills may contribute to this initial tendency to avoid verbal pursuits and focus on maintaining motor skills as long as possible. Also, the progressive nature of the motor loss creates a situation that is both physically and emotionally quite different from a static loss. With the progression of the disease, the adaptive value of choosing motor tasks diminishes. A tendency to focus subsequently on verbal pursuits is suggested by the Prosser et al. study's (1969) finding of a significant increase in verbal IQ with increasing age.

The psychiatric symptomatology identified in DMD children has been varied. It includes such behavioral problems as negativism, excessive verbal aggressiveness, poor relationships with peers, achievement problems, excessive shyness and withdrawal from others, night terrors, temper tantrums, poor self-esteem, immaturity, overdependence, and an inordinate reliance on fantasy for basic satisfaction. Many investigators find few instances where the emotional problems were simply a reaction to physical disability. Rather, the stress of muscular dystrophy tends to exaggerate to a pathologic degree the problems of both the parents and the child. Children with serious behavioral problems most often come from families with marked conflicts. Of great interest, however, is the finding that as many as 50 percent of DMD children show little or no psychopathology. The major problems the children express are in controlling aggression and hostility, a not surprising finding given the poor prognosis and disability created by the disease. Clinically, preadolescent DMD children show little overt anxiety and depression, while adolescents often show significant depression, social isolation, and apprehensiveness about their condition (Bayrakal, 1975). An excessive reliance on fantasy as both a source of vicarious satisfaction and an outlet for tension is often observed. The children also show a preoccupation in personality testing (e.g., projective tests; play therapy) with destructive forces over which they have no control, with bodily injury, and with catastrophic events leading to death. With progressive muscular weakness, the adolescent can become very isolated, withdraw from the school setting, and rely even more heavily on fantasy. Clinical interview material rarely reveals any discussion about sexual concerns, although in a prolonged group therapy experience adolescents did briefly discuss their concerns in this area. Since death typically occurs in late adolescence or early adulthood, often after a prolonged period where little if any ambulation is possible, the improbability of achieving sexual intimacy likely accounts for their silence in this regard. Such silence does not necessarily suggest a lack of interest; rather it may reflect hopelessness and depression over the anticipated loss of this experience (Bayrakal, 1975).

Increasing preoccupation with the disease and the predominant use of emotional energy to ward off concomitant painful feelings can block the use of energy for intellectual and interpersonal pursuits. Consequently, the educational achievements of many of these children have been low in comparison to their abilities. Apathy and lack of motivation present problems in completing schoolwork. Sherwin and McCully (1961) also observed that in the school setting, many children tended to respond to situations in an exaggerated way, with passive nonparticipation or sudden, impulsive aggressiveness. Poor control over their behavior in groups or with individuals, combined with limited understanding of or ability to attend to the needs of others, further interfere with peer relationships.

The impact of this chronic disease on family relationships is great. While occasionally rejection of the DMD child has been noted, by far the more common pattern is guilt, overprotection, self-abnegation and, at times, psychological neglect of the unaffected children. Tragically, many of the patients come from families with multiple cases within a family and generations of affected individuals. It is often difficult for the parents to consider the broader aspects of their child's life. Understandably, they focus primarily on the disease itself. In later stages of the disease, the physical care of the child leaves little time free for the mother or primary caretaker for attention to the other children, social activities, or periods alone (Travis, 1976). Muscular dystrophy associations have provided invaluable support and relief in this respect.

The DMD child can also be overly demanding, noncompliant, or intentionally guilt-provoking for secondary gains. These and other behavioral problems are difficult for the parents, since punishment and limit setting are often hard to enforce on a child with such a debilitating illness (Mearig, 1973). Acceptance of the diagnosis and its implications is often quite difficult for both parents and child. While there is often conscious understanding of the immediate physical limitations, when the future is considered, denial of disability often alternates with acceptance (Sherwin & McCully, 1961). Many DMD children are aware they may live only until their early twenties. Direct questions about death are usually asked only in the beginning of the illness. Later the subject is anxiously avoided, though preoccupation with the death of others or bodily injury to others may come out in play or in group therapy (Bayrakal, 1975).

Treatment Considerations

All investigators emphasize the need for intervention for these children and their families. Therapeutic and educational interventions might delay and/or diminish the tendency for these children to fall behind emotionally and intellectually. More active social pursuits and the opportunity to develop various interests and hobbies are essential in furthering closer relationships with others. Such interaction with other children, if successful, will offer the opportunity to develop feelings of self-worth and competence, so essential to personal satisfaction. Remaining in school is also of obvious importance in facilitating both cognitive and interpersonal competencies.

In order to maintain optimal levels of functioning, an active exercise program to improve muscle strength is essential. Involving both parents and child from the onset and stressing the importance of exercise and the danger of immobility can help promote more positive coping with the disease and may prevent or reduce the obesity that can develop. Social service support and registration with the Muscular Dystrophy Association may help the family identify ways of modifying their home environment to accommodate a wheelchair and provide avenues for financial assistance and emotional support. While at present there is no medical treatment to reverse the muscular dystrophy, the goal of educational, psychological, and social services for these children should be to maximize their total development for whatever life span they have (Mearig, 1973). When the cure for this disease is discovered, each DMD child must also be prepared emotionally, educationally, and socially for the future.

Later treatment goals. In addition to providing educational and psychotherapeutic supports for the child with muscular dystrophy, the needs of the parents and siblings must also be responded to. The parents often need to obtain some respite from the daily demands of caring for their progressively weaker and more dependent child. Special schools and camps for children with muscular dystrophy can play an important role in providing this much needed relief. Siblings are often burdened by the physical care demands. Their conflicting emotions can create considerable conflict. Worry, grief, and sadness over the eventual death of their dystrophic brother can precipitate severe guilt about their own good fortune. Alternatively, the constant attention the dystrophic child receives from the mother or caretaker can result in resentment, anger, and feelings of deprivation. If a therapist can establish a trusting relationship with the various family members, the opportunity to discuss their worries, resentment, guilt, and sadness can provide great relief, comfort, and support. Travis (1976) emphasized that the mother's defenses and ways of coping should be respected: "Opportunity to unburden, not confrontation or destruction of what she hides behind, is to be sought" (p. 419). Parent, patient, and sibling support groups also can provide an opportunity for the family members to unburden themselves and receive guidance and support from others struggling to cope with the devastating reality of this disease.

References

Hemophilia

Agle, D. Psychological factors in hemophilia—the concept of self-care. *Annals of the New York Academy of Science*, 1975, *240*, 221-225.

Agle, D.P., & Mattsson, A. Psychological complications of hemophilia. In M.W. Hilgartner (Ed.), *Hemophilia in children*. Littleton, Massachusetts: Publishing Sciences Group, Inc., 1976.

Biggs, R., & MacFarlane, R.G. (Eds.). *Treatment of haemophilia and other coagulation disorders*. Philadelphia: F.A. Davis Co., 1966.

Desforges, J.F. AIDS and preventive treatment in hemophilia. *The New England Journal of Medicine*, 1983, *308*(2), 94–95.

Fajardo, R.A. Psychosocial aspects. In D. Green (Ed.), *Hemophilia: A manual of outpatient management*. Springfield, Illinois: Charles C. Thomas, 1973.

Lazerson, J. Hemophilia home transfusion program: Effect on school attendance. *The Journal of Pediatrics*, 1972, *81*, 330–332.

Markova, I., MacDonald, K., & Forbes, C. Impact of haemophilia on child-rearing practices and parental co-operation. *Journal of Child Psychology and Psychiatry and Allied Disciplines*, 1980, *21*, 153–162.

Mattsson, A., & Gross, S. Adaptational and defensive behavior in young hemophiliacs and their parents. *American Journal of Psychiatry*, 1966a, *122*(12), 1349–1356.

Mattsson, A., & Gross, S. Social and behavioral studies on hemophilic children and their families. *The Journal of Pediatrics*, 1966b, *68*(6), 952–964.

Olch, D. Personality characteristics of hemophiliacs. *Journal of Personality Assessment*, 1971, *35*(1), 72–79.

Ragni, M.V., Lewis, J.H., Spero, J.A., & Bontempo, F.A. Acquired-immunodeficiency-like syndrome in two haemophiliacs. *The Lancet*, 1983, *1*, 213–214.

Salk, L., Hilgartner, M., & Granich, B. The psycho-social impact of hemophilia on the patient and his family. *Social Science and Medicine*, 1972, *6*, 491–505.

Spencer, R.F. Psychiatric impairment versus adjustment in hemophilia: Review and five case studies. *Psychiatry in Medicine*, 1971, *2*, 1–12.

Steinhausen, H.-C. Hemophilia: A psychological study in chronic disease in juveniles. *Journal of Psychosomatic Research*, 1976, *20*, 461–467.

Thurber, F.W. Potential stresses during toddler years: Irreversible alterations in health status. In J.J. Tackett & M. Hunsberger (Eds.), *Family-centered care of children and adolescents: Nursing concepts in child health*. Philadelphia: W.B. Saunders Co., 1981.

Wright, L., Schaefer, A.B., & Solomons, G. *Encyclopedia of pediatric psychology*. Baltimore: University Park Press, 1979.

Muscular Dystrophy

Bayrakal, S. A group experience with chronically disabled adolescents. *American Journal of Psychiatry*, 1975, *132*(12), 1291–1299.

Dubowitz, V. *Muscle disorders in childhood*. Philadelphia: W.B. Saunders Co., 1978.

Karagan, N.J., & Zellweger, H.U. Early verbal disability in children with Duchenne muscular dystrophy. *Developmental Medicine and Child Neurology*, 1978, *20*, 435–441.

Kübler-Ross, E. *On death and dying*. New York: Macmillan, 1969.

Marsh, G.G., & Munsat, T.L. Evidence for early impairment of verbal intelligence in Duchenne muscular dystrophy. *Archives of Disease in Childhood*, 1974, *49*, 118–122.

Mearig, J.S. Some dynamics of personality development in boys suffering from muscular dystrophy. *Rehabilitation Literature*, 1973, *34*(8), 226–243.

Moosa, A. Muscular dystrophy in childhood. *Developmental Medicine and Child Neurology*, 1974, *16*, 97–111.

Prosser, E.J., Murphy, E.G., & Thompson, M.W. Intelligence and the gene for Duchenne muscular dystrophy. *Archives of Disease in Childhood*, 1969, *44*(234), 221–230.

Sherwin, A.C., & McCully, R.S. Reactions observed in boys of various ages (ten to fourteen) to a crippling, progressive, and fatal illness (muscular dystrophy). *Journal of Chronic Diseases*, 1961, *13*(1), 59–68.

Tackett, J.J.M., & Hunsberger, M. (Eds.). *Family-centered care of children and adolescents: Nursing concepts in child health*. Philadelphia: W.B. Saunders, Co., 1981.

Travis, G. *Chronic illness in children: Its impact on child and family*. Stanford, California: Stanford University Press, 1976.

Wright, L., Schaefer, A.B., & Solomons, G. *Encyclopedia of pediatric psychology*. Baltimore: University Park Press, 1979.

|10| Concluding Remarks

Throughout this book the importance of considering three interrelated systems, the biological, psychological, and social, has been emphasized in providing comprehensive care for chronically ill children. This "biopsychosocial" model (Engel, 1977) provides an integrated framework for understanding the impact of illness and the multiple factors and processes (physiologic, developmental, intrapsychic, and interpersonal) that relate to the child's subsequent adaptation. In-depth consideration of factors in each of these areas will allow us to tailor our psychological and medical intervention not only to the disease and its specific management requirements, but also to the specific characteristics of the child and family with whom we are dealing.

This book provides an overview of the types of stresses that can be potentiated by specific illnesses and the medical and physical treatments required. The importance of evaluating illness through a stress and coping perspective has been underscored throughout. This book emphasizes the importance of exploring the adaptive capacities of the child and family to respond positively to these stresses as well as specific vulnerabilities that may result in poor adjustment. In chronic pediatric illness, the added complexity of the child's changing developmental status during prolonged treatment must be considered. Normal cognitive, emotional and social stages of development must be well understood before the possible distortions superimposed upon this normal developmental process from chronic illness can be appreciated (Drotar, 1981). The impact of the child's illness on the parents, the stability and cohesiveness of the parents' marriage, and the effect of the illness on siblings in the family are critical social factors that strongly influence the eventual adaptation that the chronically ill child may make.

The Need to Identify Children "At Risk"

Previous research on chronically ill children has focused on the differences between normal and chronically ill children and has attempted to identify specific psychopathological characteristics in the child or in the parent-child interaction. Recent comparative studies have not, however, found any evidence of a specific emotional or social disturbance for a specific illness group (Drotar, 1981; Pless & Pinkerton, 1975; Tavormina, Kastner, Slater, & Watt, 1976). In the Tavormina et al. (1976)

study, comparisons were made between children with diabetes, asthma, and cystic fibrosis. These investigators found that the majority of the children displayed normal coping patterns and responses rather than deviant or pathological responses. Heterogeniety of response within illness group was, by far, the more typical finding. As noted by Pless and Pinkerton, the effect of an illness on behavior is not necessarily adverse. Some children's behavior worsens whereas other children's behavior improves. Psychopathologic responses appear to be characteristic of only a minority of children with chronic illness.

Such variability in response suggests that having a chronic physical condition does not, by itself, determine psychological outcome (Bedell, Giordani, Amour, Tavormina, & Boll, 1977). Not all chronically ill children are equally at risk for social and emotional maladaptive function. Although the determinants of an individual child's outcome are extremely complex and difficult to predict, our task is to identify those children who are most vulnerable at the earliest possible time so that appropriate interventions may be provided.

Identification of Successful Coping Patterns

Before appropriate interventions can be provided, however, we need a clearer understanding of the specific factors which contribute to successful coping with chronic illness. The typical focus in research and clinical practice on the adverse outcome of *some* chronically ill children has not facilitated the exploration of factors that might mitigate the adverse impact of chronic illness on the child and family (Drotar, 1981). Before suggestions can be made about interventions for children who are vulnerable or at risk for disturbance, it is important to understand which coping responses are most effective for specific individuals, specific types of problems and in specific situations (Cohen & Lazarus, 1979). Such an understanding can only come from comprehensive longitudinal study of children and families who have coped successfully with a specific disease. Garmezy (1982) comments that it is a "recurrent paradox that we in our *mental health* professions are more wedded to psychopathology than we are to well-being, to concern with those who fail rather than to those who succeed, to children who capitulate to stress rather than to those who resist its debilitating effects" (p. 25). Thus, before we can make progress in selecting appropriate interventions for children, a dramatic change in our orientation is necessary. We must expand our efforts to study not only individual vulnerabilities and indications of risk, but also stress mitigating protective factors that enhance and facilitate adjustment to various illnesses (Garmezy, 1982).

Such an approach will require a multi-factorial approach to development. The child's genetic endowment, predisposition to specific disease, neurological integrity, and early individual differences in temperament must be examined in relationship to subsequent environmental influences (family, school, medical resources available in the community, and other support services). Variations relating to the specific temporal nature of the illness, for example whether the stress presented by the illness decelerates (as can occur following successful open heart surgery), accelerates (as in muscular dystrophy and other degenerative diseases) or is chronic and intermittent (as in asthma, epilepsy, diabetes, and JRA) have received little attention. In each of these areas the type of coping response that is effective likely changes over time and it is important to document the tasks and potential successful coping techniques that are present at each stage.

Table 10-1 presents many of the psychological issues commonly encountered in chronic illness. Perhaps one way to make progress in developing effective psychosocial interventions would be to look systematically and longitudinally at the characteristics of children and families who are able to cope successfully with these psychological issues. Such a study could provide much needed understanding of the successful coping strategies employed by these children and their parents to meet the difficulties that arise from the stress of chronic illness. The adaptive mechanisms of children and parents living with a specific chronic illness could then be compared to those exposed to different types of chronic physical illnesses as well as to other psychosocial stresses. Such research could provide much needed information regarding normality and coping in the face of a physical stress that has biological as well as psychological and social components.

Family coping. Research directed at family coping has remained relatively sparse and the development of reliable and valid family measures remains a priority for future research (Drotar, 1981). Measures such as Moos's (1974) Family Environment Scale, McCubbin, McCubbin, and Cauble's (1979) Coping-Health Inventory for Parents and Holroyd's (1974) Questionnaire on Resources and Stress are relatively new research instruments which appear to have special promise in documenting

TABLE 10-1

Psychological Issues Common to Most Chronic Illnesses

Pain and malaise
Frequent medical crises
Medical and surgical procedures
Hospitalization
Fear of death or disfigurement
Activity limitations
Diet restrictions
Heightened dependency on parent(s) during acute episodes
Family disruption
Sibling rivalry and resentment
Financial burdens
Frequent school absences
Peer isolation

coping processes in families who have a physically ill member. In addition, the Holmes and Rahe (1967) Life Stress Scale for adults and Coddington's (1972) and Garmezy, Tellegen, and Devine's (1981) modification of this scale for children provide useful indices of the level of stress experienced by a family in the previous year.

The importance of assessing life stress in relation to illness was highlighted in a recent study by Bedell et al. (1977). They found that when chronically ill children were divided into two groups, those who had experienced either low or high recent environmental stress, the level of stress was a significant determinant of current functioning. High-stress children experienced more acute episodes of illnesses related to their chronic disease and also perceived themselves in a more negative light. For example, they believed that they were "more poorly behaved, less physically attractive, less able at schoolwork, less popular, and less satisfied with themselves in general" (p. 241).

The effect of a chronic illness on marital stability and sibling adjustment has received even less study. Clinical reports have documented both negative and positive impact. Whereas some children become more resentful, anxious and prone to feelings of rejection when the parents' time and energy is spent in caring for the chronically ill child, other parents report that some siblings respond favorably to the added responsibilities in the family. Lavigne and Ryan (1979) conducted a major study exploring the variation in sibling adjustment among three groups of siblings: 1. those whose brothers or sisters had required plastic surgery (predominantly for cleft lip, cleft palate); 2. siblings of children with congenital heart disease; and 3. siblings of children with blood disorders (primarily leukemia). The adjustment of these siblings was then compared to that of a healthy control group. Several significant major findings and interaction effects were obtained. First, the illnesses seemed to differ in the extent to which they were associated with subsequent adjustment problems in the siblings. Although more siblings of patients were likely to show symptoms of irritability, social withdrawal and fearfulness than siblings of healthy children, the younger (ages 3–6 years) siblings of children under going plastic surgery demonstrated the highest level of general psychopathology. This finding was somewhat in contrast to the expectation that severity of illness would correspond to the degree of manifest emotional problems. The siblings of patients with leukemia, for example, did not demonstrate as significant a disturbance as those of patients requiring plastic surgery, despite the significantly greater severity of this disorder. Similarly, when severity of illness was assessed within the congenital heart defect group, no relationship between severity and subsequent sibling adjustment problems was found. Male siblings in the 7- to 13-year-old age group of patients with leukemia were more likely to show signs of emotional disturbance than females. Other significant age and sex effects were also obtained. In general, younger female siblings of patients had more problems than did younger male siblings whereas older female siblings demonstrated fewer problems than did older male siblings.

How illness, developmental, and sex factors interact to produce such effects remains somewhat unclear. Lavigne and Ryan speculated that differences in sex roles may partially account for the findings. For example, they speculated that in this culture, dependency is more encouraged among female children and for that reason, younger female siblings of patients may be particularly vulnerable because of the diminished attention that they may receive if another child in the family is chronically ill. In contrast, older girls were thought to respond more positively to the responsibility of caring for a younger ill sibling because of their more accustomed experience in providing care and managing household tasks at the older age level. Older male siblings, in contrast, may experience difficulty because the tasks assigned to them are viewed less favorably, or are tasks for which they are poorly prepared.

Psychologist's Role

The psychologist engaged in clinical work with chronically ill children and their families may be called on to provide interventions in a variety of areas: 1. prevention of long term adverse sequelae; 2. acute interventions such as preparing the child for medical experiences, reducing hospital related stress reactions, providing clinical interventions to help the child cope with pain, discomfort and other illness related problems; 3. treatment of emotional, behavioral and psychosocial problems arising secondarily from the illness; 4. helping the children and families cope with death and dying; 5. consultation with medical and nursing staff to develop comprehensive care programs for children with chronic illnesses; and 6. identification of effective techniques for improving adherence to medical regimens.

To date, some interventions specifically designed to prepare nonchronically ill children for hospitalization and minor surgeries have been developed and evaluated (Melamed & Siegel, 1980). Few, if any studies, however, have been completed which evaluate such interventions with chronically ill children. Petrillo and Sanger (1980) provide specific guidelines for preparing children for various surgeries, but specific outcome data regarding the benefits of such preparation and the types of children and problems for whom it is most beneficial is not yet available.

Intervention approaches that have been attempted with children in the illness categories covered in this book are briefly summarized in the Appendix. A quick perusal of these studies reveals that a majority are case reports or reports on small samples of children with a specific disease. Inspection of these tables also indicates that often the same intervention procedures have been applied across a wide range of physical problems. In a number of instances, multiple techniques have been attempted either simultaneously or in succession (see pertinent illustrations in Appendix tables A-6 and A-2 on diabetes and tic disorders, respectively). Currently, clinical case study and research outcome data have not successfully identified specific techniques that are most effective with specific disorders.

Different approaches have been utilized consistently, however, with certain purposes in mind. Behavioral contracts, positive reinforcement, response cost and time out procedures, aversive conditioning procedures, and modeling procedures have often been successfully employed to alter maladaptive behaviors that have developed concomitantly with the illness (Russo & Varni, 1982). These techniques have been particularly successful in dealing with aggressive or self-injurious behaviors (see Appendix tables on rumination (A-7), epilepsy (A-1), asthma (A-8), and encopresis (A-7) for illustrative examples), improving the child's compliance with treatment recommendations (see Appendix table A-6 on diabetes), and increasing the frequency of adaptive behaviors such as improved school attendance and more effective peer interaction (see Appendix table A-8 on asthma). Specific training programs have also been developed to improve children's skill in relating interpersonally and in handling stress. Such approaches include assertion training, social skills training, and peer and parent support groups (illustrative examples are contained in the Appendix tables on peptic ulcer (A-7), hemophilia (A-9), and irritable bowel syndrome (A-7)). Self-control procedures, such as biofeedback, systematic muscular relaxation and hypnosis have been used with a variety of illnesses (see Appendix tables on asthma (A-8), epilepsy (A-1), diabetes (A-6), encopresis (A-7)) with varying success. Finally, interventions designed to alter intrapsychic processes have been attempted as well. These include individual psychotherapy, systematic desensitization, behavioral rehearsal and other cognitive-behavioral approaches. Combinations of cognitive-behavioral therapies and self-control therapies have achieved some success in facilitating patient's confidence in handling anxiety related to asthmatic attacks, coping with the pain accompanying the illness, and dealing with other depressive or anxiety-provoking thoughts related to the illness. Russo and Varni (1982) emphasize the importance of developing treatment programs that are individually tailored to each child's particular need, medical condition and life situation. The task for future researchers in this area will be to establish empirically which treatment interventions are most effective for specific illnesses and/or at specific phases of disease progression. Seifert and Lubar's (1975) and Sterman, Macdonald, and Stone's (1974) work on biofeedback in patients with epilepsy (see table A-1 in the Appendix) provides an excellent beginning in the effort to differentiate types of patients who would benefit most directly from a specific technique.

Approaches to helping a child initially cope with the diagnosis of a disease are beautifully illustrated by Geist (1979). His overview of psychotherapeutic interventions with chronically ill children provides rich clinical examples of the types of difficulties encountered as well as specific suggestions for intervention. Adaptive coping mechanisms such as intellectualization, identification with the medical staff, denial in the service of hope, and idiosyncratic rituals are highlighted as well as maladaptive responses requiring further intervention. Geist's review is also relatively unique in providing a sensitive discussion of the personal impact on nursing and mental-health staff resulting from prolonged care of chronically ill children. His discussion of feelings of personal guilt, helplessness, and depression that can ensue when dealing with a chronic, debilitating, or life-threatening illness is particularly helpful for those working closely with such children.

Another area in which psychologists have become increasingly active has been in developing intervention programs designed to improve patient adherence to medical regimens (for illustration, see Table A-6 on diabetes in the Appendix). In a comprehensive review of this area, Epstein and Cluss (1982) report that approximately one-half of all patients with a chronic disease do not adhere to their treatment program. The unfortunate consequences of noncompliance can be increased morbidity and mortality, more frequent medical emergencies, and potential exposure to toxic drug levels or more potent drugs if dosage or type of drug is changed in an effort to control symptoms.

Specific interventions that have been shown to be successful in improving compliance have included drug-level feedback, reinforcement of medication use and reinforcement of improved symptom control. Self-monitoring of symptoms has not been shown to be as effective as reinforcement or feedback approaches. Epstein and Cluss emphasize, however, that adherence (or compliance) and clinical response to treatment are factors that must be examined separately. They report that in one study patients who adhered to a *placebo* showed more improvement than patients who did not adhere. Obviously, since a placebo was given, the patients were not responding to the pharmacologic effects of a drug. This finding raised the possibility that there may be specific characteristics of people who adhere that produce positive health effects and that we should direct our efforts toward identifying these characteristics. Epstein and Cluss speculate that patients who adhere may either not be as sick as patients who do not adhere or that adherent patients may have more ordered lives and better health related behaviors. They suggest that the process of adhering, in and of itself, may influence outcome. For example, adhering may allow a patient to meet well-defined goals, provide the patient with self-control strategies which may diminish feelings of helplessness, depression or anxiety that can accompany chronic illness, or may alter the patient's ability to make other health changes that might improve their health status (Epstein & Cluss, 1982). It is significant to note, however, that there is often a modest correlation between adherence and outcome. Many patients who do adhere are not under good clinical control and some who are under clinical control do not adhere. Epstein and Cluss caution against insistence on adherence to a medical program when the basic efficacy of the treatment is in dispute or has not been demonstrated, and they conclude that it is not always appropriate to attribute poor treatment results to poor compliance. As indicated in earlier chapters, it may be the treatment that is failing the patient, not the patient that is failing treatment (Levine & Bakow, 1976).

Recent studies have also identified social support as a potential moderator of the stress of illness (Cobb, 1976; Dean & Lin, 1977). Presence of social support has been associated with reduced amounts of medication required by the patient, an accelerated recovery period, and increased compliance with prescribed treatment programs. The association between social support and compliance is of particular interest. Cobb reports that patients who are not socially isolated and who are well supported stay in treatment longer and are more cooperative and consistent in following medical recommendations. Social isolation and lack of affiliation with others were significantly related to noncompliance. The importance of examining social support as a buffer against succumbing to illness is further highlighted in Dean and Lin's (1977) comment that "although it may not be possible to obviate routine life stresses or modify genetic or constitutional factors, it might be possible to mobilize social-support systems into community health services" (p. 413). Further documentation of the role of social support as a protective factor in illness susceptibility could have important implications for primary prevention.

References

Bedell, J.R., Giordani, B., Amour, J.L., Tavormina, J., & Boll, T. Life stress and the psychological and medical adjustment of chronically ill children. *Journal of Psychosomatic Research*, 1977, *21*, 237–242.

Cobb, S. Social support as a moderator of life stress. *Psychosomatic Medicine*, 1976, *38*(5), 300–314.

Coddington, R.D. The significance of life events as etiologic factors in the diseases of children: A survey of professional workers. *Journal of Psychosomatic Research*, 1972, *16*, 7–18.

Cohen, F., & Lazarus, R.S. Coping with the stresses of illness. In G.C. Stone, F. Cohen, & N.E. Adler (Eds.), *Health psychology: A handbook*. San Francisco: Jossey-Bass Publishers, 1979.

Dean, A., & Lin, N. The stress-buffering role of social support: Problems and prospects for systematic investigation. *The Journal of Nervous and Mental Disease*, 1977, *165*(6), 403–417.

Drotar, D. Psychological perspectives in chronic childhood illness. *Journal of Pediatric Psychology*, 1981, *6*(3), 211–228.

Engel, G.L. The need for a new medical model: A challenge for biomedicine. *Science*, 1977, *196*, 129–136.

Epstein, L.H., & Cluss, P.A. A behavioral medicine perspective on adherence to long-term medical regimens. *Journal of Consulting and Clinical Psychology*, 1982, 50(6), 950–971.

Garmezy, N. *Stress-resistant children: The search for protective factors*. Unpublished manuscript, University of Minnesota, 1982.

Garmezy, N., Tellegen, A., & Devine, V.T. *Project competence: Studies of stress-resistant children*. Technical Reports, University of Minnesota, 1981.

Geist, R.A. Onset of chronic illness in children and adolescents: Psychotherapeutic and consultative intervention. *American Journal of Orthopsychiatry*, 1979, *49*(1), 4–23.

Holmes, T.H., & Rahe, R.H. The social readjustment rating scale. *Journal of Psychosomatic Research*, 1967, *11*, 213–218.

Holroyd, J. The questionnaire on resources and stress: An instrument to measure family response to a handicapped family member. *Journal of Community Psychology*, 1974, *2*, 92–94.

Lavigne, J.V., & Ryan, M. Psychologic adjustment of siblings of children with chronic illness. *Pediatrics*, 1979, *63*(4), 616–627.

Levine, M.D., & Bakow, H. Children with encopresis: A study of treatment outcome. *Pediatrics*, 1976, *58*(6), 845–852.

Melamed, B.G., & Siegel, L.J. *Behavioral medicine: Practical applications in health care*. New York: Springer Publishing Company, 1980.

McCubbin, H.I., McCubbin, M.A., & Cauble, E. *CHIP: Coping-Health Inventory for Parents*, 1979, Form B, Available from Family Social Science, University of Minnesota, St. Paul, Minnesota 55108.

McCubbin, H.I., McCubbin, M.A., Patterson, J.M., Cauble, A.E., Wilson, L.R., & Warwick, W. *CHIP: Coping-Health Inventory for Parents: An assessment of parental coping patterns in the care of the chronically ill child*. Unpublished manuscript, University of Minnesota, 1981.

Moos, R. *Family Environment Scale and preliminary manual*, 1974. Available from Consulting Psychologists Press, 577 College Avenue, Palo Alto, California 94305.

Moos, R.H., & Moos, B.S. A typology of family social environments. *Family Process*, 1976, *15*, 357–370.

Petrillo, M., & Sanger, S. *Emotional care of hospitalized children: An environmental approach* (2nd ed.). Philadelphia: J.B. Lippincott Company, 1980.

Pless, I.B., & Pinkerton, P. *Chronic childhood disorder: Promoting patterns of adjustment*. London: Henry Kimpton Publishers, 1975.

Russo, D.C., & Varni, J.W. Behavioral pediatrics. In D.C. Russo & J.W. Varni (Eds.), *Behavioral pediatrics. Research and practice*. New York: Plenum Press, 1982.

Seifert, A.R., & Lubar, J.F. Reduction of epileptic seizures through EEG biofeedback training. *Biological Psychology*, 1975, *3*, 157–184.

Sterman, M.B., Macdonald, L.R., & Stone, R.K. Biofeedback training of the sensorimotor electroencephalogram rhythm in man: Effects on epilepsy. *Epilepsia*, 1974, *15*, 395–416.

Tavormina, J.B., Kastner, L.S., Slater, P.M., & Watt, S.L. Chronically ill children: A psychologically and emotionally deviant population? *Journal of Abnormal Child Psychology*, 1976, *4*, 99–110.

Appendix

TABLE A-1

Epilepsy

Authors and Date	Type of Epilepsy	Sample Size	Age	Treatment	Outcome	Follow-Up	Comments
Fabisch & Darbyshire, 1965	Self-induced (nonconvulsive) by hyperventilation	1	2½ yrs.	*Aversive Conditioning* Spontaneous remission after self-induced seizures resulted in vomiting	Cessation of habit for 6 months	Resumption of over-breathing; minor nonconvulsive seizures	Aversive conditioning may be effective treatment for self-induced seizures
Scholander, 1972	Generalized and partial complex	1	14 yrs.	*Aversive Conditioning* Treatment for compulsive neck gripping: 1) massed practice which led only to temporary improvement; 2) electric shock for one month	Neck gripping extinguished	9 months still symptom free	Treatment also resulted in a decrease in epileptic symptoms and increase in self-esteem
Adams et al., 1973	Grand mal & petit mal; nonepileptic falls	1	14 yrs.	*Behavior Therapy* Punishment and reinforcement of alternative appropriate behaviors	No nonepileptic falls after 6 weeks of treatment	1 month no falls	Falls not related to true seizures, but to social reinforcement; improvement in self-management and social interaction evident after successful treatment
Balaschak, 1976	Organically based	1	11 yrs.	*Behavior Therapy* Positive reinforcement of seizure-free period	30% reduction	Return to baseline	Verbal praise and candy given by teacher if child is seizure free

Study	N	Seizure type	Age	Treatment	Results	Follow-up	Comments
Gardner, 1967	1	Psychogenic	10 yrs.	*Behavior Therapy* Contingency management	Seizures stopped; decrease in tantrums	6 months–few tantrums; occasional somatic complaints	Parents instructed to ignore tantrums and reward positive behavior with attention
Ince, 1976	1	Petit mal & grand mal	12 yrs.	*Behavior Therapy* Relaxation; anxiety desensitization; conditioning of seizure response	Dramatic reduction	Seizure free at 9 months	Child had developed secondary psychologic problems and psychosomatic complaints
Wright, 1973	1	Self-induced by hand waving and blinking	5 yrs.	*Behavior Therapy* Aversive conditioning (electric shock)	90% reduction in eye blinking; 100% reduction in hand waving	Decrease maintained at 7 months	Child mentally retarded
Zlutnick et al., 1975	5	Tonic-clonic minor motor (2) and absence; major motor	4–17 yrs.	*Behavior Therapy* Contingent interruption of seizure chain. Reinforcement of behavior incompatible with seizures	+4/5	6–12 months	Environmental manipulation especially useful when typical preseizure behavior is identified
Finley, 1977	2	Akinetic psychomotor	13, 24 yrs.	*Biofeedback* EEG biofeedback of sensorimotor rhythm	+2/2	–	Investigator outlines a number of methodological advances
Johnson & Meyer, 1974	1	Grand mal	18 yrs.	*Biofeedback* Relaxation and EMG training; EEG biofeedback of 3 brain rhythms	46% reduction	Decrease maintained at 3 months	Subject able to return to school after 6 years of home tutoring
Lubar et al., 1981	8	Tonic-clonic (3) partial complex (2) and absence	13–52 yrs. ($x=25$)	*Biofeedback* EEG biofeedback of 3 types of frequency bands	49% decrease in 5/8	–	Majority of subjects had mental deficiency

TABLE A-1 **Epilepsy** (*continued*)

Authors and Date	Type of Epilepsy	Sample Size	Age	Treatment	Outcome	Follow-Up	Comments
Lubar & Shouse, 1978	Generalized myoclonic; partial complex (3); atonic mixed	6	15–19 yrs. 30 yrs.	*Biofeedback* EEG biofeedback training	++4/6 +2/6	At varying intervals	Two patients were able to achieve complete seizure control
Seifert & Lubar, 1975	Grand mal; myoclonic; psychomotor; petit mal	6	12–19 yrs.	*Biofeedback* EEG biofeedback of sensorimotor rhythm	+5/6	Subjects still in training	Subjects had varying degrees of mental retardation
Sterman & Macdonald, 1978	Mixed (5) Generalized (2) Partial focal motor (1)	8	8–24 yrs.	*Biofeedback* EEG feedback training for various frequency bands	6/8 demonstrated a reduction in seizures	—	Maximum seizure reductions noted after at least 6 months training
Sterman et al., 1974	Mixed; focal onset, generalized tonic-clonic	4	6, 18, 23, 46 yrs.	*Biofeedback* EEG biofeedback of sensorimotor rhythm	All patients obtained seizure reduction	—	Changes not observed until 2–3 months regular training. Training session extended over 1 year period
Gardner, 1973	Petit mal variant disturbance at age 3 yrs; currently having psychogenic seizures	1	8 yrs.	*Hypnotherapy* Hypnosis in conjunction with play therapy; 18 sessions over 3 months	Decrease in eye blinking spells from 113 in a 15 minute period to 0–10 in a 15 minute period.	—	Also increase in IQ scores from 72 to 103 after treatment; improved school and home behavior

| Glenn & Simonds, 1977 | Psychogenic (although EEG indicated right temporal slowing) | 1 | 13 yrs. | *Hypnotherapy* Hypnotherapy and psychotherapy in inpatient setting | No seizures after first week of hospitalization | 2 years no seizures | All anticonvulsant medication discontinued |

Epilepsy Table (A-1)
References

Adams, K.M., Klinge, V., & Keiser, T.W. The extinction of a self-injurious behavior in an epileptic child. *Behaviour Research and Therapy*, 1973, *11*, 351–356.

Balaschak, B.A. Teacher-implemented behavior modification in a case of organically based epilepsy. *Journal of Consulting and Clinical Psychology*, 1976, *44*(2), 218–223.

Fabisch, W., & Darbyshire, R. Report on an unusual case of self-induced epilepsy with comments on some psychological and therapeutic aspects. *Epilepsia*, 1965, *6*, 335–340.

Finley, W.W. Operant conditioning of the EEG in two patients with epilepsy: Methodologic and clinical considerations. *Pavlovian Journal of Biological Science*, 1977, *12*(2), 93–111.

Gardner, G.G. Use of hypnosis for psychogenic epilepsy in a child. *The American Journal of Clinical Hypnosis*, 1973, *15*(3), 166–169.

Gardner, J.E. Behavior therapy treatment approach to a psychogenic seizure case. *Journal of Consulting Psychology*, 1967, *31*(2), 209–212.

Glenn, T.J., & Simonds, J.F. Hypnotherapy of a psychogenic seizure disorder in an adolescent. *The American Journal of Clinical Hypnosis*, 1977, *19*(4), 245–250.

Ince, L.P. The use of relaxation training and a conditioned stimulus in the elimination of epileptic seizures in a child: A case study. *Journal of Behavior Therapy and Experimental Psychiatry*, 1976, *7*(1), 39–42.

Johnson, R.K., & Meyer, R.G. Phased biofeedback approach for epileptic seizure control. *Journal of Behavior Therapy and Experimental Psychiatry*, 1974, *5*, 185–187.

Lubar, J.F., Shabsin, H.S., Natelson, S.E., Holder, G.S., Whitsett, S.F., Pamplin, W.E., & Krulikowski, D.I. EEG operant conditioning in intractable epileptics. *Archives of Neurology*, 1981, *38*, 700–704.

Lubar, J.F., & Shouse, M.N. Use of biofeedback in the treatment of seizure disorders and hyperactivity. In B.B. Lahey & A.E. Kazdin (Eds.), *Advances in clinical child psychology* (Vol. 1). New York: Plenum Press, 1978.

Scholander, T. Treatment of an unusual case of compulsive behavior by aversive stimulation. *Behavior Therapy*, 1972, *3*, 290–293.

Seifert, A.R., & Lubar, J.F. Reduction of epileptic seizures through EEG biofeedback training. *Biological Psychology*, 1975, *3*, 157–184.

Sterman, M.B., & Macdonald, L.R. Effects of central cortical EEG feedback training on incidence of poorly controlled seizures. *Epilepsia*, 1978, *19*, 207–222.

Sterman, M.B., Macdonald, L.R., & Stone, R.K. Biofeedback training of the sensorimotor electroencephalogram rhythm in man: Effects on epilepsy. *Epilepsia*, 1974, *15*, 395–416.

Wright, L. Aversive conditioning of self-induced seizures. *Behavior Therapy*, 1973, *4*(5), 712–713.

Zlutnick, S., Mayville, W.J., & Moffat, S. Modification of seizure disorders: The interruption of behavioral chains. *Journal of Applied Behavior Analysis*, 1975, *8*(1), 1–12.

TABLE A-2

Tics

Authors and Date	Sample Characteristics	Treatment	Outcome	Follow-Up	Comments
Caine et al., 1979	12 subjects 12–54 yrs.	*Drug Treatment* 1) Double blind crossover clozapine or placebo for 4–7 weeks. 1 subject received only clozapine. 2) subjects received clozapine 3–5 weeks	*Tourette's* 5/7 showed no change; 2/7 showed slight decrease *Huntington's* 2/3 showed decrease in abnormal involuntary movement; 1/3 showed no change *Dyskinesia* 2/2 showed no change	—	Tourette's Syndrome, Huntington's disease and drug induced dyskinesia. 2 subjects with Huntington's experienced significant side effects. Clozapine was not effective
Cohen et al., 1979	8 subjects 10–16 yrs.	*Drug Treatment* Clonidine 0.05 mg daily increased in two stages to 0.15 mg daily	Decrease in tics; better frustration tolerance; able to write	Subjects treated for one year with clonidine with no serious side effects	Tourette's Syndrome: Subjects previously treated unsuccessfully with haloperidol or developed significant side effects
Golden, 1977	15 subjects 7–17 yrs.	*Drug Treatment* Received 1–5 mg daily of haloperidol	3/15 subjects had mild symptoms and did not require medication; 9/12 good response 2/12 fair response 1/12 inadequate response	—	Tourette's Syndrome: Side effects occurred in 5 subjects; 2 subjects required anti-Parkinsonian agents for extrapyramidal reaction
Shapiro et al., 1973	21 subjects	*Drug Treatment* Haloperidol 6–180 mg/day; all subjects received anti-Parkinsonian agents to reverse side effects	85% improvement	*12 months* 90% improvement *18 months* 95% improvement	Only subjects with diagnosed Tourette's Syndrome included. Required dosage of haloperidol stabilized after one year

TABLE A-2 **Tics** (continued)

Authors and Date	Sample Characteristics	Treatment	Outcome	Follow-Up	Comments
Yaryura-Tobias & Neziroglu, 1977	20 subjects 5–52 yrs.	*Drug Treatment* 1) 15 subjects received chlorimipramine (CLI); 2) 10/15 received CLI for 5 months; placebo 2 weeks and CLI 2 weeks	Group 1–80–90% control of symptoms; Group 2– 4/5 cases in which Tourette's recurred while subjects receiving placebo	—	Tourette's Syndrome: Prior haldol treatment unsuccessful or associated with severe side effects. CLI appears to be effective, with fewer side effects than haloperidol
Cohen et al., 1980	25 subjects 9–50 yrs.	*Drug Treatment* Clonidine hydrochloride of 0.15 mg gradually increased to 0.30 mg	70% responded positively. No serious side effects	—	Tourette's Syndrome: Haloperidol previously unsuccessful. Clonidine worked best in alleviating compulsive, aggressive, behavioral and attentional symptoms
Cohen & Marks, 1977	1 subject 11 yrs.	*Operant Conditioning* Reward with stars and money for vocal tic-free periods; required vocal tic-free time was gradually lengthened	No verbal tics after 6 weeks of treatment	*6 months* No vocal tics; frequency and severity of motor tics still at baseline level	Tourette's Syndrome
Thomas et al., 1971	1 subject 18 yrs.	*Reciprocal Inhibition and Drug Treatment* 1. Baseline 2. Treatment: a. Self-monitoring of tics b. Reciprocal inhibition (RI) c. Haloperidol	With RI and haloperidol, tics decreased to nearly zero; when haloperidol was discontinued tics increased	—	Tourette's Syndrome: Prior to behavioral therapy, medication was only partially successful

Doleys & Kurtz, 1974	1 subject 14 yrs.	*Selective Reinforcement* 1. Baseline 2. Treatment (5 months) a. Reinforcement of incompatible behavior during experimental task b. Reinforcement of social behaviors (eye contact and self-hygiene)	1. Increase in eye contact 2. Increase in social behaviors and self-hygiene. 3. Reduction in gutteral sounds	—	Tourette's Syndrome: Reduction in symptoms thought to be related to the low rate of reinforcement of vocal tics and reinforcement of adaptive behaviors
Friedman, 1980	1 subject 11 yrs.	*Self-Control and Relaxation* 1. Baseline 2. Treatment a. Control obscenities by having subject substitute a "clean" word b. Modified Jacobson's relaxation training with positive imagery	Baseline: verbal tics 150/hr. After treatment almost no coprolalic expressions, but muscular movements and tics still present	*4-18 months* Drug treatment also initiated. Only two occasions of coprolalia	Tourette's Syndrome: Medication more effective for muscle tics and movements; self-control strategies effective for coprolalia
Schulman, 1974	1 subject 14 yrs.	*Extinction* 1. Baseline 2. Mother told to ignore tics 3. Family therapy	Baseline = 3–15 tics/minute during mother-child conflict; after 9 weeks of treatment 2–3/week	*2 months* Tics occurred 3–4/week	Subject had multiple tics. Tics primarily occurred in mother's presence. Serious family conflict evident. Therapy was terminated prematurely
Canavan & Powell, 1981	1 subject 24 yrs.	*Massed Practice* 1. Massed practice of a single obscenity and relaxation 2. Massed practice of multiple obscenities	1. No change 2. No change	—	Tourette's Syndrome: Massed practice was not beneficial. It encouraged habit strength

TABLE A-2 Tics (*continued*)

Authors and Date	Sample Characteristics	Treatment	Outcome	Follow-Up	Comments
		3. Oral feedback ("No") whenever an obscenity occurred 4. Feedback ("No") and time-out following 1 min. of silence	3. Significant immediate effect, but did not carry through treatment session 4. Immediate within treatment session improvement was not maintained after 4 sessions		
Hollandsworth & Bausinger, 1978	1 subject 18 yrs.	*Massed Practice* For treatment of copralalia a $30 deposit was made; subject received $2 for each session completed. Monetary fines if target word used	Increased and improved articulation of coprolalia as treatment progressed; terminated therapy after 8 sessions	*6 months* Return to baseline	Tourette's Syndrome: Subject had both motor tics and coprolalia. Haloperidol and supportive therapy also unsuccessful
Tophoff, 1973	1 subject 13 yrs.	*Massed Practice* 1. Baseline 2. Massed practice and assertiveness training 3. Parents instructed to ignore tics.	Decrease in verbal tics to 0. Motor tics also disappeared	*4 months* Subject still symptom-free; functioning well socially	Tourette's Syndrome: Prior treatment with haloperidol, psychotherapy, and relaxation unsuccessful
Azrin & Nunn, 1973	12 subjects 5–64 yrs.	*Self-Monitoring* 1. Describe and enact habit 2. Alert subject to occurrence 3. Detect preliminary signs 4. Tense muscles incompat-	All subjects attained at least 90% reduction in the nervous habit after 1–2 sessions. 10/12 subjects had no nervous habits after 3rd week of treatment	*5 months* 7/12 subjects *2 months and 5 months* For 2/12 subjects (both required 1	Treatment for a variety of nervous habits (e.g., head jerking, lisping, nail biting, thumb or gum sucking). Follow-up not adequately documented

Study	Subject	Procedure	Results	Follow-up	Comments
		ible with habit 5. Explication of situations in which habits occur 6. Discuss social stigma of habit 7. Praise and reminders to practice			additional treatment session)

Hutzell et al., 1974	1 subject 11 yrs.	*Self-Monitoring*
		1. Baseline
		2. Treatment
		  a. Therapist observes and demonstrates tics; subject models
		  b. Self-monitoring using a hand held cumulative counter
		  c. Same procedure for barking
			1. Baseline for head jerks: 1.20/min. After treatment, 1.03/min
			2. Baseline for barking: 1.58/min. After treatment, 0.21 barks/min
				12 months
				Both parents and teacher reported no symptoms but experimenter observed that improvement maintained at treatment level
					Tourette's Syndrome: Both haloperidol and positive reinforcement procedure tried without success. Therapy more successful for vocal tics

Tic Table (A-2)
References

Azrin, N.H., & Nunn, R.G. Habit-reversal: A method of eliminating nervous habits and tics. *Behaviour Research and Therapy*, 1973, *11*, 619–628.

Caine, E.D., Polinsky, R.J., Kartzinel, R., & Ebert, M.H. The trial use of clozapine for abnormal involuntary movement disorders. *American Journal of Psychiatry*, 1979, *136*(3), 317–320.

Canavan, A.G.M., & Powell, G.E. The efficacy of several treatments of Gilles de la Tourette's Syndrome as assessed in a single case. *Behaviour Research and Therapy*, 1981, *19*, 549–556.

Cohen, D., & Marks, F.M. Gilles de la Tourette's Syndrome treated by operant conditioning. *British Journal of Psychiatry*, 1977, *130*, 315.

Cohen, D.J., Detlor, J., Young, J.G., & Shaywitz, B.A. Clonidine ameliorates Gilles de la Tourette Syndrome. *Archives of General Psychiatry*, 1980, *37*, 1350–1357.

Cohen, D.J., Young, J.G., Nathanson, J.A., & Shaywitz, B.A. Clonidine in Tourette's Syndrome. *Lancet*, 1979, *2*, 551–553.

Doleys, D.M., & Kurtz, P.S. A behavioral treatment program for the Gilles de la Tourette Syndrome. *Psychological Reports*, 1974, *35*, 43–48.

Friedman, S. Self-control in the treatment of Gilles de la Tourette's Syndrome: Case study with 18-month follow-up. *Journal of Consulting and Clinical Psychology*, 1980, *48*(3), 400–402.

Golden, G.S. Tourette Syndrome: The pediatric perspective. *American Journal of Diseases of Children*, 1977, *131*, 531–534.

Hollandsworth, J.G., Jr., & Bausinger, L. Unsuccessful use of massed practice in the treatment of Gilles de la Tourette's Syndrome. *Psychological Reports*, 1978, *43*, 671–677.

Hutzell, R.R., Platzek, D., & Logue, P.E. Control of symptoms of Gilles de la Tourette's Syndrome by self-monitoring. *Journal of Behavior Therapy and Experimental Psychiatry*, 1974, *5*, 71–76.

Schulman, M. Control of tics by maternal reinforcement. *Journal of Behavior Therapy and Experimental Psychiatry*, 1974, *5*, 95–96.

Shapiro, A.K., Shapiro, E., Wayne, H.L., Clarkin, J., & Bruun, R.D. Tourette's Syndrome: Summary of data on 34 patients. *Psychosomatic Medicine*, 1973, *35*(5), 419–435.

Thomas, E.J., Abrams, K.S., & Johnson, J.B. Self-monitoring and reciprocal inhibition in the modification of multiple tics of Gilles de la Tourette's Syndrome. *Journal of Behavior Therapy and Experimental Psychiatry*, 1971, *2*, 159–171.

Tophoff, M. Massed practice, relaxation and assertion training in the treatment of Gilles de la Tourette's Syndrome. *Journal of Behavior Therapy and Experimental Psychiatry*, 1973, *4*, 71–73.

Yaryura-Tobias, J.A., & Neziroglu, F.A. Gilles de la Tourette Syndrome: A new clinico-therapeutic approach. *Progress in Neuro-Psychopharmacology*, 1977, *1*, 335–338.

TABLE A-3

Intellectual Development in Children with Congenital Heart Defects

Author (Year)	Heart Group	N	x̄ Age in Years	Tests Given	x̄ IQ	Range	Comments
Linde et al., 1967	Cyanotic	98	3.6	Cattell, Gesell or Stanford-Binet	96.1	49–145	Although cyanotic children also showed a significant delay in motor development, such physical incapacity alone did not correlate positively with IQ
	Acyanotic	100	4.9		104.4	67–137	
	Normal Sib	81	5.3		110.2	81–170	
	Normal Control	40	2.9		111.9	82–158	
Feldt et al., 1969	Cyanotic	34	2–17 (Range)	Cattell or Stanford-Binet	95.7	47–154 SD=24.1	Incidence of MR 44% in cyanotic vs. 9% in acyanotic children. No relationship between severity of defect and psychometric score
	Acyanotic	44			103.6	24–142 SD=19.4	
Silbert et al., 1969	Cyanotic	15	5.8	Stanford-Binet (other tests not listed)	105.2	87–131	Significant differences found also favoring acyanotics on Frostig Perceptual Quotient and tests for gross motor performance
	Acyanotic w/congestive failure	12	6.0		114.9	100–137	
	Acyanotic w/o congestive failure	15	6.0		118.5	97–146	

TABLE A-4

Operated Versus Nonoperated CHD Children

Author (Year)	Heart Group	N	x̄ Age in Years	Preop IQ	Postop IQ	Comments
Finley et al., 1974	Tetralogy of Fallot	16, Blalock 21, No Blalock	8.75 6.75	106.1 97.0	110.5 98.2	Stanford-Binet given. Children who had a palliative operation (Blalock) prior to corrective surgery had higher preop IQ and made greater gains
Linde et al., 1970	Acyanotic op Acyanotic no op Cyanotic op Cyanotic no op Sibling Well baby	35 45 33 45 68 39		*1st Test* 102.3 105.2 99.9 94.6 110.3 112.8	*2nd Test* 103.3 109.9 105.2 95.1 113.9 114.5	Gesell, Cattell, and Stanford-Binet given. Greatest improvement in intellectual functioning, psychological adjustment, and physical ability occurred for operated cyanotic children
Honzik et al., 1969	Variety of heart defects	60 males 58 females	*Age Range in Years* 5–16	105 101	105.1 97.4	Stanford-Binet given preoperatively, WISC given postoperatively. Startling reversal of typical sex difference findings. Cardiac girls' verbal IQ was lower than boys' and performance IQ was higher than verbal IQ both before and after surgery
Cravioto et al., 1971	Acyanotic heart defects	22 Acyanotic, Mexican males 22 Matched, normal males 41 Acyanotic,	5–12	71.9 81.5	— —	WISC given. Reverse finding regarding sex differences to that of Honzik et al. Male cardiac patients had significantly lower IQ scores than controls, while female cardiac patients did not differ

Study	CHD type	Sample	Age			Comments
		Mexican females		79.1	--	
		39 Matched, normal females		76.2	—	
Honzik et al., 1976	Variety of CHDs	78 males	1–17 (majority were 4–8)	103.3	106.5	Stanford-Binet given. Cardiac children's IQ distribution is essentially normal. The IQ sex difference favoring the males is greatest in the low SES families. Pre- & postop perceptual motor deficits were suggested by the children's poor Bender-Gestalt scores
		77 females		100.0	100.8	

TABLE A-5

Intellectual Deficits Following Reparative Open Heart Surgery

Author (Year)	Cardiac Surgery	N	Mean Age in Years	Tests	IQ Scores & Ranges			Comments
					Preop	Postop	Range	
Whitman et al., 1973	Cardiopulmonary bypass	11	9.0	WISC	106.1	110.7	89–138 Pre / 88–142 Post	No apparent deleterious effect on IQ
	Other method	7	8.0		107.6	105.7	94–128 Pre / 91–131 Post	
Haka-Ikse et al., 1978	Deep hypothermia with circulatory arrest	17	2.25	Yale Developmental Scale	–	92.5 ± 12.7 (Developmental Quotient (DQ))		Duration of cardiorespiratory arrest did not negatively influence outcome. DQ of cardiac patients lower than siblings
Dickinson & Sambrooks, 1979	Deep hypothermia with circulatory arrest	38	4.16	WPPSI, WISC-R or Merrill-Palmer	Cyanotics 99.0 ± 19.5 Acyanotics 99.7			Wide variation in SD of IQ score as duration of arrest increased. No relationship to $\bar{x}$ age or weight at operation
Messmer et al., 1976	Deep hypothermia & arrest	11	7.0	Variety	SON 107 ± 32			Study did not find $\bar{x}$ differences between groups, but did find significantly different variances
	Other method	11	6.5		HAWIK 101 ± 28			
					Normal Physical	Normal Intel		
Wright et al., 1979	VSD continuous perfusion	15	–	Developmental assessment	80%	80%		Authors suggest need for more careful assessment of sequelae of deep hypothermia with arrest
	VSD deep hypothermia with arrest	17	–		41%	53%		

Wagner & Subramanian, 1978	Deep hypothermia with arrest	36	—	Binet Wisconsin Rating	Bright *Postop* 19.4% Average 61.1% Dull 11.1% EMR 8.3%	Authors stress need for careful monitoring of growth, development, behavior, and scholastic performance
Stevenson et al., 1974	Surface induced hypothermia with arrest	9 21 (includes above 9) 11	— — —	Variety Variety Denver Developmental	*Preop* *Postop* 103 95 Cyanotics 107 Acyanotics 91 9 pts ≥ CA 2 pts ≤ CA	Infants w/cyanotic defects were corrected at sufficiently young ages that adverse effects of hypoxia may have been reduced. 7/32 or 22% of sample performed at EMR level or below

Congenital Heart Defects Tables (A-3, A-4, A-5)
References

Cravioto, J., Lindoro, M., & Birch, H.G. Sex differences in I.Q. pattern of children with congenital heart defects. *Science*, 1971, *174*, 1042–1043.

Dickinson, D.F., & Sambrooks, J.E. Intellectual performance in children after circulatory arrest with profound hypothermia in infancy. *Archives of Disease in Childhood*, 1979, *54*, 1–6.

Feldt, R.H., Ewert, J.C., Stickler, G.B., & Weidman, W.H. Children with congenital heart disease: Motor development and intelligence. *American Journal of Diseases of Children*, 1969, *117*, 281–287.

Finley, K.H., Buse, S.T., Popper, R.W., Honzik, M.P., Collart, D.S., & Riggs, N. Intellectual functioning of children with tetralogy of Fallot: Influence of open-heart surgery and earlier palliative operations. *The Journal of Pediatrics*, 1974, *85*(3), 318–323.

Haka-Ikse, K., Blackwood, M.J., & Steward, D.J. Psychomotor development of infants and children after profound hypothermia during surgery for congenital heart disease. *Developmental Medicine and Child Neurology*, 1978, *20*, 62–70.

Honzik, M.P., Buse, S.T., Fitzgerald, L.H., & Collart, D.S. Psychologic development. In L.J. Bayer & M.P. Honzik (Eds.), *Children with congenital intracardiac defects: A pictorial atlas of individual somatic and neuropsychologic development before and after open heart surgery*. Springfield, Illinois: Charles C. Thomas, 1976.

Honzik, M.P., Collart, D.S., Robinson, S.J., & Finley, K.H. Sex differences in verbal and performance IQ's of children undergoing open-heart surgery. *Science*, 1969, *164*, 445–447.

Linde, L.M., Rasof, B., & Dunn, O.J. Mental development in congenital heart disease. *The Journal of Pediatrics*, 1967, *71*, 198–203.

Linde, L.M., Rasof, B., & Dunn, O.J. Longitudinal studies of intellectual and behavioral development in children with congenital heart disease. *Acta Paediatrica Scandinavica*, 1970, *59*, 169–176.

Messmer, B.J., Schallberger, U., Gattiker, R., & Senning, A. Psychomotor and intellectual development after deep hypothermia and circulatory arrest in early infancy. *The Journal of Thoracic and Cardiovascular Surgery*, 1976, *72*(4), 495–502.

Silbert, A., Wolff, P.H., Mayer, B., Rosenthal, A., & Nadas, A.S. Cyanotic heart disease and psychological development. *Pediatrics*, 1969, *43*(2), 192–200.

Stevenson, J.G., Stone, E.F., Dillard, D.H., & Morgan, B.C. Intellectual development of children subjected to prolonged circulatory arrest during hypothermic open heart surgery in infancy. *Circulation*, 1974, *49–50* (Suppl. II), 54–59.

Wagner, H.R., & Subramanian, S. Deep hypothermia in infant cardiac surgery. *Pediatrics*, 1978, *61*(3), 479–483.

Whitman, V., Drotar, D., Lambert, S., VanHeeckeren, D.W., Borkat, G., Ankeney, J., & Liebman, J. Effects of cardiac surgery with extracorporeal circulation on intellectual function in children. *Circulation*, 1973, *48*, 160–163.

Wright, L., Schaefer, A.B., & Solomons, G. *Encyclopedia of pediatric psychology*. Baltimore: University Park Press, 1979.

TABLE A-6

Diabetes

Authors and Date	Sample Characteristics	Assessment	Outcome	Comments
Johnson et al., 1982	151 children 6–18 yrs. 179 parents	*Assessment of Knowledge of Diabetes* 1) General information (39 multiple choice questions) cause, terms, facts; 2) What to do in diabetes problem situations (36 multiple choice questions)	1) Understanding of relationship between insulin, exercise, and stress often not sufficient to make accurate management decisions; 2) 15–18 yr. olds knew more than 9–14 yr. olds who did not differ; 6–8 yrs. evidenced poorest performance; 3) mothers knew more than fathers; girls more accurate than boys	8 content areas examined; diet, insulin, urine testing, insulin reactions, illness, exercise, anxiety/excitement, miscellaneous. Duration of diabetes was not significantly related to knowledge
Etzwiler, 1962	74 children 6–17 yrs.	*Assessment of Knowledge of Diabetes* 15 multiple-choice questions on fundamental concepts and management	1) Significant difference in knowledge regarding insulin, blood sugar, cause, etc., between children 6–11 yrs. and those 12 and older; 2) meaning and interpretation of urine tests not understood until child over 10 years old	Self-care may be forced on the diabetic child before he has the cognitive maturity to understand the fundamental relationships between insulin, blood sugar, and food intake
Collier & Etzwiler, 1971	129 children 12–18 yrs. 141 parents	*Assessment of Knowledge of Diabetes* 34 multiple choice questions	1) Parents gave higher proportion of correct answers, although parent-child pairs were highly correlated; 2) poor knowledge recognizing acidosis, understanding insulin time reactions, testing for acetone, and dietary management; 3) no relationship found between grade level, duration of diabetes, and mother's education level	Contrary to expectation, diabetic children having diabetic parents actually knew *less* about their illness than those not having had a family history. Information given primarily by pediatrician or family physician to the parent

TABLE A-6 **Diabetes** (*continued*)

Authors and Date	Sample Characteristics	Assessment	Outcome	Comments
Etzwiler & Robb, 1972	66 children 9–18 yrs. 114 parents	*Programmed Instruction on Knowledge of Diabetes* 1) Initial Diabetes Knowledge Test; 2) Assessment of academic achievement; 3) Pre- and post-fasting blood sugar and 24 hour urine collection; 4) Auto-Tutor machine programmed education	1) Pretest diabetes knowledge positively correlated with chronological age; 2) knowledge increased following programmed instruction; retained at 3 month follow-up; 3) No significant changes in fasting blood glucose levels or amount of urinary glucose excreted after instruction; 4) parent's knowledge did not differ from that of child's	Increased knowledge did not result in increased control as measured by fasting, blood sugar and urine collection. Vocabulary used in instruction judged difficult for 9–12 yr. olds; Short (6–12 months) and long (> 5 yr) duration associated with greater knowledge
Malone et al., 1976	220 children 54 cooperated completely 7–18 yrs.	*Accuracy of Urine Glucose Testing and Assessment of Diabetic Control* Child tested urine sample 3x/day for urine reducing sugar concentration (URS). 2 specimens on 2 days kept for lab tech to check; blood specimens before breakfast and 2 hrs. after eating in afternoon tested for plasma glucose level; 24 hr. collection of total urine voided tested for URS	1) 74% complied with request to determine URS; 2) 51% of urines tested by child agreed with lab tech; 3) in 41% of the disagreements the child reported a lower URS value; 4) good control in 18/54 subjects	Plasma glucose levels taken in morning and afternoon varied in 50% of the children. Correlations between 24 hr. excretion of reducing sugar inconsistent. These measures do not reflect consistent or accurate metabolic state
Sönksen et al., 1978	64 subjects 15–53 yrs.	*Assessment of Blood Glucose Concentration* Subjects taught to measure glucose in capillary blood with Dextrostix and Eyetone meter. Blood was obtained by finger prick with disposable needle	64% of subjects were able to maintain good diabetic control; 80% of blood glucose readings ≤ 10 mmol/1; adjustments of insulin dosage and type was easier and more predictable; hypoglycemic episodes were less frequent	11 subjects did not cooperate fully. Results suggest that self-monitoring of blood glucose achieved better diabetic control than urine-glucose analysis. 70% of subjects preferred blood tests

Walford et al., 1978	69 subjects 14–65 yrs.	*Assessment of Blood Glucose Concentration* Subjects taught to measure blood glucose with reflotest strips and relfomat machine. Blood samples taken at preset intervals throughout day and evening. When possible urine tests were taken simultaneously	48% of subjects achieved good diabetic control (only 1 blood-glucose value exceeded 10 mmol/1). Self-monitoring was helpful in highlighting problems in control, preventing hypoglycemia and managing pregnancy. Urine and blood glucose often correlate poorly and isolated blood glucose measurements often are unrepresentative	Subjects participating included pregnant women (8), subjects with good control (17), subjects poorly controlled (26), and subjects with significant complications or problems (18). Blood glucose testing was preferred by subjects and could be employed even by those with limited education
Johnson et al., 1982	151 children 6–18 yrs.	*Accuracy of Urine Glucose Testing* Children were asked to test a 7% sugar urine (sugar content unknown to child), sample, and prepare to self-inject insulin. The test was marked pass or fail by the examiner	1) Over 80% of children made one or more serious error on urine test. Most common error was incorrect timing on test for acetone. 2) 40% made one or more serious error on the self-injection test. Most common error was bubbles in insulin. 3) Girls more accurate than boys and older children more accurate than younger children on both tests.	Skill level of children with diabetes is poor and current instruction is inadequate for home management. Recommended instruction in self-injection at age 9, but not complete responsibility for urine testing until at least age 12
Epstein et al., 1980 Part I	81 children 6–17 yrs.	*Accuracy of Urine Glucose Testing* Children were presented 3 prepared glucose solutions and asked to determine glucose concentration using the Clinitest method	Children were correct 45.7% of the time across all concentrations; errors were in timing or difficulty in discriminating colors; accuracy decreased as concentrations approached 1% glucose; 93% of the errors were underestimates	Accuracy improves at extreme values of negative or 5%. Tendency to underestimate glucose concentrations may be an attempt to minimize the seriousness or lack of control of urine glucose
Epstein et al., 1980 Part II	12 adults	*Accuracy of Urine Glucose Testing and Feedback Training* Pretraining assessment of urine glu-	In pretraining subjects were correct 61% of the time; with training they were correct 84% of the	Improvement in accuracy was statistically significant. Training can be readily adapted for in-

TABLE A-6 **Diabetes** (*continued*)

Authors and Date	Sample Characteristics	Assessment	Outcome	Comments
		cose testing in 10 nurses and 2 technicians; visual discrimination training with feedback. Subjects told if correct; if incorrect, shown true concentration	time and showed a reduction in underestimates	structing children in self-regulation
Epstein et al., 1981b	73 children 6–17 yrs.	*Accuracy of Urine Glucose Testing and Feedback Training* Pretraining assessment of urine glucose testing in 10 samples; children obtaining at least 50% inaccuracy were given either extended practice or feedback training	*Pre and Post Assessment* Mean number of correct responses 5.17 (SD = 2); Mean number of correct responses was 3.8 for extended practice and 7.2 for feedback	Extended practice resulted in a deterioration in performance, whereas informational feedback resulted in an increase in accuracy from 36% to 72%
Epstein et al., 1981a	19 children 6–12 yrs.	*Instruction and Behavioral Management* 1) Instruction in insulin reactions, adjustment and self-administration of injections, exercise, diet, and stress management 2) Use of point economy and praise to reward appropriate self-monitoring 3) Parent check on reliability of child's urine testing using identification of placebo tablets	1) Increase in % of negative urines and glycosylated hemoglobin (GHb) 2) No change in blood glucose or units of insulin/kg body weight 3) % of negative urine and GHb significantly correlated 4) All children learned self-administration *2 months* 1) increase in % of negative urines and % GHb values maintained 2) Significant increase in cholesterol level 3) % negative urines and GHb no longer correlated	Multiple baseline across groups design. Significant change in % of negative urine not associated with improvement in diabetic control. More precise measures such as blood glucose monitoring may be needed to appropriately adjust insulin to metabolic needs

Seeburg & DeBoer, 1980	1 subject 24 yrs.	*Frontalis EMG Biofeedback* 1) Three 25 min. sessions/ week for 8 weeks. 2) 6 months no treatment 3) EMG biofeedback 1 week	1) 25% reduction in insulin dosage after 8 weeks 2) Treatment discontinued due to hypoglycemic symptoms 3) Reinstating biofeedback led to severe insulin reaction	*12 months* Subject restabilized at a lower total amount of insulin	Subject had juvenile onset diabetes. Biofeedback was associated with change to poorer control. Caution is suggested in using this technique with diabetic patients
Fowler et al., 1976	1 subject 20 yrs.	*Frontalis EMG Biofeedback* 1) Baseline for one semester 2) 30–40 min. sessions 2x/ day for one semester using a portable EMG unit and relaxation tapes	1) Decrease in baseline level of 85 units of insulin/day to 44 units/day 2) Decrease in urine sugars	*6 months* 52 units/day of insulin required; decrease in urine sugars	Juvenile onset diabetes. Subject experienced severe insulin reaction during treatment due to rapid decrease in insulin requirements. During training subject rated herself as less emotional and in more stable diabetic control

Diabetes (Table A-6)
References

Collier, B.N., Jr., & Etzwiler, D.D. Comparative study of diabetes knowledge among juvenile diabetics and their parents. *Diabetes*, 1971, *20*(1), 51-57.

Epstein, L.H., Coburn, P.C., Becker, D., Drash, A., & Siminerio, L. Measurement and modification of the accuracy of determinations of urine glucose concentration. *Diabetes Care*, 1980, *3*(4), 535-536.

Epstein, L.H., Beck, S., Figueroa, J., Farkas, G., Kazdin, A.E., Daneman, D., & Becker, D. The effects of targeting improvements in urine glucose on metabolic control in children with insulin dependent diabetes. *Journal of Applied Behavior Analysis*, 1981a, *14*(4), 365-375.

Epstein, L.H., Figueroa, J., Farkas, G.M., & Beck, S. The short-term effects of feedback on accuracy of urine glucose determinations in insulin dependent diabetic children. *Behavior Therapy*, 1981b, *12*, 560-564.

Etzwiler, D.D. What the juvenile diabetic knows about his disease. *Pediatrics*, 1962, *29*, 135-141.

Etzwiler, D.D., & Robb, J.R. Evaluation of programmed education among juvenile diabetics and their families. *Diabetes*, 1972, *21*(9), 967-971.

Fowler, J.E., Budzynski, T.H., & VandenBergh, R.L. Effects of an EMG biofeedback relaxation program on the control of diabetes. *Biofeedback and Self-Regulation*, 1976, *1*(1), 105-112.

Johnson, S.B., Pollak, R.T., Silverstein, J.H., Rosenbloom, A.L., Spillar, R., McCallum, M., & Harkavy, J. Cognitive and behavioral knowledge about insulin-dependent diabetes among children and parents. *Pediatrics*, 1982, *69*(6), 708-713.

Malone, J.I., Hellrung, J.M., Malphus, E.W., Rosenbloom, A.L., Grgic, A., & Weber, F.T. Good diabetic control—a study in mass delusion. *The Journal of Pediatrics*, 1976, *88*(6), 943-947.

Seeburg, K.N., & DeBoer, K.F. Effects of EMG biofeedback on diabetes. *Biofeedback and Self-Regulation*, 1980, *5*(2), 289-293.

Sönksen, P.H., Judd, S.L., & Lowy, C. Home monitoring of blood-glucose: Method for improving diabetic control. *The Lancet*, 1978, *1*, 729-732.

Walford, S., Gale, E.A.M., Allison, S.P., & Tattersall, R.B. Self-monitoring of blood-glucose: Improvement of diabetic control. *The Lancet*, 1978, *1*, 732-735.

TABLE A-7

Gastrointestinal Disorders
RUMINATION

Authors and Date	*Sample Characteristic*	*Treatment*	*Outcome*	*Follow-Up*	*Comments*
Cunningham & Linscheid, 1976	1 infant 9.5 months rumination	*Aversive Conditioning* Electric shock given when subject ruminated; terminated when rumination stopped. Treatment was conducted in different environments	Decrease in rumination and amount of emesis. Weight gain and improvement in social behavior	*3 months* Motor, mental, and speech development normal *6 months* Weight gain; no rumination	Infant severely malnourished. Previous treatments had been ineffective
Flanagan, 1977	1 infant 8 months rumination	*Positive Reinforcement* Staff fed child a regular diet. Staff played with child for about 1 hour after eating	Increase in weight; decrease in rumination	*6 months* Child still gaining weight and almost no vomiting	Mother followed and supported by nurse and social worker after child discharged from hospital
Lang & Melamed, 1969	1 infant 9 months rumination	*Aversive Conditioning* Shock was delivered as soon as vomiting occurred, until that response was terminated. The treatment was continued until there were 3 sessions in which no vomiting occurred. 2 days after treatment terminated, there was a	Marked reduction in rumination and vomiting behavior (almost no vomiting observed). 26% increase in body weight	*1 month; 5 months* Weight gain continued. Vomiting had not recurred *12 months* Follow-up pediatric exam was normal	Vomiting and rumination were judged to be life threatening. Only after all previous treatments had failed was aversive conditioning attempted. EMG recording during treatment documented mouth and throat movement preceding vomiting

TABLE A-7 RUMINATION (continued)

Authors and Date	Sample Characteristic	Treatment	Outcome	Follow-Up	Comments
		resumption of rumination and this required 3 more treatment sessions			
Linscheid & Cunningham, 1977	1 infant 9 months rumination	*Aversive Conditioning* Baseline. Electric shock until rumination ceased. Treatment reversal. Reinstate electric shock	Decrease in rumination and crying; increase in weight gain and social interaction. Reversal resulted in increase in rumination	*9 months* No rumination	Infant was hospitalized with severe weight loss, malnutrition and medical problems. Shock intensity elicited a startle reaction, but no crying
Murray et al., 1976	1 infant 6 months rumination	*Reinforcement and Aversive Conditioning* Thicken subject's food. Affection during feeding. No physical contact during emetic episode. Punishment: Tabasco sauce in mouth when subject rolls tongue. Child picked up when tongue rolling ceases	Rumination under control; weight gain; decrease in punishment; decrease in volume of vomitus; subject more alert, active, and sociable	*4 months* Weight gain; no vomiting	Effective treatment requires combination of positive reinforcement and punishment procedures. Weight increased in 11 days; total treatment was 3 weeks
Toister et al., 1975	1 infant 7½ months rumination	*Aversive Conditioning* Baseline. Shock contingent on vomiting	Reduction in vomiting, stereotyped rocking and hand posturing. Increase in social behavior and weight	*8 months* No vomiting, continued weight gain and normal development	Subject unsuccessfully treated with thickened feedings, postprandial posturing, parental counseling and increased attention

Wright et al., 1978	1 infant 9 months rumination and failure to thrive	*Time Out* Baseline. Treatment: staff and parents instructed to put subject down and leave room when rumination occurs, and to return 3 minutes later to wipe mouth	After 68 days of treatment, rumination eliminated; subject growth increased and weight increased from 4th percentile to 18th percentile	*251 days* Weight at 55th percentile	If condition is life threatening electroshock may produce more rapid remission. Reinforcement procedure although effective, required considerable time in the hospital; family pathology also requires intervention
Sajwaj et al., 1974	1 infant 6 months rumination	*Aversive Conditioning* Baseline. Lemon juice squirted in mouth when movements associated with rumination occurred. Reversal Reinstatement of lemon juice therapy	54% increase in weight. Decrease in rumination and tongue movements. Increased interest in environment. Baby discharged to foster home after 8 weeks of therapy in hospital	*12 month period* (7 visitations); 2 brief episodes of rumination; weight continued to increase although weight at one year follow-up only at 25th percentile	Previous hospitalization for feeding problems due to cleft lip and palate; child previously neglected, from an unstable family

TABLE A-7
ENCOPRESIS

Authors and Date	Sample Size	Age	Treatment	Outcome	Follow-Up	Comments
Engel et al., 1974	7	1 child 6 yrs. 6 adults	Biofeedback	4 patients completely continent since their last lab studies; 2 improved; 1 withdrew	6 months–5 yrs.	Child had myelomeningocele and also received positive reinforcement (verbal and toy)
Olness et al., 1980	50	4–18 yrs.	Biofeedback and Education	47 learned to have voluntary bowel movements and 30 eliminated soiling accidents	6 months–3 yrs.	Sample consisted of children with histories of chronic soiling and constipation (40) and 10 children with repair of imperforate anus
Hardin et al., 1982	32	5–18 yrs. x̄ = 8.8 yrs.	Biofeedback (11) Laxative Therapy (21)	45% of subjects improved (36% no soiling; 9% < 3 times/week) with 3 months biofeedback. 62% improved (24% no soiling; 38% < 3 times/week) with 3 months laxatives	After 6 months, 54% improved with biofeedback alone, 62% with laxative alone; 73% with both	Biofeedback did improve rectal sensation, but standard laxative therapy more effective for control of soiling. Compliance significantly related to treatment success
Olness, 1976	5	3½–5 yrs.	Autohypnosis (self-hypnosis using coin induction method)	4 children developed the ability to control bowel movements; 5th child not treated due to organic cause	1 year	All children in the study had undergone long periods of medical and surgical management without improvement
Peterson & London, 1965	1	3 yrs.	Hypnosis attempted and positive reinforcement (popsicle and verbal praise)	3 therapy sessions and 75 days of positive reinforcement resulted in no soiling	1 year: remission complete	Formal hypnosis unsuccessful

	N	Age	Treatment	Results	Follow-up	Comments
Silber, 1968	9	5–9 yrs.	*Hypnosis* with imagery and enemas initially	All responded quickly and successfully to treatment	1 child required 2 repeat sessions after initial treatment	Details reported on only one case
Davidson et al., 1963	119	children	*Pediatric Management:* enemas and laxatives; toilet-training; follow-up	Approximately 90% of those without organic disease developed regular bowel habits	80 out of 119 remained symptom free at follow-up (6 months–7 yrs.)	Classic description of pediatric management of this problem
Levine & Bakow, 1976	127	$\bar{x}$ = 8.16 yrs.	*Pediatric Management:* education; bowel catharsis; laxatives; bowel training	51% no accidents for more than 6 months; 27% marked improvement, rare episodes of incontinence; 14% some improvement; 8% no improvement	1 year outcome on 110 patients	Pediatric management successful in 75% of cases; severity of incontinence and constipation, compliance and multiple additional problems were characteristic of treatment failures.
Young, 1973	24	4–10 yrs.	*Pediatric Management:* Medical exam; enemas; gastro-ileal reflex training (toilet training); Senokot tablets daily	92% successful; 19 subjects successfully completed treatment in less than a year; 3 subjects successfully completed treatment in over 1 year's time. 2 subjects no response	6 months–6 yrs. symptoms recurred in 4 subjects	Combination of physiologic and behavioral approaches successful without requiring hospitalization
Ashkenazi, 1975	18	3–12 yrs.	*Pediatric Management & Behavior Therapy* After meals glycerine suppository given; 15–20 minutes later, subject sent to toilet. If elimination occurs receives praise and toy.	16/18 successful treatment	3–6 months; no relapse	1 group of children had potty or toilet phobia; the phobic reaction was deconditioned. Duration of encopresis in those successfully treated was 4 months–3 years. Purpose of treatment is to make rectal distention a dis-

TABLE A-7 ENCOPRESIS (*continued*)

Authors and Date	*Sample Size*	*Age*	*Treatment*	*Outcome*	*Follow-Up*	*Comments*
			If no soiling at end of day, given a small toy; After 5 consecutive days of no soiling, suppository is discontinued. If no bowel action one day, then suppository given next day. Mother phases out toys and praise intermittently			criminitive stimulus for elimination (by using suppository)
Neale, 1963	4	7½–10 yrs.	*Pediatric Management & Behavior Therapy* Abdominal rectal exam. Laxative given if needed. Diagnosis of behavioral etiology of encopresis. Operant conditioning (praise, candy, treats given following bowel movement)	1 child failed to become continent	4 months–3/4 still continent, but not normal (rectum not empty)	Children were selected from a children's psychiatric inpatient unit
Nilsson, 1976	5	5–7 yrs.	*Pediatric Management & Behavior Therapy* enemas and token economy; 8–14 weeks of treatment	4/5 no soiling after implementation of token economy; 1 child showed decrease	1 year–3/5 required reimplementation of token economy	Pretreatment assessment should include evaluation of neurologic factors, bowel impaction, and psychopathology

	N	Age	Method	Results	Follow-up	Comments
Wright, 1975 (see also Wright & Walker, 1977)	14	3–9 yrs.	*Pediatric Management & Behavior Therapy* Exam by M.D.; enemas; Positive and negative reinforcement; Parental instruction	14 subjects showed no soiling after 10–38 weeks	6 months–1 patient regressed	Problem typically alleviated after 15–20 weeks of treatment Hospitalization not required. Treatment given by parents and monitored by technician. Practical and cost effective
Wright, 1973	36	children	*Pediatric Management & Behavior Therapy* (See Above)	Soiling decreased 75–90%	10–15% regression following completion	(See Above)
Doleys & Arnold, 1975	1	8 yrs.	*Behavior Therapy* 1. Shaping (positive reinforcement; imitation of peers toileting) 2. Food and verbal reinforcement of independent toileting 3. Toilet training each hour for 10 mins. 4. Punishment (verbal displeasure and self-cleaning and washing of soiled underwear)	Bowel control at end of 16th week of treatment	6 months–soiling once a week	Trainable mentally retarded child. Program required hourly monitoring by parents which was difficult to sustain. Reinforcement occurred at home and school
Doleys et al., 1977	3	4–9 yrs.	*Behavior Therapy* 1. Periodic pant and/ or toileting checks 2. Reinforcement for appropriate toileting 3. Full cleanliness training (FCT) contingent upon soiling (displeasure expressed; child scrubs undergarments and bathes in cold water)	Bowel control after 8 weeks of treatment	8 months–2 soilings for 1 subject; 3–6 months–2 subjects bowel control	FCT may increase negative confrontations between parents and child; to encourage a child to take responsibility for behavior, author describes a "verbal rationale" which could be used in addition to punishment procedure

TABLE A-7 ENCOPRESIS (continued)

Authors and Date	Sample Size	Age	Treatment	Outcome	Follow-Up	Comments
Edelman, 1971	1	12 yrs.	*Behavior Therapy* Operant conditioning employing punishment and negative reinforcement	1. Punishment alone—decrease in mean soiling rate/week from 6.31 to 3.73 2. Punishment and avoidance—decrease in mean soiling rate/week from 6.31–0.93	3 months—complete suppression of soiling	First 10 weeks punishment alone. After this, no soiling was also reinforced by allowing child to avoid aversive task
Gelber & Meyer, 1965	1	13 yrs.	*Behavior Therapy* Operant conditioning in hospital setting. Positive reinforcement (i.e., time off ward) and punishment (deduction from earned time off)	Continent after 45 days and 62 days of inpatient treatment.	6 months—incontinent twice in first 3 months; no soiling in next 3 months.	Prior to treatment child seen in weekly psychotherapeutic sessions; mother seen by psychiatric social worker
Keehn, 1965	1	5 yrs.	*Behavior Therapy* Reinforcement—chocolate given upon elimination in toilet	No soiling	2 months—no relapse	Informal treatment program. Frequency of chocolate reinforcement greatly reduced
Logan & Garner, 1971	1	7 yrs.	*Behavior Therapy* Operant conditioning buzzer alarm system; positive reinforcement	Striking decrease in number of soiling incidents/day, until several weeks without soiling	Next school year no problems	Prior to treatment subject underwent surgery for Hirschprung's disease. Entire class rewarded for his success

	N	Age	Treatment	Results		Comments
McDonagh, 1971	1	12 yrs.	*Behavior Therapy* Operant conditioning, positive reinforcement (praise, candy, social contact)	Decrease in frequency of soiling until last week when subject was to be transferred to mental hospital	—	Premature withdrawal of support and treatment due to transfer to a state hospital resulted in considerable increase in encopresis despite initial success.
Ringdahl, 1980	13	children	*Behavior Therapy* Program for hospital setting; behavior modification, individual, group, occupational and and family therapy concurrently	12 improved or no soiling; 1 mother refused to cooperate	12 months–2 children had a recurrence of symptoms; problem remitted with hospitalization	Behavior modification used positive reinforcement techniques; serious family conflict in all cases (10/13 divorced)

TABLE A-7

INCONTINENCE AND COLITIS

Authors and Date	Sample Characteristics	Treatment	Outcome	Follow-Up	Comments
Whitehead et al., 1981	8 subjects 5–15 yrs. myelomeningocele fecal incontinence	*Biofeedback* 1. Assessment of rectal distention sensory threshhold 2. Taught to contract external anal sphincter when not distended, when distended, and during internal sphincter inhibition 3. Feedback provided by polygraph training	5/8 continent 1/8 80% reduction 2/8 not continent (subjects could not contract external anal sphincter) Most subjects discontinued use of suppositories and enemas after treatment	*13–24 months* 4/5 continent or accident once/month or less 1/8 maintained 80% reduction 2/8 unchanged	Treatment for fecal incontinence. Verbal feedback gradually replaced visual feedback. Failures may have been due to subject's young age and cognitive immaturity
Mitchell, 1978	1 subject 37 yrs. spastic colitis	*Relaxation* Baseline. Self-management. Stage 1. Train client to identify antecedents of anxiety Stage 2. Progressive muscle relaxation by audiotape for 6 weeks. Stage 3. Four 30 minute audiotapes which taught techniques for control of worry, fear and anxiety	At end of Stage 2: 57% reduction in muscle tension and 41% reduction in frequency of colitis attacks At end of Stage 3: 59% reduction in intrusive cognitions and 85% reduction in frequency of colitis attacks	*3 months* Improvements maintained. 60% reduction in intrusive cognitions; 94% reduction in colitis attacks	Combination of muscle relaxation training and cognitive control particularly helpful in reducing both tension and anxiety about academic success as well as the frequency of colitis attacks

| Susen, 1978 | 1 subject 35 yrs. ulcerative colitis | *Relaxation* Relaxation training with emphasis on abdominal relaxation. Later subject was taught to induce relaxation at onset of pain | Pain and symptoms extinguished after 3 months | *12 months* Symptoms have not recurred | Symptom onset appeared related to stress of a new job situation. Patient had experienced symptoms for about 4 years |

TABLE A-7

IRRITABLE BOWEL SYNDROME AND ULCERS

Authors and Date	Sample Characteristics	Treatment	Outcome	Follow-Up	Comments
Heefer et al., 1978	31 subjects 18–76 yrs. Irritable Bowel Syndrome	*Drug Treatment* 14 subjects received 150 mg daily desipramine hydrochloride (tricyclic antidepressant) 17 subjects received placebo medication	Depression frequently associated with IBS. The placebo alone was associated with some improvement in depressive symptoms, GI disturbances, and level of daily functioning. The tricyclic antidepressant medication resulted in greater improvement in daily activities. Improvement in GI symptoms and depression not statistically different between drug and placebo groups	Data available only on a subsample	Of 44 initial subjects, 13 did not complete the study. 3 patients had medication side effects. Zung Self-Rating Depression Scale employed. Medication recommended primarily for IBS patients in which depression is an important symptom
Garrick, 1981	1 subject 40 yrs. Irritable Bowel Syndrome	*Psychotherapy* Baseline of activities and pain. Treatment: communication skills training to facilitate marital interaction	After 16 biweekly sessions: No diarrhea No pain Off medication Occasional abdominal tenseness	*4, 18, 24 months* No diarrhea, but occasional abdominal tenseness	Therapist thought pain was associated with marital problems. After 1 year subject divorced husband
Wise et al., 1982	20 subjects 23–70 yrs. Irritable Bowel Syndrome	*Group Therapy* 6 group therapy sessions 90 minutes in length. (Education, diet, stress, coping techniques, relaxa-	15–30% improvement in gaseousness, cramping, constipation, and diarrhea. 50% of subjects changed their diet. 40% rated relaxation	*6 months* Improvements maintained	Psychological changes most evident in symptoms of interpersonal sensitivity, depression, anxiety, hostility, and obsessive-compulsiveness. Group

Study	Subjects	Treatment	Results	Follow-up
		tion, and behavioral diaries)	exercises as helpful. Significant reduction in psychological stress	therapy most beneficial for patients characterized as field dependent and external in their locus of control
Brooks & Richardson, 1980	22 adults, Duodenal Ulcers	*Assertiveness Training* Group 1: 11 subjects—emotional skills training included assertiveness training and anxiety management in 8 60–90 minute sessions. Group 2: 11 subjects attention placebo treatment	Treatment group had less severe symptoms and fewer symptomatic days than controls. Treatment group took significantly less antacid than controls. Treatment group reported lower levels of general anxiety and were more assertive than controls	*3½ years* Significantly lower rate of ulcer recurrence in the treatment group; i.e., 1/9 treatment subjects and 5/8 placebo subjects had a recurrence of duodenal ulcer	Results based on patient's responses to 3 questionnaires (state-trait anxiety, constriction and assertiveness) as well as an examination of medical records

Gastrointestinal Disorders (Table A-7)
References

Ashkenazi, Z. The treatment of encopresis using a discriminative stimulus and positive reinforcement. *Journal of Behavior Therapy and Experimental Psychiatry*, 1975, *6*, 155–157.

Brooks, G.R., & Richardson, F.C. Emotional skills training: A treatment program for duodenal ulcer. *Behavior Therapy*, 1980, *11*, 198–207.

Cunningham, C.E., & Linscheid, T.R. Elimination of chronic infant ruminating by electric shock. *Behavior Therapy*, 1976, *7*, 231–234.

Davidson, M., Kugler, M.M., & Bauer, C.H. Diagnosis and management in children with severe and protracted constipation and obstipation. *The Journal of Pediatrics*, 1963, *62*, 261–275.

Doleys, D.M., & Arnold, S. Treatment of childhood encopresis: Full cleanliness training. *Mental Retardation*, 1975, *13*(6), 14–16.

Doleys, D.M., McWhorter, A.Q., Williams, S.C., & Gentry, W.R. Encopresis: Its treatment and relation to nocturnal enuresis. *Behavior Therapy*, 1977, *8*, 77–82.

Edelman, R.I. Operant conditioning treatment of encopresis. *Journal of Behavior Therapy and Experimental Psychiatry*, 1971, *2*, 71–73.

Engel, B.T., Nikoomanesh, P., & Schuster, M.M. Operant conditioning of rectosphincteric responses in the treatment of fecal incontinence. *The New England Journal of Medicine*, 1974, *290*(12), 646–649.

Flanagan, C.H. Rumination in infancy—past and present with a case report. *Journal of Child Psychology and Psychiatry and Allied Disciplines*, 1977, *16*, 140–149.

Garrick, T.R. Behavior therapy for irritable bowel syndrome: A case report. *General Hospital Psychiatry*, 1981, *3*, 48–51.

Gelber, H., & Meyer, V. Behaviour therapy and encopresis: The complexities involved in treatment. *Behaviour Research and Therapy*, 1965, *2*, 227–231.

Hardin, T.M., Kerzner, B., & McClung, H.J. The role of biofeedback training for the control of fecal soiling. Unpublished manuscript, Ohio State University, 1982.

Heefner, J.D., Wilder, R.M., & Wilson, I.D. Irritable colon and depression. *Psychosomatics*, 1978, *19*(9), 540–547.

Keehn, J.D. Brief case-report: Reinforcement therapy of incontinence. *Behaviour Research and Therapy*, 1965, *2*, 239.

Lang, P.J., & Melamed, B.G. Avoidance conditioning therapy of an infant with chronic ruminative vomiting. *Journal of Abnormal Psychology*, 1969, *74*(1), 1–8.

Levine, M.D., & Bakow, H. Children with encopresis: A study of treatment outcome. *Pediatrics*, 1976, *58*, 845–852.

Linscheid, T.R., & Cunningham, C.E. A controlled demonstration of the effectiveness of electric shock in the elimination of chronic infant rumination. *Journal of Applied Behavior Analysis*, 1977, *10*(3), 500.

Logan, D.L., & Garner, D. Effective behavior modification for reducing chronic soiling. *American Annals of the Deaf*, 1971, *116*, 382–384.

McDonagh, M.J. Is operant conditioning effective in reducing enuresis and encopresis in children? *Perspectives in Psychiatric Care*, 1971, *9*(1), 17–23.

Mitchell, K.R. Self-management of spastic colitis. *Journal of Behavior Therapy and Experimental Psychiatry*, 1978, *9*, 269-272.

Murray, M.E., Keele, D.K., & McCarver, J.W. Behavioral treatment of ruminations: A case study. *Clinical Pediatrics*, 1976, *15*(7), 591-596.

Neale, D.H. Behaviour therapy and encopresis in children. *Behaviour Research and Therapy*, 1963, *1*, 139-149.

Nilsson, D.E. Treatment of encopresis: A token economy. *Journal of Pediatric Psychology*, 1976, *4*, 42-46.

Olness, K. Autohypnosis in functional megacolon in children. *The American Journal of Clinical Hypnosis*, 1976, *19*(1), 28-32.

Olness, K., McParland, F.A., & Piper, J. Biofeedback: A new modality in the management of children with fecal soiling. *The Journal of Pediatrics*, 1980, *96*(3), 505-509.

Peterson, D.R., & London, P. A role for cognition in the behavioral treatment of a child's eliminative disturbance. In L.P. Ullmann & L. Krasner (Eds.), *Case studies in behavior modification*. New York: Holt, Rinehart & Winston, Inc., 1965.

Ringdahl, I.C. Hospital treatment of the encopretic child. *Psychosomatics*, 1980, *21*(1), 65-71.

Sajwaj, T., Libet, J., & Agras, S. Lemon-juice therapy: The control of life-threatening rumination in a six-month-old infant. *Journal of Applied Behavior Analysis*, 1974, *7*(4), 557-563.

Silber, S. Encopresis: Rectal rebellion and anal anarchy? *Journal of the American Society of Psychosomatic Dentistry and Medicine*, 1968, *15*(3), 97-106.

Susen, G.R. Conditioned relaxation in a case of ulcerative colitis. *Journal of Behavior Therapy and Experimental Psychiatry*, 1978, *9*, 283.

Toister, R.P., Condron, C.J., Worley, L., & Arthur, D. Faradic therapy of chronic vomiting in infancy: A case study. *Journal of Behavior Therapy and Experimental Psychiatry*, 1975, *6*, 55-59.

Whitehead, W.E., Parker, L.H., Masek, B.J., Cataldo, M.F., & Freeman, J.M. Biofeedback treatment of fecal incontinence in patients with myelomeningocele. *Developmental Medicine and Child Neurology*, 1981, *23*, 313-322.

Wise, T.N., Cooper, J.N., & Ahmed, S. The efficacy of group therapy for patients with irritable bowel syndrome. *Psychosomatics*, 1982, *23*(5), 465-469.

Wright, D.F., Brown, R.A., & Andrews, M.E. Remission of chronic ruminative vomiting through a reversal of social contingencies. *Behaviour Research and Therapy*, 1978, *16*, 134-136.

Wright, L. Handling the encopretic child. *Professional Psychology*, 1973, *4*, 137-144.

Wright, L. Outcome of a standardized program for treating psychogenic encopresis. *Professional Psychology*, 1975, *6*, 453-456.

Wright, L., & Walker, C.E. Treatment of the child with psychogenic encopresis. *Clinical Pediatrics*, 1977, *16*(11), 1042-1045.

Young, G.C. The treatment of childhood encopresis by conditioned gastro-ileal reflex training. *Behaviour Research and Therapy*, 1973, *11*, 499-503.

TABLE A-8

Asthma

Authors and Date	Sample Size	Age	Treatment	Outcome	Follow-Up	Comments
Creer, 1970	2	10 yrs.	*Behavior Therapy* 1) 6 week baseline; 2) time out from positive reinforcement; 3) reversal; 4) time out reinstituted	Both first and second time out procedure led to a decrease in number and duration of hospitalizations. With reversal there was an increase in both	—	Children are residents at Children's Asthma Research Institute and Hospital (CARIH). Had become "favorites" of the nurses and received much attention and positive reinforcement in the hospital
Creer & Miklich, 1970	1	10 yrs.	*Behavior Therapy* Videotape made and child role played appropriate and inappropriate behavior	Child responded appropriately after 3rd viewing session	6 months–child still behaving appropriately	Child is a resident at CARIH. Presenting problems were immaturity, nonassertive behaviors, poor peer relationships, and tantrums
Creer & Yoches 1971	2	7 yrs. 9 yrs.	*Behavior Therapy* Response-cost technique: Patients started each session with 40 points and lost 1 point for each 30 seconds they were distracted. Prizes awarded based on points	Significant decrease in nonattending behaviors and an increase in attending behaviors	6 months–children performing at satisfactory levels in the classroom	Children are residents at CARIH; both frequently absent from school; had inefficient work habits, poor attention, were disruptive, and underachieving
Creer et al., 1974	1	10 yrs.	*Behavior Therapy* 1) Time out applied during 2 different treatment sessions; when hospital-	After first treatment session mean number of days hospitalized decreased from 11.1 to	1 year after discharge from residence gains still maintained	Child is a resident at CARIH; excessive time spent in this facility thought to be related to

Author	N	Age	Treatment	Results	Follow-up	Comments
			ized, child was placed in a room by himself, no visitors, only school books allowed, all meals eaten alone in room. 2) Systematic shaping of appropriate classroom behaviors	6.8 in a 6 month period After second treatment session mean number of days hospitalized decreased from 6.8 to 3.9 in a 9 month period and stabilized at 2.5 days		avoidance of difficult school and peer relationships
Gardner, 1968	1	6 yrs.	*Behavior Therapy* 1) Withdrawal of attention for inappropriate behavior (hyperactivity, facial tics, body twitches); 2) reinforcement (toys) for normal activity and appropriate behaviors; 3) alternative responses to stress developed in therapy; 4) placebo medication given	Asthma attacks decreased from 3–4/week to 1–2/week; attacks became less intense; hyperactivity decreased	6 months—only 2 asthma attacks; no hospitalizations; behavioral improvement maintained	Severely emotionally disturbed child with very severe asthma
Hochstadt et al., 1980	7	8–13 yrs.	*Behavior Therapy* Time out from positive reinforcement upon admission to hospital: (private room, no visitors, no TV, or use of hospital recreation facilities). Discharge when acceptable peak expiratory flow rate (PEFR) reached	Mean length of hospitalization reduced from 18.3 days/year to 9.0 days/year; mean number of days to reach optimal PEFR reduced from 3.5–16 days to 2–7 days	Followed in outpatient clinic for medical care	Children were overusers of the hospital; all children were from families receiving public assistance; use of recreational facilities at hospital allowed during entire afternoon of outpatient visits if symptom free
Miklich, 1973	1	6½ yrs.	*Behavior Therapy* 1) Operant conditioning	Decrease in asthma panic; hyperventilation	8 months—maintained reduction	Child is a resident at CARIH

TABLE A-8 **Asthma** (*continued*)

Authors and Date	Sample Size	Age	Treatment	Outcome	Follow-Up	Comments
			to shape quiet, relaxed chair sitting; 2) time out following misbehavior; 3) reinforcement for maintaining relaxed posture during desensitization	during attacks was reduced and treatment not resisted	in asthma panic, but hyperkinetic behaviors returned to pretherapy level	
Moore, 1965	12	6 adults 6 children	*Behavior Therapy* 3 types of treatment. Each subject received 2 different types: 1) relaxation; 2) relaxation and suggestion; 3) relaxation and reciprocal inhibition	Only relaxation with reciprocal inhibition produced objective improvement (e.g., number of asthma attacks decreased from 3/week to 0.5/week)	—	Subjective improvement occurred with all three treatments
Neisworth & Moore, 1972	1	7 yrs.	*Behavior Therapy* Operant treatment: 1) parents discontinued attention and medicine during bedtime asthmatic attacks; 2) reinforcement of incompatible behavior (i.e., lunch money if child coughed less night before); 3) reversal procedure; 4) operant treatment reinstated	Reduction in duration of nighttime asthmatic attacks	11 months—remained at treatment level	Severe asthma since infancy
Miklich et al., 1977	26	Mean=11 yrs.	*Behavior Therapy* Systematic desensitization for 19 children. No inter-	Only measure significantly differentiating the groups was morning	6 weeks	Twice daily pulmonary measures taken, as well as tabulation of medica-

Study	N	Age	Treatment / Protocol	Results	Follow-up	Comments
			...vention for 7 controls. Protocol included 1) 16 week baseline; 2) 10 week treatment; 3) 9 week post treatment assessment; 4) 11 week interum; 5) 6 week follow-up	lung function. This seemed related to decline in controls flow rate, rather than improvement in treatment group		tion requirements, number of hospital admissions, and daily symptom severity
Feldman, 1976	4	10–16 yrs.	*Biofeedback*	Statistically significant improvement in all 3 measures of airway obstruction; neither biofeedback or isoproterenol brought respiratory values to normal	—	Each child had an allergic and emotional component to his illness; no data collected to determine if use of this technique results in clinical improvement
Khan et al., 1974	20 — 10 reactors (bronchospasm to saline); 10 nonreactors	8–15 yrs.	*Biofeedback* (positive reinforcement) 1) 5 sessions children tried to increase their forced expiratory volume (FEV) in absence of bronchospasm when given biofeedback; 2) 10 sessions used to overcome experimentally induced bronchial constriction; 3) 5 sessions refresher training period after 1, 2, 3, and 6 months	Improvement in experimental group greater than in control group in frequency of attacks, number of emergency room visits, and amount of medication; no treatment analyses performed between reactors and nonreactors	8–10 months	Sample selected from an Allergy Clinic; reactors initially had more hospitalizations, although nonreactors tended to have more severe asthma. No data provided on the children's actual success in increasing FEV's
Kotses et al., 1976	36	8–16 yrs.	*Biofeedback* Operantly produced frontalis muscle relaxa-	Only contingent group's PEFRs improved substantially after treat-	—	All children diagnosed as severe chronic asthmatics; respiratory

TABLE A-8 Asthma (continued)

Authors and Date	Sample Size	Age	Treatment	Outcome	Follow-Up	Comments
			tion: 1) contingent feedback group; 2) noncontingent feedback group; 3) 2 no treatment control groups	ment. Frontalis muscle tension decreased in contingent group, whereas muscle tension increased in noncontingent group		improvement seemed to relate to frontalis relaxation. Noncontingent feedback may have been quite frustrating for children
Scherr et al., 1975	44	6-15 yrs.	Biofeedback Control group (22) no treatment. Experimental group (22) relaxation training EMG feedback	Experimental group had greater improvement in: 1) behavior ratings; 2) improved peak flow rates; 3) decrease in number of asthma attacks; 4) decrease in infirmary visits; 5) decrease in steroid usage	10 months	Caution in interpretation of findings. Need more rigorous controls. Behavior ratings and medical evaluations performed without knowledge of group status
Khan, 1977	80	8-15 yrs.	Biofeedback and Counter Conditioning 1) Reactors identified by bronchoconstriction to saline inhalation. 2) Biofeedback and counter conditioning employed with both groups. 3) Controls contained reactors and nonreactors.	68% of subjects in experimental groups were able to decrease their airway resistance by 10-15% within 5 sessions; 20% had a 10% decrease in airway resistance after isoproterenol use; 12% could not achieve criteria even after use of isoproterenol	1 year reduction in frequency, duration, and severity for both experimental groups and control reactor group	Follow-up assessment included number and duration of attacks, number of emergency room visits, number of hospital admissions, amount of medication, and severity of asthma
Davis et al., 1973	24	6-10 yrs. 11-15 yrs.	Biofeedback and Relaxation Group 1: Jacobsonian re-	Group 1 achieved a reduction in airway resistance that was greater than con-	Relaxation training with or without biofeedback had no	Subjects residents at CARIH. Relaxation therapy with biofeed-

			laxation and biofeedback; Group 2: Jacobsonian relaxation training; Control group: Given assorted reading material and told to relax. All subjects had five ½ hour treatment sessions.	trol group. No significant difference was found between treatment conditions for severe asthmatics. Age had no effect on response to treatment.	long term effect on symptom improvement.	back resulted in reduction of symptoms for subjects with mild asthma, but not for those with severe asthma requiring steroids.
Aronoff et al., 1975	17	6–15 yrs.	*Hypnosis*	Average improvement at end of ½ hour period was greater than 50% using peak flow, dyspnea, wheezing, and subjective ratings by subjects as outcome data	—	Severe chronic asthma in all subjects. Over 50% were receiving steroids. Hypnosis thought to be effective in reducing anxiety associated with attack
Collison, 1975	121	8–73 yrs.	*Hypnosis*	*Excellent:* 21% became completely asthma free; no drug therapy. *Good:* 33% had a decrease in frequency and severity of asthma attacks. *Mild:* 22% showed some improvement. *No Change:* 24%	—	Those less than 30 yrs. responded best to hypnotherapy; trance depth related to improvement; subjective improvement in well-being noted among patients showing little or no objective improvement
Maher-Loughnan et al., 1962	55	6–59 yrs.	*Hypnosis* 1 month observation for all subjects: Experimental group (27): hypnotic induction procedure; symptom removal suggestions. Control group	Experimental group evidenced significantly greater reduction in wheezing, use of medication, and pump	—	Patients under 30 yrs. old, those with milder asthma, and those who had a shorter duration demonstrated most improvement. Asthma triggered by emotional

TABLE A-8 Asthma (*continued*)

Authors and Date	Sample Size	Age	Treatment	Outcome	Follow-Up	Comments
			(28) given symptomatic treatments not used before			factors responded best, but allergic and infective types also benefitted
Renne & Creer, 1976	4	7–12 yrs.	*Instructions and Reinforcement* Experiment I: Intermittent Positive Pressure Breathing (IPPB) instructional training (eye fixation, facial posturing, and diaphragmatic breathing) and positive reinforcement for using IPPB apparatus during attacks, or no more asthma during hospitalization	Significant improvements in use of IPPB: 41% effectiveness before training; after training, 82.25% effective use	6 months–3/4 children used IPPB apparatus correctly. 1 child reverted to inappropriate response but later corrected response.	Subjects are residents at CARIH. Proper use of IPPB apparatus diminished need for more intensive treatment such as steroids. hospitalizations, etc.
Renne & Creer, 1976 (continued)	2	8–9 yrs.	Experiment II: same as above except 8 nurses experimenters/observers	Subjects used IPPB apparatus correctly	1 month–continued to use equipment appropriately	Operant procedures facilitated the nurse's teaching of proper inhalation procedures.
Danker et al., 1975	6	9–12 yrs.	*Operant Conditioning* Baseline assessment made. Reinforcement trials administered (red light turns on if child achieves higher PEFR than criterion; child told red light means "good")	No evidence of any conditioned increase in PEFR	—	Children were residents at CARIH. Operant conditioning of PEFR (using biofeedback) was unsuccessful in reducing asthma in both studies. In one child the vigorous breathing exacerbated

Study	N	Age	Procedure	Results		Comments
	5	8–11 yrs.	Baseline assessment then reinforcement sessions as above, except a new criterion was set for each session	3/5 showed an increase in PEFR within treatment session. Only 1 displayed intersession improvement.	—	his condition. Authors suggest use of noneffortful techniques
Alexander, 1972	25	10–15 yrs.	*Relaxation* 5 sessions sitting quietly. 5 sessions taught to relax using modified Jacobsonian relaxation training.	Greater improvement in PEFR during relaxation than during sitting quietly sessions. Effect of relaxation on PEFR was greater for children with emotional factors	—	Children were residents at CARIH. Neither change in anxiety or degree of "trait anxiety" related to improvement of PEFR with relaxation.
Alexander et al, 1972	36	10–15 yrs.	*Relaxation* 20 subjects had 3 sessions of modified Jacobsonian systematic relaxation training; 16 subjects sat quietly	Significant increase in PEFR in the relaxation group; no change in the control group. 11% increase in PEFR for total relaxation group; 10 children demonstrated 32% improvement	—	Children were residents at CARIH. Relaxation training may provide relief from asthma only for children able to achieve substantial PEFR improvement
Philipp et al., 1972	20	14–49 yrs.	*Relaxation* Sequence included: 1) baseline; 2) inhaling methylcholine or saline; 3) suggestions for inhalants; 4) relaxation training; 5) relaxation and inhalant	Intrinsic asthmatics (no allergic component, N=10) reacted to both saline and methylcholine. Extrinsic asthmatics (known allergic sensitivity, N=10) responded only to latter. Relaxation training in-	—	Results support cognitive mediation of breathing response. Intrinsics particularly benefited from relaxation.

TABLE A-8 **Asthma** (*continued*)

Authors and Date	Sample Size	Age	Treatment	Outcome	Follow-Up	Comments
				creased tolerance for methylcholine and enhanced respiratory efficiency for both groups		
Alexander et al., 1979	14		*Relaxation* Sequence included baseline resting, relaxation training, and relaxation sessions. Sessions initiated just before next dose of medication was to be given. 8 children trained individually; 6 trained in groups of 3	During resting there was a decline in pulmonary function. During relaxation, pulmonary function (PEFR and airway resistance) maintained despite length of time since receiving medication. EMG, heart rate, and blood pressure tended to be lower	—	Children thought to be at the end of their response to the previous medication. Comprehensive pulmonary function assessment as well as frontalis EMG, heart rate, respiration rate, skin conductance, and skin temperature measures taken

Asthma Table (A-8)
References

Alexander, A.B. Systematic relaxation and flow rates in asthmatic children: Relationship to emotional precipitants and anxiety. *Journal of Psychosomatic Research*, 1972, *16*, 405–410.

Alexander, A.B., Cropp, G.J., & Chai, H. Effects of relaxation training on pulmonary mechanics in children with asthma. *Journal of Applied Behavior Analysis*, 1979, *12*(1), 27–35.

Alexander, A.B., Miklich, D.R., & Hershkoff, H. The immediate effects of systematic relaxation training on peak expiratory flow rates in asthmatic children. *Psychosomatic Medicine*, 1972, *34*(5), 388–394.

Aronoff, G.M., Aronoff, S., & Peck, L.W. Hypnotherapy in the treatment of bronchial asthma. *Annals of Allergy*, 1975, *34*, 356–362.

Collison, D.R. Which asthmatic patients should be treated by hypnotherapy? *The Medical Journal of Australia*, 1975, *1*, 776–781.

Creer, T.L. The use of a time-out from positive reinforcement procedure with asthmatic children. *Journal of Psychosomatic Research*, 1970, *14*, 117–120.

Creer, T.L., & Miklich, D.R. The application of a self-modeling procedure to modify inappropriate behavior: A preliminary report. *Behaviour Research and Therapy*, 1970, *8*, 91–92.

Creer, T.L., Weinberg, E., & Molk, L. Managing a hospital behavior problem: Malingering. *Journal of Behavior Therapy and Experimental Psychiatry*, 1974, *5*, 259–262.

Creer, T.L., & Yoches, C. The modification of an inappropriate behavioral pattern in asthmatic children. *Journal of Chronic Diseases*, 1971, *24*, 507–513.

Danker, P.S., Miklich, D.R., Pratt, C., & Creer, T.L. An unsuccessful attempt to instrumentally condition peak expiratory flow rates in asthmatic children. *Journal of Psychosomatic Research*, 1975, *19*, 209–213.

Davis, M.H., Saunders, D.R., Creer, T.L., & Chai, H. Relaxation training facilitated by biofeedback apparatus as a supplemental treatment in bronchial asthma. *Journal of Psychosomatic Research*, 1973, *17*, 121–128.

Feldman, G.M. The effect of biofeedback training on respiratory resistance of asthmatic children. *Psychosomatic Medicine*, 1976, *38*(1), 27–34.

Gardner, J.E. A blending of behavior therapy techniques in an approach to an asthmatic child. *Psychotherapy: Theory, Research and Practice*, 1968, *5*(1), 46–49.

Hochstadt, N.J., Shepard, J., & Lulla, S.H. Reducing hospitalizations of children with asthma. *The Journal of Pediatrics*, 1980, *97*(6), 1012–1015.

Khan, A.U. Effectiveness of biofeedback and counter-conditioning in the treatment of bronchial asthma. *Journal of Psychosomatic Research*, 1977, *21*, 97–104.

Khan, A.U., Staerk, M., & Bonk, C. Role of counter-conditioning in the treatment of asthma. *Journal of Psychosomatic Research*, 1974, *18*, 89–92.

Kotses, H., Glaus, K.D., Crawford, P.L., Edwards, J.E., & Scherr, M.S. Operant reduction of frontalis EMG activity in the treatment of asthma in children. *Journal of Psychosomatic Research*, 1976, *20*, 453–459.

Maher-Loughnan, G.P., MacDonald, N., Mason, A.A., & Fry, L. Controlled trial of hypnosis in the symptomatic treatment of asthma. *British Medical Journal*, 1962, (5301), 371–376.

Miklich, D.R. Operant conditioning procedures with systematic desensitization in a hyperkinetic asthmatic boy. *Journal of Behavior Therapy and Experimental Psychiatry*, 1973, *4*, 177–182.

Miklich, D.R., Renne, C.M., Creer, T.L., Alexander, A.B., Chai, H., Davis, M.H., Hoffman, A., & Danker-Brown, P. The clinical utility of behavior therapy as an adjunctive treatment for asthma. *Journal of Allergy and Clinical Immunology*, 1977, *60*(5), 285–294.

Moore, N. Behaviour therapy in bronchial asthma: A controlled study. *Journal of Psychosomatic Research*, 1965, *9*, 257–276.

Neisworth, J.T., & Moore, F. Operant treatment of asthmatic responding with the parent as therapist. *Behavior Therapy*, 1972, *3*, 95–99.

Philipp, R.L., Wilde, G.J.S., & Day, J.H. Suggestion and relaxation in asthmatics. *Journal of Psychosomatic Research*, 1972, *16*, 193–204.

Renne, C.M., & Creer, T.L. Training children with asthma to use inhalation therapy equipment. *Journal of Applied Behavior Analysis*, 1976, *9*, 1–11.

Scherr, M.S., Crawford, P.L., Sergent, C.B., & Scherr, C.A. Effect of bio-feedback techniques on chronic asthma in a summer camp environment. *Annals of Allergy*, 1975, *35*, 289–295.

TABLE A-9

Hemophilia

Authors and Date	Problem	Sample Size	Age	Treatment	Outcome	Follow-Up	Comments
Varni, 1980	Persistent behavior problem	Case study	4½ yrs.	Contingency management	Increase in appropriate behavior at school and home; decrease in misbehavior	+12 month period	Findings consistent with behavioral management techniques with non-hemophilic children
LaBaw, 1975	Anxiety about possible bleeding	20 hemophilics 10 experimental 10 control	children and adults	Group and self-hypnosis for 30 months	Significant decrease in need for blood transfusion in experimental group	—	Patients appeared to achieve a sense of self-control which helped to relieve anxiety
LaBaw, 1970	Tension and anxiety regarding bleeding	7	latency-adolescence	Suggestive therapy (group and individual)	Clinical case reports of improvement and reduced hospitalizations	+	Technique employed by children prior to and during dental extractions, in hospital, for reducing tension, etc.
Handford et al., 1980	Effect of emotional state on use of antihemophilic factor (AHF) concentrate	Case study	15 yrs.	Psychiatric intervention: family, individual, and group therapy	50% reduction in use of AHF from baseline	+15 months 43% reduction	Also number of hemorrhages, infusions, and days using infusions declined
Caldwell et al., 1974	Psychological stress in families with hemophilic member	5 couples: 3 males with hemophilia; 2 parents with hemophilic child	adults	8 months group psychotherapy	Significant changes in feelings of self-worth and satisfaction	—	Tennessee Self Concept Scale used to assess self-satisfaction and perceived self-worth as a family member

TABLE A-9 **Hemophilia** (*continued*)

Authors and Date	Problem	Sample Size	Age	Treatment	Outcome	Follow-Up	Comments
Mattsson & Agle, 1972	Parent-child relationships	10 parents	adults	25 weekly meetings	Increase in self-esteem & confidence in handling severe bleeding episodes	+2 years	Also outlines common methods of coping and adapting to the stress of raising a child with hemophilia

Hemophilia Table (A-9) References

Caldwell, H.S., Leveque, K.L., & Lane, D.M. Group psychotherapy in the management of hemophilia. *Psychological Reports*, 1974, *35*, 339–342.

Handford, H.A., Charney, D., Ackerman, L., Eyster, M.E., & Bixler, E.O. Effect of psychiatric intervention on use of antihemophilic factor concentrate. *American Journal of Psychiatry*, 1980, *137*(10), 1254–1256.

LaBaw, W.L. Regular use of suggestibility by pediatric bleedings. *Haematologia*, 1970, *4*(3–4), 419–425.

LaBaw, W.L. Auto-hypnosis in haemophilia. *Haematologia*, 1975, *9*(1–2), 103–110.

Mattsson, A., & Agle, D.P. Group therapy with parents of hemophiliacs: Therapeutic process and observations of parental adaptation to chronic illness in children. *American Academy of Child Psychiatry*, 1972, *11*, 558–571.

Varni, J.W. Behavioral treatment of disease-related chronic insomnia in a hemophiliac. *Journal of Behavior Therapy and Experimental Psychiatry*, 1980, *11*(2), 143–145.

Index of Names

Index of Names

266

Tizard, J., 8, 70
Todd, T., 110
Toister, R.P., 234, 247
Tophoff, M., 217, 220
Topoff, M., 64, 72
Torres, F., 83, 92
Tourette, Gilles de la, 57
Tourette Syndrome Association, 60
Travers, R.D., 70
Travis, G., 76, 78, 92, 97, 99, 101, 107, 110, 112, 150, 153, 154, 159, 165, 168, 171, 175, 178, 190, 193, 197, 199
Tsu, V.D., 7
Tuma, J.M., 6, 8
Tutihasi, M., 7, 70
Twiggs, J.T., 167
Tyler, H.R., 82, 93

VanHeeckeren, D.W., 226
Vanden Belt, R.J., 74, 93
VandenBergh, R.L., 111, 232
Vandersall, T.A., 136, 138–139, 140, 149
Varni, J.W., 8, 208, 259, 260
Volpe, J.J., 81, 93

Wagner, H.R., 225, 226
Walford, S., 229, 232
Walker, C.E., 147, 247
Walsh, M.E., 7, 26
Waltz, J.M., 69
Warnberg, L., 102, 112
Watt, S.L., 8, 208
Wayne, H.L., 220
Weber, F.T., 232
Wedgwood, R.J., 179
Weidman, W.H., 226
Weinberb, E., 166, 257
Weiner, H., 130, 131, 133, 134, 148
Weisnagel, J., 167
Weiss, J.M., 134, 148
Westman, J., 91

White, J.L., 146
Whitehead, W.E., 115, 116, 127, 128, 130, 134, 138, 146, 147, 148, 149, 242, 247
Whitman, V., 224, 226
Whitmore, K., 8, 70
Whitsett, S.F., 214
Wiener, C.L., 172, 180
Wilde, F.J.S., 258
Wilder, R.M., 246
Williams, R.B., Jr., 91
Williams, S.C., 147, 246
Williams, D.T., 5, 8, 41, 70, 71
Wilson, I.D., 246
Wise, T.N., 243, 247
Wolcott, G.J., 71
Wolf, L., 148
Wolff, B.B., 174, 180
Wolff, P.H., 91, 92, 226
Woodruff, R.A., Jr., 149
Woodward, K.L., 25, 27
Worley, L., 247
Wright, D.F., 116, 146, 234–235, 247
Wright, F.S., 28, 46, 47, 71, 74, 83, 92, 93
Wright, L., 34, 52, 65, 67, 117, 120, 122, 123, 125–126, 129, 147, 171, 172, 182, 190, 198, 199, 211, 214, 224, 226, 239, 247
Wright, L.A., 72

Yalom, I., 148
Yaryura-Tobias, J.A., 216, 220
Yoches, C., 166, 257
Young, G.C., 237, 247
Young, J.G., 220
Young, S.J., 142, 149
Yule, W., 167

Zavanella, C., 82, 93
Zellweger, H.U., 198
Zimsky, E.P., Jr., 72
Zlutnick, S., 211, 214

Subject Index

275

for muscular dystrophy, 196–197
for rumination, 115–117
for seizure control, 51–54
for tic disorders, 62–64, 215–220
(table)
for ulcerative colitis, 139–140
intervention approaches for, 204–207
Psycho-Motor seizure. *See* Complex partial seizure
Psychosexual development, 10 (table)
Psychosocial impacts
of asthma, 158–160, 165
of CHD on children, 85–90
of CHD on parents, 76–77, 85–90
of diabetes mellitus, 106–107
of epilepsy, 36–37
of muscular dystrophy, 190, 193–196
of tic disorders, 60
Psychosomatic diseases, "core," 173
Psychotherapy
for hemophilia, 259 (table)
for irritable bowel syndrome, 244 (table)
for tic disorders, 62
Punishment
for seizure control, 52
illness as, 13, 18
in encopresis treatment, 126–127

Questionnaire on Resources and Stress, 202

Rage outburst. *See* Intermittent explosive disorder(s)
Rate of disturbance
relationship to disorder type, 2
Reciprocal inhibition
for tic disorders, 216 (table)
Reflux
and rumination, 113
Relaxation therapy
for asthma, 163–164, 252–253 (table), 255–256 (table)
for colitis, 242–243 (table)
for peptic ulcer, 135
for seizure self-control, 52
for tic disorders, 62, 217 (table)
Retinopathy
resulting from diabetes mellitus, 101
Reward management
for seizure control, 52

Rochester Child Health Survey, 1
"Rooming In," 11, 12
Rumination
characteristics of, 114 (table)
definition and diagnosis of, 113, 115
etiology of, 115
prognosis, 115
psychological treatment for, 115–117
review of literature on, 233–235 (table)

Seashore Tonal Memory Test, 37
Security
during toddler period, 12
Seizure(s)
and somatization disorders, 40–41
causes of, in children, 31
classification of, 32–33 (table)
definition of, 28
diagnostic guidelines for, 41, 44–45
environmental determinants of, 38–39
impact on learning, 34–36
in cases of CHD, 83
pseudoseizures and neurogenic, 39–40
precipitated by stress, 39, 41
prevalence of, 31
psychotherapeutic strategies for, 51–54
Seizure Disorders Survey, 38
Selective reinforcement
for tic disorders, 217 (table)
Self-Control techniques
for asthma management, 162–164
for juvenile rheumatoid arthritis, 177–178
for seizure control, 52
for tic disorders, 62, 217 (table)
loss of, during seizures, 36
Self-Hypnosis
for encopresis treatment, 128, 236 (table)
See also Hypnotherapy
Self-Identity
development of, in adolescence, 21
Self-Monitoring
for tic disorders, 218–219 (table)
Separation anxiety
and CHD, 85